ULTIMATE WARRIOR

THE DEAN BELL STORY
RICHARD BECHT

VICTOR GOLLANCZ
LONDON

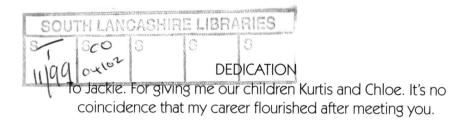
DEDICATION

To Jackie. For giving me our children Kurtis and Chloe. It's no coincidence that my career flourished after meeting you.

Acknowledgements

Many thanks to Cameron and Janice Bell for their assistance, as well as the 10 other key people who provided their insights into Dean's life in league— Graham Lowe, Arthur Beetson, Hugh McGahan, Ellery Hanley, Maurice Lindsay, Andy Platt, Frano Botica, Denis Betts, Va'aiga Tuigamala, John Kirwan and John Monie.

Several books and publications were used for reference purposes, including the following: *Rugby League Week, Big League, Rothmans Rugby League Yearbook* (various editions), *The A–Z of Rugby League, Lion Red New Zealand Rugby League Annual* (various editions), *Modern Rugby League Greats, The Encyclopedia of Rugby League Players, New Zealand Herald, Sunday News* and *Sunday Star-Times*.

Special thanks are also due to all the photographers whose work appears in the book.

First published in Great Britain 1995
by Victor Gollancz
An imprint of the Cassell Group
Wellington House, 125 Strand, London WC2R 0BB
Published in association with David Bateman Limited

A catalogue record for this book is
available from the British Library.

ISBN 0 575 06162 6

Book design by Chris O'Brien/Pages Literary Pursuits
Printed in Hong Kong by Colorcraft Limited

Contents

10 march 1995

The difference between the possible and the impossible lies in a man's determination.

Scene One: Wembley Stadium, London

Wigan's famous colours overpower the visual senses, and the stadium is transformed into an ocean of cherry and white as the fans salute their team's entrance to one of sport's greatest arenas.

And there, filing out in the Wigan team, are five New Zealanders: one is coach Graham Lowe, the other four all players—brothers Kevin and Tony Iro, Adrian Shelford and Dean Bell. It's a first for all of them—Challenge Cup final day, 30 April 1988, before a capacity crowd of 94,273. The day after his 26th birthday, Dean Bell is nervous, very nervous.

Scene Two: Eden Park, Auckland

New Zealand's home of rugby is utterly crammed for another test match. That's not unusual—but this match is. It's a *rugby league* test being played at Eden Park, the 1988 World Cup final no less.

A few minutes before the 4.00 p.m. kick-off on 9 October, a black-clad figure appears at the players' tunnel, the same tunnel which has been used by the world's great rugby union and cricket internationals, but never a rugby league player. Kiwi captain Dean Bell changes history, leading his team into a cauldron packed with 47,363 spectators. There with him the same Wigan team-mates—the Iros and Adrian Shelford—who were with him at Wembley a little over five months earlier. And Dean Bell is nervous, very nervous.

Scene Three: Ericsson Stadium, Auckland

It used to be known as Mt Smart Stadium; now it rings to the name of Ericsson Stadium, courtesy of the age of selling naming rights. It's not the same ground in appearance either. It has been totally transformed to suit its new purpose as a rugby league arena. And a few minutes before 8.30

p.m. on 10 March 1995, it's counting down not just to rugby league history but an important chapter in New Zealand sporting history.

Lining up in a tunnel in the north-east corner of the ground waiting to be fêted by 31,500 spectators, are the players who'll generate a sporting phenomenon, led by the Aucklander who has returned home from England to lead the Warriors—Dean Bell. And, even at 32, he's nervous, very nervous.

He had played 26 tests for New Zealand, and 36 matches in all for the Kiwis. He could count seven Challenge Cup final appearances at Wembley among his 253 matches for Wigan, plus 40 Winfield Cup appearances for Eastern Suburbs. Not to mention stints with Carlisle and Leeds, appearances for Oceania and the Rest of the World, Auckland and the New Zealand Maori. But those moments, those precious moments on the night of 10 March 1995, found Dean Bell as nervous as he had ever been.

Which wasn't altogether surprising because this was no ordinary match. It was an occasion and, as far as games go, as momentous as they come. Auckland, indeed New Zealand, and Australia, too, had waited for this— to see New Zealand's first fully professional sporting team enter a competition regarded as the pinnacle in its code. The one the coaches and players always call "the toughest in the world".

And the Warriors' organisation, as it would on many other occasions during this debut season, ensured the Winfield Cup debut had memorable touches throughout. Not least among them was the innovative idea to use that tunnel as a special entry point for the Warriors. The visitors would run onto the field from the more conventional entrance under the main grandstand—while the Warriors would make their entrance on a grand scale.

In fact, in a year which produced indelible sporting images of Peter Blake hoisting the America's Cup and Jonah Lomu charging through and over England fullback Mike Catt, the Warriors added to the tapestry. It was captured in those moments when Dean Bell led his team through a flame-flanked guard of honour onto Ericsson Stadium.

Timing was everything. The operation had to be synchronised for maximum effect. An event which had been hyped up beyond belief for weeks still had more in store, reaching its crescendo with the dynamic entrance. The crowd went delirious. Dean Bell was overwhelmed.

"Standing there at the tunnel I could hear and almost feel the roar. There had been such a build-up and finally we were there," says Bell.

"Now I'm more experienced I do allow myself to take in these things. There was an overwhelming feeling of pride knowing what was happening. And experienced as I am, I did have to physically hold the tears back

The moment of truth arrives for Dean Bell as he leads the Warriors out of the tunnel for their debut Winfield Cup outing against Brisbane. Nigel Marple (Fotopress)

walking through the flames. It was very emotional. It dawned on me that this was why I came back home. I knew I'd made the right decision.

"Using the tunnel was a great idea. It gave us that sort of grand entrance, especially with the way they have the two lines of flames. It makes you feel like you're walking out onto your stage. I knew we were going to come out from that tunnel the very first time I had a look at the ground when I came home. And I went through that in my mind every time I trained. I would look at it and picture in my mind how we were going to come through it.

"But I was incredibly nervous, so nervous I nearly tripped over as I ran onto the field—which would have gone down really well with the crowd. There's a slight rise up from the track to the field and I stumbled on it with the sprigs of my boots.

"The Brisbane match was very much like my first Challenge Cup final appearance at Wembley [in 1988]. That feeling of going into the unknown. Going out onto the Wembley arena was something I'd never done before. Going out onto Ericsson that night was just the same. I'd never played a Winfield Cup game with those players before. We just didn't know how things were going to go."

It wasn't quite a feeling of helplessness. Bell realised he and his players could determine their destiny that night—but there was fair reason for a hint of fear. The fear of being involved in a debacle after such an astonishing build-up. Bell had been through it all before.

Before returning for Operation Warriors, Dean Bell hadn't played at home since 1988, when he played with the Kiwis in their World Cup final appearance at Eden Park. That in itself said enough.

"What we went through all added up to the same sort of scenario as the 1988 World Cup final. And I did think about that, too," he says. "It could go two ways. We could have been thrashed or we could have been competitive."

The ghost of 1988 had also been unintentionally revived by Bell's former Kiwi team-mate Hugh McGahan. He rang Bell on 10 March 1995 to do the decent thing, only to regret it afterwards when he realised the last time he'd made a best wishes call to Bell was the day the Kiwis had been savaged 25–12 in the 1988 World Cup final.

That was then. This was now, and in the months, weeks and days before the Warriors' real arrival, there had been all sorts of traumas and tribulations as well as considerable personal doubt.

Most observers wouldn't readily classify Dean Bell as a footballer who would be subject to any personal doubts. He has such an overt iron will on the field, an ultimate warrior who shirks nothing and seems so assured in all he does. But underneath Dean Bell's combative veneer there is, surprisingly, the slightest hint of vulnerability.

"While, I try to be positive about myself, there was always that big

Dean Bell had personal doubts about his form, but they weren't obvious as he used his guile to get outside his Brisbane opposite Michael Hancock. (Fotopress)

doubt, personally as much as anything," says Bell. "I'm not deaf. I knew a lot of people were doubting whether I could still do it at 32 going on 33. I'd heard people saying, 'He's too old, why did they bring him over?' Even though you might have confidence in yourself, you wouldn't be human if it didn't affect you.

"I thought that after all the good seasons I'd had, I'd hate to come back home and look just a shadow of myself. I could have taken the easy way out and finished on a high at Wigan, allowing me to use that reputation. Then there would have been the questions about whether I could have handled it in the Winfield Cup. I once said I didn't have anything to prove to Australians about playing in the Winfield Cup, but deep down inside I knew I did.

"I had so many personal doubts I was very close to getting on the phone to John [Monie] to tell him I didn't think I could go through with it."

The root cause of Bell's pessimism could instantly be found in his recent track record of injury. Injury haunts plenty of footballers. Many succumb to it, beaten by the odds of a complaint which simply won't allow them to operate; others possibly lack the will to fight through. Not Dean Bell. He's had to live and survive as a footballer with injury a constant, if unwanted, companion. Not just one serious injury either, but a multitude of them.

Five operations were needed during or after the 1993–94 English season. One was for a torn ligament in his right thumb, there was another for a severe problem with his right shoulder, an arthroscope on a troublesome knee and, most crucially, two groin operations.

"The shoulder caused me loads of concern. It had nagged me for a couple of years and I was worried about it after my first couple of Warriors training sessions with the ball. I'd go home and my shoulder was giving me so much agony, just from catching the ball and passing it.

"In the end, I thought if I'm going to break down I'm going to break down trying to do it [playing for the Warriors]. I couldn't live with myself if I hadn't tried."

The Warriors had announced Bell's signing as captain in August 1993, so his dispiriting 1993–94 season with Wigan created both real and imagined reservations.

"I know Ian [Robson] was also beginning to worry about me because I'd been out of action so long in that 1993–94 season," says Bell. "Ian and John were at Central Park the night I did my groin. Ian had been back since and saw I still wasn't playing so it was no surprise to know he was worried. I started to wonder whether Ian was having second thoughts about bringing me to Auckland, so I actually had to ring the coach a couple of times to ensure everything was okay."

The seriousness of his groin injury could never be overstated. It might easily have ended his career as he tried to tolerate it despite being bothered by internal bleeding every time he ran. It certainly put a major dent in his activity that season, keeping him out of action for several months. When he returned, he was far from fit but still utterly determined to help at the business end of proceedings. And he did, helping Wigan clinch the first division championship and then the Challenge Cup once more before ending his season in favour of the operating table.

At its worst, the groin worry had prevented almost all movement to the point where Bell couldn't even jog.

"In the end I had another hernia operation on it [he'd had one in the late 1980s]. To me, the symptoms were similar to the first time around.

"The doctor was a bit sceptical. He said there was a little movement in the groin which suggested it might be a hernia, but he didn't think it was bad enough that surgery was required. So I virtually forced him into it because I'd been through a lot of problems with my groin in my second season at Wigan and didn't want to go through all the hassles again.

"Having had the operation, I thought that'll be fine. I'll be right in about four weeks. I wasn't, though, so after trying everything to get it right for a few months, I saw Wigan's orthopaedic surgeon whom I possibly should have seen in the first place.

"He thought I had an adductor tear and cut me open. What he found was an absolute mess inside. Everything had congealed and was all getting a little septic. He tidied that up and I haven't looked back since."

An example of Bell's typically understated manner of accounting for an injury which would have seen many footballers walk away from the game. It's also a typical example of why coaches have so valued the man. And it is why he was able to run onto Ericsson Stadium for one of the most important dates in New Zealand league's history.

There'd been no shortage of reminders about the day either. The players had been subjected to a demanding promotional programme over and above their training requirements. Shooting the Tina Turner advertisement and the Warriors' own effort had frayed tempers at times, Bell insisting the requirements, while accepted, tended to be far more time-consuming than they ought to have been.

And no matter what he did, he couldn't hide from the hype. "The night before the game John had asked us to relax and do something unrelated to the game," says Bell. "So I went out to the movies and, when I came home, I flicked the television on to watch the news. Well, there was something on about the Warriors and, when I changed channel, there was something else about the game. Surely it couldn't have been on a third channel? Sure enough, the Warriors were on again. There was just no escaping it."

Bell's match-day ritual was no different than usual. A late morning video movie as a diversion plus keeping to himself as much as possible, his wife Jackie ensuring son Kurtis and daughter Chloe were out of the frame much of the time. And, typically, eating was a worry.

"I don't eat much on match day—not because I don't want to. Because I can't. I spew it up all the time," says Bell. "Right from when I was a kid I've been a chucker like that. I tried much harder to force some food down this year and it benefited me. I still had my chunders and, true to form, I dry retched before the Brisbane game. It's a weekly event. No one likes getting changed next to me because they don't know what's coming."

Dean Bell knew what was coming his way in the match, however. He'd be marking the abrasive Michael Hancock instead of Brisbane's splendid centre Steve Renouf, who'd been ruled out with injury—a decided bonus.

But once the game started, the Warriors very soon found themselves wondering what was in store for them as, within 14 minutes, Brisbane bolted to a 10–0 lead through a dubious Willie Carne try and a converted Chris Johns touchdown.

Yet, just when the Warriors were threatened with a woeful baptism, they transformed the contest and made the night even more memorable than it had already been.

The Australian connection had a say. Centre Manoa Thompson's great

*Australian Phil Blake, the man who created a slice of
history by scoring the Warriors' first Winfield Cup try.*
Nigel Marple (Fotopress)

pass created room for his winger Whetu Taewa to carve up Brisbane down
the left flank and find Phil Blake inside for a dazzling try. The Warriors
first in Winfield Cup football and it had gone to an Australian.

Before the half was out, Dean Bell's angled run and inside ball to Sean
Hoppe had laid on another try and second rower Tony Tatupu had a third
Auckland try to give the home side a 16–10 half-time lead.

Even with Phil Blake in the sin bin, the Warriors were dictating affairs
in the second half; Hitro Okesene putting replacement Tea Ropati over
and Gene Ngamu's conversion stretching the lead to what seemed
tantalisingly close to a match-winning 22–10.

Just when the perfect result promised to top the night, a little man with
tons of talent changed the course of the match. Allan Langer, restricted for
much of the game, suddenly started running the show as he scored two
tries, and the Broncos escaped with a 25–22 win.

"I think deep down not many people thought we'd win but they wanted
us to be at least competitive in defeat," says Bell. "Once the game had
finished I was bitterly disappointed. It doesn't matter who you are, or

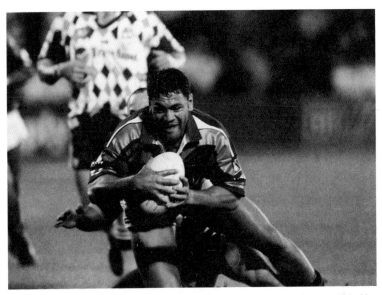

Former Kiwi Tea Ropati came off the bench to score early in the second half, stretching the Warriors' lead to what should have been a match-winning margin. Ross Land (Fotopress)

how long you've been together, when you get that sort of lead, you should finish a team off. The adrenalin should be running so much that no side should be able to get back into the game. A lesson learnt and, at the end of the day, relief that we didn't disgrace ourselves, that we'd been competitive.

"There were still so many positives to erase the doubts I'd had. While I was annoyed with the defeat, when I sat down and thought about it, I saw plenty of good points in the performance. If you could ever have a moral victory when losing, that was it.

"Still, I couldn't believe the reaction from some of the Australian experts who, on the strength of one game, were saying we were definitely top eight material, probably even top three. I wasn't thinking that."

Among the doubts erased that night were Dean Bell's own misgivings about his ability. If it had been waning, which he suggested it had been, there was no hint of it in this game. Maybe not quite as quick any more— and at 32 no one would expect him to be—but his all-round class was so obvious. On defence, he was exceptional. On attack, inspirational, as he worked a try for Hoppe and also provided a fabulous ball to Hoppe behind Michael Hancock. He was unmistakably the Warriors' man of the match.

He had to collect the award after the match with an obvious legacy from the battle—a stitched top lip, courtesy of some special attention from Michael Hancock. "Hancock copped me a good one late in the match. I think it happened when I put Sean away with that pass around behind Hancock. He just caught me and had the cheek to ask, 'Are you alright

Dean?' It didn't worry me, because if I had the chance I would have done the same thing. Some people might think he was concerned about my health but I didn't detect too much concern in his voice."

There was some concern in the way the Warriors had surrendered a winning lead but none about the night on a wider scale. The Warriors had delivered everything to the New Zealand sporting public short of a win.

And Dean Bell had made a triumphant return, at a venue new to him as a rugby league ground but fittingly close to the territory he calls home. The boy had been taken out of South Auckland—but South Auckland hadn't been taken out of the boy.

the kid from otara

I hope that I may always desire more
than I can accomplish.

In this sensitive new age, there are people who resent being told they live in South Auckland. Some vehemently object, insisting the reference to "South Auckland" has sinister undertones, that the name immediately implies an association with racial tension and crime. The truth is that this heavily populated area of New Zealand's largest city boasts a vibrant smorgasbord of Polynesian races and cultures, not always combining too harmoniously. Crime is an unwanted problem and there is some racial strife.

But, whatever it might be, it's still South Auckland to Dean Bell. It's also the place he calls home.

As a born and bred product of the area, he never thought there was a class structure or system in New Zealand, certainly not in Auckland. Not in the way there so obviously is in England where the "haves" and "have nots" are so readily identifiable—something he has seen for himself.

But when he returned home in 1994 for his one-off year with the Warriors he sensed some change, that there were clear signs of a division. When he rationalised his thinking, Bell realised why—he himself had changed. After years of being cocooned in South Auckland and the way of life there, his horizons had broadened. He hadn't lived in New Zealand for any length of time for about 10 years and, when he and his family looked for a place they would call home for a year, they settled on a middle class Auckland suburb bordering the Remuera Golf Club.

Still, it was South Auckland life which framed the man who graduated to captain the Kiwis, Wigan and the Warriors. It gave him blue collar values, a working class perspective on life; rugby league and its overseas opportunities polished him.

It was also rugby league which brought a more worldly Dean Bell back home, making Ericsson Stadium his 1995 base, a venue which stands on

*Angel-faced and chubby-cheeked; the pocket-sized version
of Dean Bell well before the battle scars began to show.*
Dean Bell Collection

the northern border of South Auckland, overlooking and even adjacent to sites which evoke so many memories for Bell.

Close to the stadium is Felix Street, where the teenage Bell once worked for a tyre retreading company, inhaling copious amounts of rubber dust and then spending hours after each day's work coughing it all up. Just a few hundred metres south of the stadium lies the once-bustling freezing works district where Dean Bell would find seasonal work in the early 1980s alongside so many of his relations.

A few kilometres to the south west, Moyle Park, the home of the Manukau Rugby League Club which so consumed Bell from his youngest years until his early twenties, when he became a rugby league professional. To the south east, East Tamaki and Otara, Bell's world from birth. The family home was on the border of the two suburbs, and not too far away are the schools he attended—Mayfield Primary, Bairds Intermediate and Hillary College.

"It was my part of town, my scene," says Bell. "I used to run around there, out the back of East Tamaki to get away from all the traffic and the fumes. I ran with my Dad originally, doing Sunday runs with him and

Cameron and Janice Bell's little darlings, Dean and Tracey. Dean Bell Collection

some of his workmates when I was really young. Later I ran around there for hours and hours on my own."

The more Dean Bell talks about it, the more his upbringing and experiences can be seen in today's product. As a footballer, there are few more intense, more committed or dedicated players; he's so utterly disciplined about his league career, and tales from the past tend to provide some explanation.

"I was only in the third form at Hillary College, and we were doing some sprint work on a grass track during a physical education lesson," he says. "The teacher was working on my sprinting style, and I was trying really hard when a bunch of classmates yelled out: 'Shame!' That was the in-word and they were giving it to me because I was trying too hard.

"The teacher went off his tree at them: 'How stupid is it to be ashamed of trying your best?' It stuck in my mind. That was the attitude problem a lot of kids had then. That incident affected me. I didn't want responsibility at that time but I did like pushing myself physically in my sports." He's never done less than that since.

He admits he had some reasonably wild cousins, but Dean Bell insists he never was too unruly as a teenager. "I never smoked and I hated drinking, up till a certain age," he says. "I didn't get into those things as early as some of my cousins.

"Mind you, I had threats from my Dad like, 'If I ever catch you smoking I'll shave your hair off.' That had a bit to do with some of my attitudes. As a 12- or 13-year-old starting to get a bit vain about his hair, that was enough to put me off smoking."

Nothing could put him off football and, not unusually, it is a mother's often unsung contribution that ensured Dean Bell's life in league maintained its constancy of purpose. Janice Bell was definitely one of those Trojan-like supporters. "When I think about it, Mum used to take me everywhere, all the trips across town to training or wherever, and she never used to complain, not at all." says Bell. "I suppose I used to accept it then, or take it for granted, but when I think about it she gave so much."

His sister Tracey, five years younger, wasn't so enamoured with the rugby league lifestyle that dominated the Bell household. "With so much focus on my football, I didn't have a lot to do with Tracey in my younger days," says Dean. "And I don't think it was that easy for her really.

"I would say we also used to get on each other's nerves because our house had only two bedrooms—and we had to share one of them. That was a little awkward and not until later, when Mum and Dad bought me a caravan, could I sleep out the back."

Mentioning the Bell family has always meant just one sport—rugby league. The Bells aren't short on numbers when it comes to a head count, either. Cameron Bell is from a family of seven brothers and five sisters, the brothers all with a background in the game. There have been times when the Bell name has totally dominated Manukau teams.

One of Dean's countless uncles, George, was a New Zealand Maori representative. Cameron's baby brother Ian was a New Zealand Maori captain and also managed something none of the other six did—he was a Kiwi. He first toured Australia and Papua New Guinea with Ron Ackland's side in 1978, making his test debut as a prop in the third test against Australia and also playing the one-off international against Papua New Guinea. After that, he found no favour at all with Ackland's successor as Kiwi coach, Ces Mountford.

Not until 1983 did he reappear in the New Zealand jersey, coincidentally when his then 21-year-old nephew Dean had just come into the side. Ian Bell's involvement was as a replacement in the Kiwis' test win at Lang Park, while his fourth and last international against Papua New Guinea created a unique record. This was the test when the Kiwis fielded an uncle and two nephews—Ian Bell, Dean Bell and Clayton Friend. That year the three relations also toured Britain with the New Zealand Maori team, Ian as captain.

Dean Bell's strongest and longest-running playing association on a family level was with his cousin Clayton, son of Cameron's sister Cathy, or Bub, as she's better known. Of his 23 tests between 1982 and 1991, Friend played 17 of them with cousin Dean in the same side.

"A big family it is with so many cousins of my age. And, from the time we were kids, we all liked the game," says Dean Bell. "It was common to us all. We used to play on the sidelines at games, or on the grass bank at Carlaw Park.

"If I went to stay somewhere and I had to sleep on a mattress in the living room, I'd play football on it using a sock as the ball. Or we'd go into the hall and play football there. They were rugged games—but a good grounding for me.

"Really, my whole life has revolved around rugby league, and that's where Jackie finds it quite boring, but it's been perfect for me. She would ask me what I used to do during the week and I told her we trained or played football. What about Saturdays? Played. Sundays? Played or went to watch a game. She couldn't believe it meant so much.

"Even in summer it was never far away. We always holidayed at Sandy Bay on the Coromandel Peninsula and had some great games of touch down there."

Naturally there was no shortage of advice for a young footballer, although it seemed to add up to a situation of too much knowledge being a dangerous thing.

"There certainly was plenty of advice—but a bit of praise would have been nice sometimes," says Bell. "Still, they all used to come along to watch and support and I've seen since, with some of my second cousins, that they can't handle relations watching them. I used to feed on it. I'd look at the sideline and say to myself, 'Oh, Uncle David's here. So is Uncle Dubbie.' And I'd want to do my best in front of them.

"Sometimes the criticism was just a bit too much. The worst was when I was a bit older and Mum would drive us home. Dad would have had a few beers and he'd start going on. Instead of letting it ride, I would snap back at him and get into all sorts of arguments.

"Even in my younger days, if I scored five tries but missed a tackle, Dad would highlight the missed tackle. Kids need a bit of praise, although it certainly never did me any harm. The same attitude has rubbed off on me. That's why I'm so critical of myself now. You can trace it back to what Dad used to say to me."

Cameron Bell insists his son's aptitude for the game was evident at an almost embryonic age. Bell used to work on the Onehunga Wharf, when being a wharfie—or a freezing worker or on the rubbish trucks—was almost part and parcel of being a rugby league player. The wharfies and their families regularly had picnics and, whenever novelty races were run, there was a little blond-haired kid who would be way ahead in the midgets' contests.

If Cameron Bell hints at some athletic prowess in the family, he finds a ready reason for it. "We're actually related to the Walkers, that is to John Walker," says Cameron Bell. "John's grandfather had the same mother as my father! She married again—that's the connection."

By the time he was four, Dean was playing organised rugby league. "He absolutely loved it," says his father. "And he had a big advantage over most of the other kids in that he was gifted with speed. If you have speed at that age, what you do is go into dummy half, grab the ball and run. You end up scoring try after try and Dean would have scored something like 60 or 70 tries in a season, maybe even more."

It's often said by those who know Dean Bell's background in the game —and Hugh McGahan's one who expounds the theory—that he was brought up in the school of hard knocks; which explains why there's such an overwhelming toughness in his approach to playing rugby league. Cameron Bell knows that too.

"Tackling was my main strength as a player and it's also been one of Dean's strengths," he says. "I used to have fun with him in the back yard, letting him use me as a target to tackle. That hardened him up. It also helped Dean and Clayton that they played football among some guys who played the game hard. Some were a little older than Dean and Clayton, which meant they were playing with others who were physically more advanced and tougher than them. I'm sure it helped them."

It didn't provide much of an advantage for a youngster aiming to make Auckland representative teams, though. In fact, there are some parallels with Gary Freeman here. Freeman was barely an attraction for age group sides. Bell was only marginally more popular and that used to irk Cameron Bell.

"I definitely couldn't understand it, not simply because he was my son," says Cameron Bell. "I don't want to besmirch anybody but, in those days, it was a case of who you knew. I saw injustices being done to a lot of players at the time, not just Dean. There always has to be someone who misses out, of course, but kids cry when it happens to them, when they believe they might have had some chance.

"That was the case with Dean, and this went on and on as he still kept missing out on representative teams. One year Dean finally made it, only after another kid was dropped, and he was the player of the tournament."

Manukau were far more willing to go with the talented youngster, the then-coach Doug Gailey organising some guest appearances for Bell in the ex-Kiwis side which played school teams. With that sort of grooming, he was playing at senior level as a 17-year-old in 1979.

"Manukau always had a reputation for playing hard, uncompromising football and that rubbed off, especially when Doug Gailey was at the club," says Cameron Bell. "When I was still playing, the plan was the same just about every game. When the first scrum went down, Doug would throw

The Bell connection shows through in Manukau's championship-winning 11th open grade side in 1977. Dean Bell was the then 15-year-old captain. His father Cameron (far left, back row) was the team's manager and his uncle Tommy (far right, back row) was the coach.
Vernon H Clarke Studio

one at his opposite prop and I'd throw one through the legs at the hooker. There'd be a brawl and that would be the end of it."

Dean Bell doubted he was ready for senior football so soon. "It was a big jump and I wondered whether it was too early," he says. "I've done so many big things in my life but making that jump from junior football to first grade felt the biggest of them all. I was worried about the physical side of it, about being smashed up."

Bell's senior debut was no gently, gently proposition either. Manukau faced Glenora which, for Bell, meant marking Kiwi winger Dane O'Hara. "It was big enough playing first grade as it was, but then doing so against Dane O'Hara made it that much more demanding. I didn't do anything spectacular, although I did hold my own against him.

"The way Manukau played it in those times, I became a very fiery player, too fiery. I was quite wild in those days and I thought, if I'm going to prove my toughness, I had to be like that—which I learnt, of course, you don't have to be.

"I recall one game against Richmond. Doug Gailey told us it would be all on from the first scrum. I think that day Ian actually started it from the second row and I ran all the way from the wing on the far side of the field to get involved in the brawl. I hit Irvine Niukapu, the Richmond winger they used to call Uncle Remus.

The real deal as "The Greatest" takes on the pretenders, Dean Bell (left) and his cousin Wayne. NZ Herald

"Looking back now, I think, 'God, how stupid was that.' But those were the things you felt you were expected to do then. Wild days. You do grow up, though."

Bell adds he could have been seen as an easy target if he didn't show some aggression in those formative years. In his words, he was "a skinny white kid". A white-skinned Maori, that is. With blond hair, too.

Not afraid to mix it with anyone, the young Dean Bell also had a certain good-natured cockiness about him, never better illustrated than during a chance meeting with the man known as "The Greatest". It's the story behind an eye-catching photo which appeared in the *New Zealand Herald* during Muhammad Ali's visit to New Zealand in the late 1970s.

"I'd been to the movies with my cousin Wayne and we noticed a big commotion on the other side of the road with a big crowd gathered," says Bell. "So, we went to check out what was going on. We soon realised what it was—The Man himself, Muhammad.

"So, we just started walking in front of him, perving on his wife. She was a real pretty sort. We were only 17 or so and couldn't help ourselves.

"All of a sudden, from behind us Muhammad Ali said, 'Hey, you two boys in front of me—I want to fight you!' We spun around. We were startled. 'What! What!' 'I want to fight you. You've been perving on my lady, haven't you?'

"In a cheeky way, Wayne said, 'Yeah, yeah.' So a reporter who was there told us all to gather around and do a bit of shadow boxing. The next day it was on the front page of the *Herald*. I remember throwing one punch which caught Ali's hand and I was just amazed how enormous his hand was."

Bell's shadow boxing exhibition earned some admiration from the great man, although it wasn't about to win him a professional boxing contract. The earliest signs in Dean Bell's rugby league career were far more propitious. Through the grades he savoured championship-winning success with a number of Manukau teams and, after initial personal reservations about such an early introduction to first grade, he was obviously accomplished in that environment as well.

So many young players have been labelled internationals in the making. Dean Bell was another swiftly tagged likewise, only in his case it seemed more certain than in most instances. And Cameron Bell was one, above all others, who sensed as much.

father and son

Cameron Bell

As a parent you're always proud of your kids. In Dean's case, the reason for that pride happens to be very public; it's there for everyone to see. Not that Janice and I are the types to idolise Dean. Nothing like that at all. Of course it's a thrill to have a son who's achieved as much as Dean has—but it is a little bothersome when people insist on introducing you as, "Dean Bell's father"!

That's why a little story involving Dean and me is one I always bring up, and Dean never forgives me for it. Janice had returned to New Zealand for a holiday one year when I had the coaching job with Carlisle and, when she flew back to England, Dean and I went to Manchester Airport to pick her up.

Well, we were waiting upstairs when a guy ran over and asked, "Can I have your autograph?" Dean asked whether he had a pen, but the guy said, "I don't what your autograph—I want this man's autograph." Meaning mine. From that day on, Dean believes I set him up, that I found someone at the airport to do it. This bloke wanted the Carlisle coach's autograph, not Dean Bell's! And I never did find out that guy's name!

Still, it was a special thrill to come home again in 1994 and be part of the Warriors' arrival in 1995; to see Dean lead them into the Winfield Cup for the first time. That was great, but there have been other moments in Dean's career which I cherish even more. One of the proudest—in fact *the* proudest—for me was when Dean won his first Kiwi test jersey in 1983, especially because it was against the Australians.

The moment that left me with wet eyes, though, came when Dean was named "Man of Steel" for his efforts with Wigan in 1991–92. Knowing how difficult it is for non-British players to win awards in England, it was just so special. Janice and I were both there that night and when Dean was announced as the winner, a lump came to my throat. I really felt that was the ultimate recognition for him.

You think that's special, and then he gets the Lance Todd Trophy as man of the match in the 1993 Challenge Cup final. We were at Wembley for that, so another lump comes to your throat—and then we were there for Dean's *This is Your Life* programme in England as well. Still, the one that means the most to me will always be Dean's first test jersey.

To us, Dean was always going to go all the way. I firmly believed he had the talent, although you could never have dreamed it would come to this. And it was always going to be rugby league as well. It was in the blood.

Rugby Union figured very little in Dean's life, although he did make an Auckland representative team as a schoolboy. It was quite a process as well with something like five trial matches before the team was selected. At one of them, I recall the manager screaming out to Dean to kick the ball. He said there was only one thing wrong with "that fellow", and that was that he ran too much!

So, really it was rugby league all the way. Always with someone from the Bell clan around, and always a connection with the Manukau club. Through Dean's younger years, either my brothers Tommy and Dubbie, Bill Williams or I coached or managed teams he played in. Ian also coached them one year.

When I was still playing I had to juggle things around myself and, with a father and son involved in the same side, there were inevitably some problems. I guess you're a little harder on your own kids to a certain extent. Parents are parents. I don't think I was a screamer on the sideline—I'd hate to think I was—but I would think I was more than a little critical of Dean. I wouldn't chastise him in front of the others, more than likely I'd wait until we got home to do that.

He developed a hard edge to his game and I suppose he did get a few high shots away when he tackled. He might have got that off me! At least I waited until I was over 30 before I started going a little bit high! In fact, one year I was sent off five times in the season, so it was fairly hard for me to tell someone I was coaching to watch how he tackled. I was no role model for my young players!

Dean also had to toughen up as a kid brought up in South Auckland. I recall one time he was having some trouble with three guys who were always picking on him. On his way home from school, Dean would walk across a pipe over an estuary and these three would always be waiting for him on the other side. If he was ever caught, I told him he just had to belt one of them and, as they were bullies, the other two would soon want to be his friend. Well, that's just what happened. Dean hit one of them and, ridiculous as it sounds, they ended up being quite friendly with each other.

He was a tough kid, and became a tough player, but, if we ever go back to Manchester Airport, it might still be a case of "Cameron Bell's son"—not "Dean Bell's father".

Cameron Bell was a long time Manukau player, but had his greatest successes as a coach. After coaching Manukau teams, he was Auckland coach in 1988 and 1989, achieving success against Great Britain and Australia as well as Winfield Cup side Eastern Suburbs. He signed as coach with Carlisle in England in 1990 before finishing up in 1994, when he returned home and took on the New Zealand Maori coaching position.

from glory to despair

Our greatest glory is not never falling —
but rising every time we fall.

Defeat doesn't always equate with shame, let alone humiliation. Many sporting losses come with honour intact, those times when maximum effort hasn't been quite enough to overcome superior opponents. Less common is the ability to savour genuine glory in defeat. Which is precisely what the Warriors were able to do despite their 25–22 reverse against Brisbane.

It added another chapter to Dean Bell's catalogue of losses which could be classed outside the norm. One of his 26 tests was like that; it was the 1985 clash against the Australians when John Ribot—who would become Super League's boss—stole what had seemed deserved and certain victory from the Kiwis with a soul-destroying try at Carlaw Park. The park had the air of a morgue, but that performance belongs among the most exceptional losing displays.

The Ericsson experience was of the same genre, if on another level. There was no funereal atmosphere after it, other than in the Warriors' dressing-room. Instead the so-called losers were hailed on all fronts; the administration for delivering an exceptional opening night's entertainment to celebrate the Warriors' arrival, and the players and coaching staff for producing an outstanding football product.

This organisation clearly had class oozing from all sides. The crowd felt satiated, with the scoreboard result not even a consideration, and the armchair viewers must have been just as suitably satisfied. After all, TV2's coverage had an average rating of 33, peaking at 37; that translated to an audience of one million, a 70 per cent share of those watching television at that time. And the match was also a ratings winner on Australian television.

There didn't seem to be a soul around who failed to extract some enjoyment from the night, but perhaps the supreme accolade came from the man who lost most through the Warriors' birth.

For years, the previously named Mt Smart Stadium had been John

Dean Bell lapped up the afterglow of the Brisbane performance, but he was realistic enough to know the Warriors weren't on easy street. Ross Land (Fotopress)

Walker's home. He'd run his 100th sub four-minute mile there, and the track had been named in his honour. The track was all but obliterated by the seating erected across it, and that wasn't something which had been too warmly received by Auckland's track and field community. John Walker excepted, that is.

He was part of the Ericsson Stadium crowd on 10 March, sitting with fellow New Zealand athlete and champion javelin thrower Mike O'Rourke. Walker certainly wasn't weeping about his track's effective demise; he was simply amazed the way the stadium had been transformed.

"So much for Mt Smart and my track," he smiled. "I think it's fabulous what they've done. It's the greatest thing that's happened to sport in Auckland. It's just a wasted complex otherwise. It's about putting bums on seats."

That was before the game. Afterwards he insisted he'd return: "It was brilliant. Everyone who came here tonight—they'll be back, too. I believe this has set an example for other sports. They need to follow it or else they're going to be left behind."

And O'Rourke's post-match analysis neatly encapsulated what everyone thought as well: "The result was as good as a win."

Indeed it was, and Dean Bell didn't begrudge anyone basking in the afterglow of the display which had put the Warriors on course. But Bell, ever the realist and hard-nosed professional, knew all the reflected glory had provided nothing tangible, outside goodwill. At the end of the day, the Warriors had started the season with a zero in the win column, a one in the loss column and no championship points. Strip it naked and a loss is still a loss.

Back in the real world, the Warriors had to wake up on the Saturday morning after Friday night's excitement and accept the reality of Winfield Cup life—and that's the fact that you have to get back up every week, whether it's after a win, draw or loss. That, almost as much as the opposition, is the test.

And even more so for the Warriors. They'd savoured and relished the comfort of playing at home. An away trip for them would be more demanding than most team's in the competition. The travel factor came into the equation. Not just a bus trip up the road somewhere but the irritating demands of international air travel, of assembling and waiting at airports and then the flight itself. It doesn't sound like much. In truth it's more exacting than might be imagined.

Of course, the matter of the opposition and their treasured home environments had to be considered as well. On the Winfield Cup scene, some away games are more threatening than others—like Newcastle at Marathon Stadium, Canberra at Bruce Stadium, Cronulla at Caltex Field, Illawarra at Steelers Stadium, Norths at North Sydney Oval and Brisbane at ANZ Stadium. The fact was, the Warriors had all of those except Bruce Stadium on their 1995 schedule. They also escaped the ordeal of travelling trans-Tasman and trans-Australia to face the Western Reds in Perth.

Coach John Monie offered his players no comfort for their second Winfield Cup outing either. "John told us a couple of days after the Brisbane match that he actually thought Illawarra were going to give us a harder game than the Broncos," says Bell. "And how right he was."

Monie knew the Winfield Cup landscape after all his years coaching at Parramatta—nine in all, including six with the Eels' first grade side from 1984–89. With that knowledge, he'd pieced together the best possible squad he could for the Warriors, but always he conceded that the unknown was how the players would overcome their collective lack of Winfield Cup experience.

In certain areas, that vital experience was there. After all, Greg Alexander could count almost 200 first grade appearances with Penrith, Phil Blake had more than 200 for a selection of clubs and Sean Hoppe, Stephen Kearney, Manoa Thompson, Gavin Hill and Dean Bell himself had all played more than 30 Winfield Cup matches.

But the first grade squad which emerged early in 1995 revealed Winfield Cup rookies in Whetu Taewa, Tony Tuimavave, Tony Tatupu, Duane Mann,

Double-teaming in the tackle as Duane Mann (top) and Tony Tuimavave (bottom) envelop Brisbane's Kerrod Walters. The Warriors didn't produce enough of the same to win their debut match. Nigel Marple (Fotopress)

Hitro Okesene and Se'e Solomona, while Gene Ngamu and Tea Ropati could boast only minimal exposure.

"John kept me informed with all the main signings when I was still in England, but, like me, he knew he wouldn't know how all the players would react until we'd all been in the trenches together," says Bell. "Okay, he knew what the Wigan players were capable of, but in the first year he was going to learn a lot about so many players who were new to him. He knew he'd have to make a decision about some players at the end of the season because they hadn't come up to the standard he'd expected.

"The most critical signing to me was Greg Alexander, first and foremost. I believe you should start your team with a quality halfback. You need a really good one and Greg fitted the bill. I came up against him when I was at Easts and he scored a freakish try for Penrith against us. I knew he was a good signing. I didn't think he would come to New Zealand but when I knew he definitely was, I was rapt. He was so obviously a class player.

"Steve Kearney was also important. I was really impressed with him

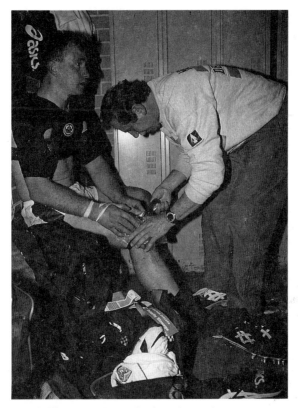

Football's an exacting and exhausting assignment at any time. But Dean Bell felt absolutely drained in the excessive heat against Illawarra in Wollongong.
Andrew Cornaga (Photosport)

when he toured Britain with the Kiwis in 1993 so his signing pleased me, and Sean Hoppe was in the same category. To get Denis Betts signed was vital as well, plus Andy Platt and Frano Botica.

"Whetu Taewa was another one. I knew him from the Kiwis' tour to Britain and France in 1989 but, when I'd asked John whether Whetu was still playing, he didn't know who I meant. The following week John had signed him!"

Taewa had excelled in the Warriors' pre-season shakedown, earning the left winger's spot in first grade and retaining it in an all but unchanged starting line-up for the Illawarra assignment. The one change was in the front row, with big former Kiwi prop Se'e Solomona replacing another former international Gavin Hill.

Steelers Stadium was a searingly hot arena for the Warriors, with the temperature reading 30 degrees plus (over 86° Fahrenheit) on Saturday, 18 March. And for too much of the time, the Aucklanders were roasted by

Illawarra's attack. Not that they were ever hopelessly out of touch on the scoreboard.

Illawarra led 22–12 at halftime, yet the Warriors had still contributed to a memorable spell of attacking football with two more Phil Blake tries. The Steelers were just a little sharper again, none more so than their large prop Darren Fritz, once regarded as the ultimate hot and cold performer in his time with Canberra.

Twice Sean Hoppe sliced Illawarra's lead to just six points in the second half and, after it had again been stretched to 12 points by the third of Brett Rodwell's four tries, replacement Tea Ropati's try again had it back to six at 34–28 with eight minutes left. A draw was on as the Warriors attacked, only for Hitro Okesene to spill the ball near the line and allow Illawarra to escape from the danger zone to lay on Rodwell's fourth of the day.

At 40–28 it was undoubtedly a thriller, 12 tries and 68 points in all, but the concern for theWarriors was that five tries wasn't enough to provide a winning edge. Clearly their defence was at fault, wilting as it did in what was excessive heat—and, to add to the embarrassment, in front of a live television audience through the ABC network.

"Starting the year off, we knew we would lose our share of games," says Bell. "What hurt about the loss to Illawarra was the manner of it— falling off tackles and basic errors. A lot of that came back to the heat. It was just so hot and I know I felt so drained. Afterwards I was gasping and I thought to myself, 'Those forwards must be finding it tough in this heat if I feel like this.'

"You would make a run and feel so drained. You couldn't recover and they kept coming at us. We couldn't keep our defensive line together. We needed to be more acclimatised to the heat but how do you do that?

"Our jerseys were also a problem. The fact we played in the blue strip against Illawarra was mentioned as a factor in how the heat affected us. The point was made that we should have been playing in our alternate white strip.

"But it really wasn't so much the colour that was the problem then, it was the fabric, and how big and heavy the jerseys were. When they got wet with sweat, they just dragged on you even more. It felt like you were playing with a great big duvet wrapped around you. It really was a problem and one that should have been addressed before the Winfield Cup itself started."

But the most significant problem for the Warriors was the largest man on the field—Darren Fritz. And that's what ate away at John Monie.

"John had said to us, 'Watch that Fritz. He can either be brilliant or he can be the most ordinary player on the field. But he has to be watched.' We didn't heed his advice and Fritz walked all over us," says Bell.

"Brett Rodwell was a problem, too. He hardly ever receives the ball in his backline position. You watch him and whoever takes the ball up in the forwards, who's next to him? It's Rodwell, ready to run off him. He backs up well. He's not often in his position but it didn't really matter that day."

Two matches, two defeats. Scratch below the surface of the results and there were redeeming features. Despite back-to-back reverses, the Warriors had immediately revealed an obvious strength—their attacking prowess; they'd totalled 50 points in the two games and scored nine tries.

But the defence? Well, it was beginning to resemble a sieve. It had yielded 65 points including 11 tries, which went right against John Monie's coaching philosophy. He approves of and encourages flexibility on attack but he's totally inflexible on defence.

"When John came to Wigan he tightened our defence up, even more so than Graham Lowe had achieved when he was coach," says Bell. "Defence has to be right, and I know there has to be so much emphasis on it if you're going to have a winning side. So John was very disappointed with the defence in those first two games, telling us we wouldn't win many games if we were going to give away that many points every time we played.

"We can all handle losses as such, but we just let in too many points, especially against Illawarra."

The pre-season build-up had actually hinted at some defensive problems, even against Canterbury and Auckland. While it had worked well enough in the Tooheys Challenge clash against Norths and also in the trial against Canberra, it was really flawed when the Warriors had another trial against the Western Reds. By halftime they trailed 40–10 and shades of that display were clearly defined at Steelers Stadium.

"It's all about application and attitude," says Bell. "And to be able to play at such a high level each week is not something many of the guys were used to. Realistically it was always going to be a problem for us, knowing how to defend and maintain those standards consistently."

But just as the try-scoring touch had been an early positive, so too was the emergence of some unlikely early-season stars. The most notable of them was unquestionably Hitro "The Hit Man" Okesene.

"Hitro had a great start to the season and even in that loss to Illawarra his effort couldn't really be faulted," says Bell. "I knew a bit about Hitro before coming home. He'd played at Carlisle when Dad was coaching there and I'd watched a couple of games he'd played there. I'd also seen some video footage of him. But he was certainly a different player from what I'd seen when he was at Carlisle. He was a bonus. He'd been signed as maybe a back-up hooker or second rower to play mainly in reserve grade, and there he was doing a good job for us at prop. He was also a real crowd pleaser from the outset with his no-fear charges—a good sort of player to have in your side."

The other notable unexpected success was Tony Tuimavave, who had played a lot of representative football for Auckland and, on earliest evidence, had shown enough promise to suggest he'd become a Kiwi test

*Fearless Hitro Okesene, an early-season surprise success
for the Warriors and one of the few players to impress in
the scratchy display against Illawarra.*
Ross Setford (Fotopress)

player. But up to 1995 that hadn't happened and, in fact, there was a general feeling that Tuimavave had become just another player; a variety of factors even saw him slide off the scene at local level. Then, in a move which generated much surprise, Tuimavave was revealed as a Warriors signing. Plenty of league people questioned the wisdom of it and almost everyone was reconciled to the fact that Tuimavave would be a reserve grade regular. How wrong.

"Again he was a player I hadn't seen an awful lot of, having been out of the country for so long and, even in a couple of early trial games, I just didn't think Tony was quite there. A good trier but that was all," says Bell. "Well, he made me eat my words, not to mention quite a few other people's as well I imagine. He just knuckled down to do some hard work and started to play some very good football for us."

In a side brimming with names like Bell, Alexander, Blake, Hoppe, Ropati, Kearney and Mann, another name which initially didn't impress those with a more general league interest was second rower Tony Tatupu. They soon changed their minds, for Tatupu was an instant eye-catcher.

"Tony was definitely a player I had earmarked. He could do things with the ball. A very elusive player, he obviously had the physique, the talent and speed to be anything. It didn't surprise to see him make the starting line-up, not like Tony Tuimavave."

The Illawarra defeat still brought more negatives than positives into focus though. And for the team management and more senior players it was a painful and rushed trip home from Wollongong.

To make their connections, the Warriors' first grade players were required to rush directly from the field to their bus—via the very quickest of showers. A dash to Sydney barely enabled them to make their connection with the plane to Auckland. It was, ultimately, a perfectly executed operation, infinitely more so than the performance at Steelers Stadium. Dean Bell felt the pain of defeat all the way to Auckland and beyond.

"I mulled over it. There were a few of us at the back of the plane who did—Sean, Gene, me and some others. We felt then that the world had ended, or was about to. Some of the others got on the drink, perhaps to drown their sorrows."

John Monie, though, proved to be more philosophical about it.

"John, as a rule, is not one to over-react but he quite surprised me after this one," says Bell. "I thought we'd be in for a right rollicking at the team meeting on Monday night but it didn't happen, and he really impressed me the way he reacted. He was so calm. He pointed out we weren't far off winning that game, which we weren't and that we all knew the problem areas in any case. I thought I had John reasonably well figured out, certainly better than most because I'd worked with him for a few years.

"While he was remarkably cool, that's not to say he had no criticism at all. What did annoy him was that all week before the game he'd mentioned Darren Fritz as the big danger, which he certainly was in the end. John had done his job by emphasising to us how important it was that we looked after Fritz but we hadn't carried out his instructions. So, he had every right to be angry.

"We didn't feel the public were too upset about the defeat, or the manner of it either. After all, they'd been conditioned not to expect the world from us, and we didn't expect too much of ourselves either. I mean, we were new to this. There was a time when I was worried about the way the Warriors were being marketed, that we were being looked at to make a huge impression. In the end, though, I think most people were understanding.

"Of course, as a professional I would have preferred to win those first two matches and every game we played. But, despite two defeats, I could see more than a glimmer of hope from what we'd done."

But even though the season was only two games old that glimmer would have to become something more tangible very soon. After all, long losing sequences hadn't been a common experience ever since he'd graduated to representative football.

creating a kiwi

Nothing can stop the man with the right mental attitude from achieving his goal; nothing on earth can help the man with the wrong mental attitude.

Wigan folk have a special affinity with New Zealand rugby league talent, which isn't the least surprising. True enough, some more than useful Australians have graced Central Park over the last 10 years or so, players like John "Chicka" Ferguson, Brett Kenny, Ian Roberts, Phil Blake, Les Davidson, Gene Miles and Andrew Farrar. And a coach by the name of John Monie, too. But the New Zealand connection has been more pronounced since the days when former Kiwi captain—and now Wigan coach—Graeme West made the club his permanent base. Howie Tamati had a brief stint there, while Kevin and Tony Iro, Adrian Shelford, Frano Botica, Sam Panapa, Va'aiga Tuigamala and Henry Paul all had, or still have, firm links. Not to mention Dean Bell, of course, or a coach by the name of Graham Lowe.

Yet, while Bell became a sporting god in the league-hungry town, there's another New Zealander who rivals his status in Wigan; some old timers argue he's even more revered. Which is why Wigan people couldn't quite work Dean Bell out when he arrived in 1986.

"The first thing people would ask was, 'Do you know Ces?' They meant Ces Mountford, who was such a hero at Central Park," says Bell.

"All I would say was, 'Yeah, I know him.' And I'd leave it at that. They wanted me to go on about him, to gush about him, but I wouldn't."

He wasn't about to explain himself either. It wouldn't have been the right thing to do. But the truth is Mountford, who was a stickler for discipline, and Dean Bell, who tended to bend the rules back then, weren't such warm friends in 1982. Without putting too fine a point on it, Mountford put an end to Bell's goal of advancing from promising player to international that year. Along with his uncle Ian and cousin Clayton Friend, the Manukau youngster had been eyeing a spot in the Kiwi team to tour

Dean Bell, Auckland club footballer. The Manukau centre
charges through Mt Albert's defence as he helps his club team
to victory in the Roope Rooster knockout competition.
Auckland Star

Australia and Papua New Guinea. And, to most observers, Dean Bell appealed as a walk-up start to be included.

He missed out, though. His fault, he readily concedes. But there has always been some lingering resentment about what happened the week he was within a beer or two of becoming a Kiwi.

"We were in camp for the Kiwi trial to pick the team for that tour," says Bell. "And, the night before the trial, all the experienced guys said, 'Let's go out for a few beers.' Apparently we were told not to, but, of course, a youngster aged 20 couldn't resist, could he? I wanted to prove I was one of the boys.

"It wasn't late when we all arrived back at the motel but Ian and I were the only ones spotted. We were singled out, unfairly we thought, although we obviously weren't about to nark on the others.

"We knew the worst the next morning when we were both reprimanded and told we'd be having only half a game each in the trial. Ian knew straight away that we had no chance of making the team so he pulled out. I wanted to do the same but he told me not to, that I still had a chance and that my career was out in front of me.

"I had a knee problem—I'd severed the posterior cruciate ligament in a club match for Manukau—but still played and thought I didn't do too badly. I genuinely believed I still had a chance so, when my name wasn't read out, I was devastated. But it was a lesson learnt."

The contrast that night at the Ellerslie Rugby League Club was all too obvious. Among the gathering were two elated mothers, Lucy McGahan and Cathy Friend, whose sons had both made the Kiwis for the first time. But Cathy Friend's elation was tempered by the fact her brother Ian and especially her nephew Dean had been given the not-to-be-picked treatment. It all helps explain why Dean Bell never was keen to shoot the breeze with Wigan people about Ces Mountford and his legendary exploits for the Riversiders in the 1940s.

"I was in the wrong, I know that—but it wasn't as though we were the only ones. I don't know whether it was the Bell name that counted against me, but I wasn't seen in a favourable light then," says Bell.

If Mountford and the Kiwi selectors didn't want him, there were other avenues open. Bell had a sizzling year for Manukau—he was Auckland's second top tryscorer with 20—and, together with Ian Bell and his cousin Clayton, he started looking for an overseas club to play for. David Robinson, one of New Zealand Rugby League's board of directors, became the key man, scouting around for an English club which would take on three New Zealanders for the 1982–83 season.

Kiwi scrumhalf Shane Varley, who had spent the 1981–82 English season with Workington Town, recommended trying Carlisle. In the far north close to the Scottish border, Carlisle had only just come into existence and, in its first year, had won promotion to the first division for the 1982–83 season.

David Robinson negotiated the deal, setting in place a Kiwi link with Carlisle which was later revived when Dean's father was coach there. At one time or another, future Warriors Hitro Okesene and Mike Dorreen were Carlisle players. Clayton Friend returned to play for his uncle and other New Zealanders contracted included Brad Hepi and Brett Iti.

For Ian and Dean Bell, plus Friend, the 1982–83 Carlisle exercise was as much a means to see some of the world as it was about playing football.

"It certainly wasn't about making money," says Bell. "They paid our air fares, gave us accommodation and provided a car between the three of us. The money was only £1,000 each after we'd played 20 games. As it was, after we'd played our 20, we had bills to pay—but they couldn't pay us our fees. The club was in that much trouble.

"We have since got that money, I must give them that. The directors honoured the debt, paying us in instalments over the years, £200 here and there."

They were known as the 'Carlisle Kiwis'. Above: Clayton Friend (left), Ian Bell and Dean Bell at their home for the 1982–83 English season. Below: Dean Bell launching for a try against Halifax, one of 11 he scored during the season for Carlisle. Dean Bell Collection

The football experience did the three of them no harm, particularly Bell, who revelled in the chance to play among some top company. Ironically, too, his first outing for Carlisle was a Lancashire Cup game—against Wigan.

"We had a fantastic time playing football—and a fantastic time when we weren't playing football," says Bell. "Our house became the main nightclub in Carlisle. It was one big party."

Those months in Carlisle also brought a more tangible reward, his wife-to-be Jackie. "It happened the very first day we were there," says Bell. "There'd been some media coverage about our arrival and we were a bit conspicuous in our tracksuits walking in the street.

"Apparently, Jackie's mate saw us and said, 'That must be those Kiwis out there,' Jackie evidently looked and said, 'Oooh, I'll have the blond one!' And hasn't that turned out to be true!"

A couple of nights later they physically met for the first time at a pub. It was the beginning of a liaison which revolved around football, both then and even more so now. Yet, ironically, Jackie had only begun to take an interest in rugby league the year before when the Carlisle club had started up.

Bell chose an unorthodox way to impress his future in-laws. The first time Jackie took them to watch Dean play was a home match against St Helens—and he obliged by being ordered off for fighting.

"It wasn't always like that, though. I did get off that one," he says. "But the football experience was vital in helping forge a reputation for myself overseas at least."

What it also did was to fortify Dean Bell for the 1983 season back home when he was desperate to achieve what Ces Mountford and the Kiwi selectors had denied him in 1982. It helped, of course, that Mountford no longer had the job.

Newly arrived as Kiwi coach was a man who would have perhaps the most profound effect of any coach on Dean Bell's footballing career— Graham Lowe. And an early chance to impress the new coach, courtesy of Bell's Aunty Bub and his father, mightn't have done him any harm.

Cameron Bell recalls: "A big help for Manukau, and especially for Dean and Clayton, was having Graham Lowe at a training run in 1983. My sister Bub told me Graham had been back home for a few weeks doing nothing and she thought I should invite him to our training. Sure, I thought! Graham Lowe, the Kiwi coach, coming to our training! I couldn't imagine it but when I rang Graham, he said he'd love to.

"What was good for Graham about that session was that there were good players, like Dean and Clayton, whom we could work with personally. He brought a knowledge with him, and a lot of things we didn't know about."

What he was as much as anything was a new face and image for New Zealand league, a coach of proven quality at club level now making the significant step up to test level. He ultimately became a unifying force for league in New Zealnd, a charismatic type who generated a new feeling of excitement.

The Kiwis hadn't beaten Australia in 13 tests, since the 24–3 Carlaw Park walkover in 1971; they hadn't managed even one try in their last four clashes against the Aussies heading into the 1983 series. By now, though, New Zealand had a collection of overseas-based professionals who promised a competitive campaign at last.

Dean Bell was hellbent on being part of it, although he still had some doubts. "Much as I wanted my first Kiwi jersey, I still didn't think Graham would put me in against Australia," he says. "I thought he might consider it too big a gamble."

He was wrong. The 21-year-old was named on the left wing for the first test at Carlaw Park, along with some of the biggest names in the game—Mark Graham, Kurt Sorensen, Dane Sorensen, Mark Broadhurst, Olsen Filipaina (who later withdrew with injury), Fred Ah Kuoi, James Leuluai, Gary Kemble and Dane O'Hara (who also withdrew). But even more daunting for Bell was the thought of marking the great Kerry Boustead, just one of the outstanding players in a power-packed Australian line-up which included Peter Sterling, Wally Lewis, Steve Rogers, Mal Meninga, Eric Grothe, Max Krilich and Paul Vautin.

"It wasn't something I told anyone about, but with that first test jersey I'd reached a goal in my mind," says Bell. "I had crawled under the fence at Carlaw Park to watch a Kiwi test one year when I was younger and thought to myself, 'I want to play in front of this sort of atmosphere one day.' So, when I ran out for that test I'd achieved that goal."

Lowe had proved an innovative coach when leading Otahuhu to championship success in 1977 and 1978. He was back home after a four-year spell with Norths in the Brisbane competition and, when he brought his first Kiwi test squad together, he seemed to put extra effort into Bell.

"He worked us so hard that week. And he really got into me about coming up into the defensive line, dropping back for kicks, then coming back into the line if they spin it. It was my positional play. He went over and over it with me, working on me so hard I even thought he was picking on me a bit."

But for all the preparation and anticipation, this Kiwi side didn't quite stay with the Australians in the first test. The five-year, four-test try drought was broken with a superb James Leuluai try off a short ball from Kurt Sorensen. With the score locked at 4–4, the decisive moment of the match came with the Kiwis deep on attack early in the second half; a pass was spilled, swooped on by the Australians and seconds later the awesome Eric Grothe was dashing 85 metres for his team's first try. A Steve Rogers try then secured Australia's 16–4 victory, although, in defeat, the young winger from Manukau had impressed.

"I was more concerned about my own game that day, about not letting the team down," says Bell. "I felt I handled Kerry Boustead fairly well. I figured he was a bit quicker than me so all I could do was make sure he didn't get too much room to move in. I was fairly quiet on attack but just happy to contain Boustead."

The watershed test for New Zealand rugby league was just weeks away. In fact, any list of famous New Zealand sporting victories over the last 20 years should automatically include the event at Brisbane's Lang Park on 9 July 1983.

Both sides had lost important players through injury. The Kiwis were without captain Mark Graham and fullback Gary Kemble, meaning Graeme West returned as captain and the volatile Nick Wright was brought in at fullback. The Australians had lost Steve Rogers and Peter Sterling, although they did have Ray Price back.

It was a test which was just about perfect for New Zealand. An early Eric Grothe try suggested gloom ahead—until the Kiwis hatched their stunning scrum move which put West over. And dazzling second half tries to James Leuluai and winger Joe Ropati had the New Zealanders hurtling to a breakthrough 19–12 win, ending the years of desolation. It was also a test which went so much further than the normal training routines and the on-the-field football. This was the match which introduced Graham Lowe as a coach on another level.

"It's the test that'll always be remembered as the 'tears of joy' test," says Bell. "Lowie showed us a tape of the New Zealand rowing eight on the victory dais at the 1972 Olympics. There was no sound, just the pictures. He wanted us to watch their faces, and their tears, telling us we could also experience the tears of joy.

"At the time I was thinking, 'Oh, come on Lowie. This is a tough rugby league player here. What are you talking about?' Little did I know that after that test I'd be absolutely bawling my eyes out.

"It's always difficult for me putting everything in perspective because I've been able to achieve so much. But looking back, that victory in 1983 and what happened afterwards was one of the most awesome feelings I've experienced in my life. To beat the Australians so early in my career was what made it so special."

Special, too, was a memorable tackle by Bell's Manukau team-mate Nick Wright, the one when he stopped a try-bound Mal Meninga. Wright was a rugby league rebel, thought to be classified "not-to-tour-again" by the New Zealand Rugby League. Lowe, though, had coached him at Otahuhu and always knew how to extract the best from him.

"Picking Nicky for that test again showed up Lowie's initiative," says Bell. "Nicky never got on with officials but Graham gave him his chance, and look what he did? Graham knew how to cope with him."

Where defence had been Bell's priority against Australia, year one as a

A family treat for the Bells, sharing in the Kiwis' shock win over the Australians at Lang Park in 1983. Back Row: Gary Prohm, Howie Tamati, Ron O'Regan, James Leuluai, Mark Broadhurst. Middle Row: Nick Wright, Shane Varley, Joe Ropati, Ian Bell, Dean Bell, Gordon Smith. Front Row: Jim Campbell (manager), Kurt Sorensen, Graeme West (captain), Graham Lowe (coach), Fred Ah Kuoi, Dane Sorensen, Glenn Gallagher (physiotherapist).
Sidney Riley

test footballer was to provide a try-scoring flourish at the end. Bell had impressed with his attacking quality for Auckland earlier in the year, playing four of their five matches and scoring six tries. He was also a potent weapon at club level, producing a magical try as Manukau beat Mt Albert to win the final of the Roope Rooster knockout competition, one of Auckland's most famous club trophies.

So, in a more attacking frame of mind, a one-off Carlaw Park test against international lightweights Papua New Guinea promised a far more comfortable ride for Bell. His hunger for tryline was quenched as he scored three times in a 60–20 win; tries which, on a scale of genuine quality, may not rate highly among Bell's 11 test touchdowns.

In the normal scheme of things, three tries would have represented a fair return whatever the opposition. Not in this particular test, though. That's because Hugh McGahan bagged a world record six himself! "That's a great achievement. It didn't matter that it was against Papua New Guinea. It was unique," says Bell. "It certainly swallowed up my effort, and I was quite proud I had scored three. But I was happy that the test helped me with my confidence on attack."

The match had another astonishing aspect. Hugh McGahan's world record stands a fair chance of being beaten as new countries enter the test arena, but the family combination the Kiwis had on the field might be more difficult to emulate, let alone surpass. This was the test which had Ian Bell in the front row, Clayton Friend at scrumhalf and Dean Bell in the centres, New Zealand boasting an uncle and two nephews in the same test side.

That was a thrill for the Bell clan, but what Dean Bell felt was most rewarding from his earliest test experiences could be summed up in the name Graham Lowe.

"The role he played as a motivator was something else," says Bell. "I'd never looked at the game the way Graham did. Sometimes it was just simple things he'd say to you like, 'If you're going to clean your car, you want to do it better than your next door neighbour—to do it the best.' He taught us to apply that attitude to our football.

"I'd never analysed the game that way, or any sport. Before I was always trying to be the best I could when I played but, with his approach and motivational ploys, he opened my eyes to why I should try to be the best.

"I had always thought coaches were meant to be there for their tactical expertise, so for Graham to come across the way he did was just so amazingly different. It gave me a new way of looking at and approaching the game.

"But don't ever let it be said that Graham Lowe was just a motivator. That's so wrong. It just happened that as well as being an outstanding tactical coach he was an exceptional motivator. He'd shown that at Otahuhu and in Brisbane [with Norths]—now he was doing it with the Kiwis."

It was but the beginning for Graham Lowe and Dean Bell, though; merely the early stages of an association which was set to continue for six years as coach and player, and which continues today as friends and mutual admirers.

the best player I ever coached

Graham Lowe

Of all the players I've been involved with, Dean Bell is the best all-round back I've coached. I say that without hesitation, and bearing in mind all the great players I've been privileged to coach at test, state and club levels.

Dean was one of the first players to come to my attention when I returned home as Kiwi coach in 1983. Bill Sorensen had said to me, "Just have a look at this kid when you get a chance." He was just class. Anyone could see that.

Dean was playing in the centres for Manukau in Auckland and I suppose he was a little too enthusiastic back then. So, we (the New Zealand selectors) decided to place him on the wing in the 1983 series against Australia, essentially because he hadn't quite reached the level of being a truly disciplined centre. I even did the same when Dean came to Wigan in 1986–87. You see, Dean was more a runner than anything then: he hadn't refined or mastered the centre's game.

All the same, there were still enormous advantages playing him on the wing, one of them being his cover defence. It was just Terminator stuff. It could have been argued that some of his tackles were questionable, but at least Dean used to stop opponents.

What always sticks in my mind was talking to Artie Beetson when he was looking for a centre for Eastern Suburbs. When he asked me what I thought of Dean I told Artie he had the potential to be another Reg Gasnier. It was probably a couple of years later that Artie told me, "I agree—but Reg Gasnier never tackled from the throat up!"

Now, Dean certainly wasn't your classic round the ankles tackler then. I'm his biggest fan, but I don't think there were too many bad calls that went against him for high shots. Normally the guy he tackled felt a lot worse than Dean did after he'd been suspended! That didn't stay with him, of course. The reason was obvious—he became a professional, and one of the best professionals in the business.

When I went to Wigan, Maurice Lindsay said I could have the choice of who I wanted to sign for the club and, rather than some big established name, I told him I wanted Dean Bell. Dean wasn't too well known at Central Park then, but within about six weeks he had become a Central Park favourite.

One of Dean's main assets as he developed was that he became such a superb communicator on the field. You noticed the difference with the Warriors when he wasn't on the field in 1995; they suffered without his communication skills. And tough? Just so tough! His ability to withstand discomfort and pain is unbelievable. For courageous acts I've seen, two stand out above all others. One was when Mark Graham went back on the field with a broken cheekbone in the first test against Great Britain at Headingley in 1985. The other involved Dean Bell earlier that year.

He'd been forced to leave the field with a serious knee injury in the second test against Australia and was given no chance by anyone of being ready for the last test just a week later. Well, he defied everyone. It took some outstanding work from our physio Glenn Gallagher as well, but it mostly came down to Dean's sheer willpower. He'd told me not to count him out and, on the morning of the match, he convinced us he would be able to play. I don't know how he managed it but he did. And that was the test we won 18–0.

What you came to appreciate when coaching Dean, was that you couldn't hope to have anyone better going into battle for you. He had an ability to look you in the eye and say, "Don't worry. We'll be right." When that happened you never had the slightest reason to doubt him. I can't recall him ever putting in a substandard performance. He wasn't capable of it, whether he was playing in front of four people or 90,000 at Wembley.

If he had one slight fault it was that he could be too hard on himself, too self-critical. And when that's the only flaw you can find, it explains why I rate Dean Bell so highly...above all the others. On the score of all-round back play, no one can compare with him. He was complete.

Graham Lowe was New Zealand coach from 1983–86, registering series wins over Great Britain and France plus test victories against Australia in 1983 and a record 18–0 success in 1985 (New Zealand's first test wins over the Aussies since 1971). He also coached Oceania (1984) and Rest of the World (1988). He was the first non-Australian to coach a State of Origin side, taking Queensland to a series win in 1991. He also coached Otahuhu in Auckland (1977–78), Norths in Brisbane (1979–82), Wigan (1986–89) and Manly (1990–92). For the 1995 World Cup, he coached Western Samoa and was signed as North Queensland Cowboys' coach for 1996.

learning to win—and count

Mistakes are a fact of life. It is the response to the error that counts.

It was a Monday morning and Dean Bell's head told him he'd had a good night. Understandably, too, because, for the first time in three attempts, he'd become a winning captain for the Warriors.

For a player whose diet at Wigan was constant success, the thought of on-going failure would have been unacceptable. So, when the Warriors cracked it against Western Suburbs in their second home game of the season at Ericsson Stadium, Bell was as elated as anyone.

The Aucklanders had shaken Brisbane and then been pummelled by Illawarra, but those results were irrelevant on 26 March 1995. The fact was the Warriors had not only delivered two Winfield Cup competition points but had done so emphatically as they scored eight tries—Phil Blake with four—to hammer Wests 46–12.

Bell, the consummate professional, isn't one to indulge in too much post-match celebrating these days but he did that Sunday night, and was paying for it the next morning. Reliving the magic provided relief as he watched a video of the game, and he couldn't help but be impressed.

"After the game I said to the boys, 'Savour the moment', because it was our first win," says Bell. "It meant a lot to all of us and we all went out and had a good night.

"I like watching a video of the game the next day, just to see what we did so I'm prepared for our Monday night team meeting when John [Monie] goes over the game.

"And I'd just finished watching it on that Monday when Jim Marr [from *Rugby League Week*] rang and said, 'I think you might have lost the points.' I said something like, 'You're joking, aren't you?', checking the date on my watch to make sure it wasn't April Fool's Day. He told me it sounded like we'd used too many replacements. I was devastated.

"Even then I didn't think it was going to cost us our points, but evidently

*Tea Ropati goes to the blood bin, forcing one of the five
replacements that led to the Warriors losing their two
competition points for their win over Western Suburbs.*
Nigel Marple (Fotopress)

there'd been two cases before and teams had been penalised."

Unbeknown to Bell, the facts had become known early on Monday morning when checks showed the Warriors had used five replacements against Wests, one more than the permitted maximum of four.

Syd Eru and Martin Moana went on as a double interchange in the first half, Manoa Thompson was a blood bin replacement for Tea Ropati, Willie Poching a blood bin replacement for Tony Tatupu and big Joe Vagana came off the interchange bench as the fifth replacement late in the match.

Warriors chief executive Ian Robson and football manager Laurie Stubbing believed the wording of the replacement rule relating to blood bin cases was ambiguous, leading to the confusion. Stubbing said the coaching staff had read, and re-read, the rules before deciding they were right to put Vagana on.

"I went to training on Monday afternoon and found everyone looking cheerful after the win—until I told a couple of them that it looked like we'd lost the points," says Bell. "The word got around and I can still see Tony Tuimavave now. He just sat down against a wall, staring for an hour without moving. He was blown away, in a state of shock.

48

"We stuffed up and that was hard to accept. I thought we'd done our job and then this happened. I wasn't looking to blame anyone. When we lost the week before, I bet our management and support staff were a bit disappointed in us, so now it was the other way around. We just had to stick together.

"I still took some personal comfort out of it because, while we were certain to lose the points, we had won on the field. After what happened against Brisbane and Illawarra it was so vital to experience the feeling of winning a game."

For a day or two, the too-many-replacements error generated a tense atmosphere at management level at Warriors headquarters. Initially Robson claimed responsibility but Monie lifted that from him by injecting a little levity into the situation. He turned up to training on Tuesday night wearing a dunce's hat and saying, "I have apologised once to the team and that will be it. We stuffed up and it is my responsibility. Usually it is the players who stuff things up for the coach. Now it is the other way around."

But, as Bell stressed, the slip-up didn't change the quality of the on-field performance against the Tom Raudonikis-coached Magpies, although there had been a degree of nervousness before that match, mainly because the Warriors had defensive deficiencies to work on after the Illawarra loss.

"John didn't panic after we'd been beaten by Illawarra," says Bell. "He maintained we weren't far off winning a game, and he wasn't about to make lots of team changes. The way he saw it, he had identified the players who were capable of doing the job and was going to retain faith in them.

"Our defence was the issue. We had to get a balance between that and our attack. Defence is a mental matter more than anything and, for the Wests game, we concentrated on getting things right in the marker area especially. That's where we had failed against Illawarra, failing to get to their runners on the advantage line and stop them before they got going.

"And our marker defence was going to be that much more important against Wests because they had Jim Sedaris who, after Steve Walters, was probably the best dummy half runner around. We had to have that part of our game right if we were to ensure we weren't exposed again."

That brought Warriors hooker Duane Mann into sharp focus. His early-season displays had provoked widespread criticism, more so because reserve grade hooker Syd Eru had been impressing and definitely looked sharper out of dummy half.

"John must have been feeling the pressure about Duane's position in the team, because he very rarely asks me about selections. He's usually fairly confident about what line-up he wants," says Bell. "This time he approached me, though, and I told him I had the greatest confidence in Duane but, because of the way Syd was playing, he might have to consider giving him a chance. As it turned out, John started with Duane.

"Although Duane wasn't on top of his game around that time, it was made to look worse because the Ericsson Stadium crowd saw Syd looking very good in the reserve grade match against Wests. Really, though, it was very unfair for parts of the crowd to turn on Duane as they did that day. No one deserves that. He's a good pro because, even though it was affecting him inside, he never let it show. He got on with his job. He even talked about giving up his job so he could train more during the day to get on top of his fitness.

"With a player of Duane's experience, you might say the criticism doesn't hurt, but it does. It's difficult. He'd obviously lost some confidence when he was playing because he wasn't making decisive decisions. He was caught in between.

"And while John started with Duane, he soon threw Syd into the game, and he had an instant impact, making dummy half runs and being involved in a few tries."

The other dramatic early-season success story was former Kiwi Tea Ropati who, after try-scoring displays off the bench in the first two games, was in the starting line-up as Bell's centres partner, scoring the Warriors' opener.

"I think John had viewed Tea more as a reserve grader and back-up for first grade when he signed him," says Bell. "But he had been looking so sharp he couldn't be ignored, really forcing his way into the side. He certainly surprised me because, while he'd had his moments at St Helens, consistency had been a problem."

Ropati's early try helped propel the Warriors to an 18–0 lead inside the first 30 minutes, but then the familiar frailties returned as they conceded two tries to lead only 18–12 at halftime. If there was a hint of vulnerability then it was utterly blown away in the second 40 minutes with five fabulous tries, including three from Blake to add to his one in the first half.

The most remarkable was a chip and chase special. Powering through a hole on the end of a Stephen Kearney pass, Blake angled away from the cover, then chipped a perfectly weighted kick back the other way, stopping it in the in-goal and winning the race for the touchdown.

"It was one of those rare days when you see a player who can do no wrong," says Bell. "That chip and chase try was just brilliant. It reminded me of the videos I used to watch in the early '80s when he was just starting with Manly and was scoring tries all over the place. When he scored that try I ran over to him and said, 'That's the Phil Blake of old!' I think he probably wondered who I was talking about."

Forgetting the probability that the Warriors would lose their two competition points for the win, the performance itself still suggested the side was in much better shape for another exacting away assignment—against North Sydney.

It was also an important weekend for one of New Zealand's greatest sportsmen, John Kirwan. After resisting the Warriors' initial offer in late

Warriors fullback Phil Blake had his full range of attacking skills on show in his four-try assault against Western Suburbs. Nigel Marple (Fotopress)

1994, the retired All Black winger had re-opened negotiations and signed the week the Warriors made their Winfield Cup debut. Now, after three rounds, the coaching staff were ready to give him a taste of reserve grade action off the interchange bench.

"When John signed, I went looking for him straight away because he's a player I've always admired," says Bell. "In many ways our careers had followed a similar path, starting at international level around the same time and also both being brought up in South Auckland.

"I thought he had a lot to offer the Warriors as far as his ability was concerned. For that trip to Sydney, I was rooming with him and I said to him as I was lying on my bed, 'Who would have thought, after all these years, I'd be in the same room, playing the same sport and for the same club as John Kirwan.' It seemed quite strange really.

"After reading his book and listening to him at the time, I knew he would regret turning down the Warriors' initial offer. My motto has always been that I wanted to finish my career having no regrets. Whether it's been right or wrong, I've done it. I think John holds similar views and obviously he did regret turning down the first offer."

Clearly, by making such a belated start, Kirwan was severely disadvantaged after missing all the pre-season training. There was also limited time to educate him on league's finer points.

The Warriors' 'Captain Courageous' Dean Bell, shadowed by North Sydney second rower Gary Larson, battles on with his right thumb broken in a futile battle at the North Sydney Oval.
Louise Rutkin (Action Photographics)

"I didn't say a lot to him. I didn't want to drown him with tips, because sometimes you can have too much coming to you at times like that," says Bell. "We knew he was a good footballer and there was no question he had the ability to come through.

"At first it blew some of the guys away having such a famous New Zealand footballer suddenly training with us, and I know John was worried how he would fit in. That never turned out to be a problem at all. His biggest problem was catching up on all the work he'd missed out on.

"When he first started training I saw him in the changing room stripped off and thought, 'Gee, he's got a lot of work to do.' But he trained like nothing on earth to push himself and never shirked anything our trainers Lano [Bob Lanigan] and Edgar [Curtis] threw at him."

Kirwan survived his league debut against Norths, although castigating himself for a couple of errors he made. But those were nothing like the pile of errors the first graders managed to make afterwards.

North Sydney were coming off a 30–0 walloping from Manly a week earlier and, after Phil Blake had given the Warriors the early lead, they were only 6–4 down at halftime. So much for being close at the break, because, in the next 40 minutes, they let in a further seven tries as Norths put on 42 points to win 48–10. It was plain miserable fare from the Aucklanders. There were few redeeming features, except in the first half.

"We felt lethargic. Bob [Lanigan] was getting flak about our fitness and I guess we started wondering whether something was wrong," says Bell. "I actually thought we'd been working well at training so we started questioning all sorts of things. Were we getting there too late for away games? Should we catch an earlier flight and give ourselves more time to acclimatise and to train?

"We hit the wall again and started falling off tackles because we were too tired to put in the extra effort in the tackle. You can't just hang on against players like that. It was really ugly, shocking. All of us were to blame for letting in so many soft tries."

There was another major negative for the skipper as well, although it also illustrated the man's resilience and tenacity.

"It was in that game that I busted my [right] hand," he says. "It felt like a bad sprain and it was giving me a lot of pain but, by then, we were being really beaten up and I thought if I went off it would look like a sign of weakness. I couldn't do that. If we were going down, then I was going to be there at the end."

After that game the storm clouds regathered over the Warriors—and they were also gathering over rugby league itself. It was on this weekend that John Monie divulged information to his senior players which ensured the game would never be the same again. Super League was born and, for the next few weeks, it would cause all sorts of distractions for Monie's men and league players all over the world. It all seemed so far removed from the times when Dean Bell started shaping his life as a professional footballer.

the fulltime pro

Life is a grindstone. Whether it grinds you down or polishes you up, depends on what you're made of.

Professional football life had an obvious appeal to Dean Bell, although it took some time for him to believe there was a real living in it. In these days of massive Super League contracts and ready talk of the elite being paid $500,000-plus a season—and a lot more if Jonah Lomu had accepted league's bait—it's pertinent to remember a professional's life was a comparatively barren existence in the early 1980s.

The deal Dean and Ian Bell and Clayton Friend had at Carlisle in 1982–83 wasn't typical. They were novices on the English scene and, in any case, they weren't chasing a fat contract, merely some pocket money so they could fund their overseas trip. But many players supposedly on good money weren't living the life of the rich; for them, league earnings had to be supplemented by another income.

By the time Dean Bell began to consider his plans for the 1983–84 English season, his emphasis on money had changed slightly, although not to the point that it really mattered to him. Furthering his football education was uppermost in his thoughts and, for his second stint in England, he was after a higher quality club. He found it, too, in Leeds, a wealthy club with an enormous reputation. It was a club, however, which was all too regularly failing to deliver.

Bell had attracted attention with his deeds for Carlisle in 1982–83 and his new-found status as a New Zealand test player made him a much better proposition even for an abbreviated 1983–84 season. But you wouldn't have thought so judging by the money being paid then.

"That season, it was something like £4,000 for the season, what was left of it for me, plus win bonuses which were probably something like £100, maybe £150," he says.

"I regarded that as reasonable money then on the basis of what I knew and my experience. Like a lot of players, though, I wondered whether I had undersold myself. I'm sure the club was happy it got me at what must have been a bargain rate. But, all the same, I was happy with what I was getting. It wasn't that important to me. I viewed it more as pocket money or spending money really."

Before he could connect with Leeds and consider his immediate professional future, Bell had further representative commitments—and this was for a rugby league cause which constantly confounds those who don't know any better. Not the cause itself, the fact that Bell qualifies to be part of it—the New Zealand Maori team.

In appearance, it's impossible for the unaware to believe Dean Bell's a Maori. Blond, blue eyes, fair skin...a Maori? Can't be. Yes, he can be and yes, he is. It's the legacy of having a father of Maori extraction and a mother of European descent. So when he lined up in a New Zealand Maori team, he did tend to stand out just a little.

That happened when the Maori team made an historic tour to Britain in late 1983, playing eight matches against amateur sides. Forgetting about the conspicuous blond-haired centre, it was a side of some quality. Included in the touring squad were past, current or future Kiwis in brothers Nick and Owen Wright, Joe Ropati, Ron O'Regan, Ricky Cowan, Dick Uluave, Nolan Tupaea and Hugh McGahan, plus the Bell connection, captain Ian Bell, Dean Bell and Clayton Friend.

"It was disappointing that we were playing only amateur sides, because we had a side good enough to play the professional clubs," says Bell.

"Being under Lummy [coach Tom Newton] was interesting too. He was a good coach; out of the old school, but a very wise man you took notice of. He had a saying that if anyone got injured you just had to rub a bit of meths on his heart to get it right!"

The combination of New Zealand's long-running domestic season, including the October test against Papua New Guinea and the Maori tour, meant Bell's plans for another off-season in Britain had to wait until mid-November—and even then he created a further distraction. His wedding!

A fast mover in a league jersey, this kid was possibly quicker when it came to an affair of the heart. Little more than a year after meeting Jackie, the pair were married. Of course, that had to be fitted in around football as well.

"We did it then because quite a few of the family were there. They'd come to follow the tour. Unfortunately, Mum and Dad weren't there—for financial reasons they couldn't make it. That was disappointing."

And, in true style, Dean Bell was on the football field the day after the wedding, for Leeds against Salford. It was part of an unbeaten run which began with Dean Bell's try-scoring debut for Leeds against Hull Kingston Rovers.

It was a handy Leeds side coached by Maurice Bamford, whom Bell and the Kiwis would face as Great Britain's coach in 1985. The Leeds playing

From Manukau to the Kiwis, cousins Dean Bell and Clayton Friend. Dean Bell Collection

staff that year included Kevin Dick, Keith Rayne, David Creasser, David Ward—later to become Leeds coach—plus Parramatta's Mark Laurie, Balmain's Steve Martin and New Zealand's Trevor Clark, who later linked with Featherstone Rovers and Bradford Northern.

The high point of that 18-match unbeaten run for Bell was helping Leeds win one of their rare titles—beating Widnes 18–10 at Central Park in the John Player Special Trophy final.

"Leeds haven't won another major title since then but the downside of the season was that we were beaten in the Challenge Cup semifinals, this time losing to Widnes, who went on to win at Wembley when Joe Lydon scored twice," says Bell.

"I was sad then that we'd missed the chance to go to Wembley but I don't think the magnitude of Wembley really hit me until I went back to start with Wigan. In my time at Leeds, I never had that same feeling about it."

In those times, New Zealand players had to make two overseas tours or play at least six tests before they were eligible for a full transfer to an overseas club; in Dean Bell's Leeds year his test tally sat on only three. The other requirement then was that an off-season stint with an overseas club couldn't start till after the New Zealand season had ended. And the player had to be back home by 31 March—which Dean Bell honoured for the 1984 New Zealand season.

"It was a big change, back to Manukau playing for $25 a win and nothing for a loss," he says. "And, if you won, the $25 went on the bar so the money went straight back into the club anyway. The man of the match award was probably a pack of meat or something like a dozen Lion Red.

"There were some clubs in Auckland then that would contract players, and I could have moved on to one of them. But I was still happy at Manukau, even without any extra payments."

When he was home in 1983 and 1984, Dean Bell would try to find a seasonal job at the freezing works to provide income. And, if no work was available, he didn't hesitate to line up for the dole.

"I spent a few months on the dole—I had no problems with that. I'd paid my dues by working from the time I left school," he says.

Preoccupying him was being reunited with Graham Lowe and the Kiwis for the 1984 home series against Great Britain. His preparation was anything but regular. Certainly turning out for Manukau wasn't unusual, nor was helping Auckland win the national interdistricts competition for the second successive season under Bob Bailey's coaching. But there was a variation on the normal theme, a trip to Paris in April as part of the Lowe-coached Oceania team to face Europe in a match celebrating the French Rugby League's 50th anniversary. Australians in the side included Mal Meninga, Kerry Boustead, Gene Miles, Wally Lewis, Steve Mortimer, Wayne Pearce and Ray Price, while the other New Zealanders were Mark Graham, Kevin Tamati, Howie Tamati, Hugh McGahan, Shane Varley and Robin Alfield.

It was a no-contest as the Oceania combination won 54–4 and, while not necessarily significant preparation for New Zealand's test programme against Great Britain, it did give a fair nucleus of the Kiwi side more exposure to Lowe's coaching methods.

By now Dean Bell was driven to succeed at international level and to establish himself as an integral player in the line-up; and, in the 1984 Great Britain side, the Kiwis could surely eye the prospect of a rare series win, their first over Great Britain since 1971.

The tourists arrived in New Zealand predictably whitewashed by Australia, bringing with them a squad which included more than a few players who would later have some impact on Bell's career—a 23-year-old Bradford Northern back by the name of Ellery Hanley, a 19-year-old Widnes centre Joe Lydon and his 22-year-old team-mate Andy Gregory, prop Brian Case and Oldham second rower Andy Goodway. Yes, they were all destined to rendezvous with Bell at Central Park over the next few years. Also in that side was the 18-year-old Garry Schofield.

The Kiwis now had an exceptional line-up, although injury had again robbed the side of Mark Graham's ability and influence. In a backline which

*Dean Bell and Ellery Hanley shape up to each other in the Kiwis' 1984
series against Great Britain. They were destined to become long-term
team-mates at Wigan.* Auckland Star

had Olsen Filipaina back in the Kiwi jersey, this time at stand-off, Fred Ah
Kuoi and James Leuluai in the centres, Dean Bell was still a test winger,
not a centre. And he wasn't upset about it either.

In the event, he was involved in an utterly compelling series effort as
the Kiwis handed the visitors another 3–0 defeat to match what happened
in Australia. The New Zealanders put together a sequence of 12–0, 28–12
and 32–16 wins, expressing themselves fully throughout. And Dean Bell
made it four victories over Great Britain in a few weeks when he turned
out for Auckland in the tour finale, the home side winning 18–16.

The more Bell played at the highest level, the more interested parties
began courting him. He heard from Balmain, from Eastern Suburbs and
from Canterbury-Bankstown.

"I was very interested in Canterbury-Bankstown because they were a
force then and I wanted to go to a strong club if I could," says Bell. "But
they weren't prepared to pay the transfer fee then, and Easts were. I was
annoyed at having the transfer fee hanging over me because it was
restricting me from going places.

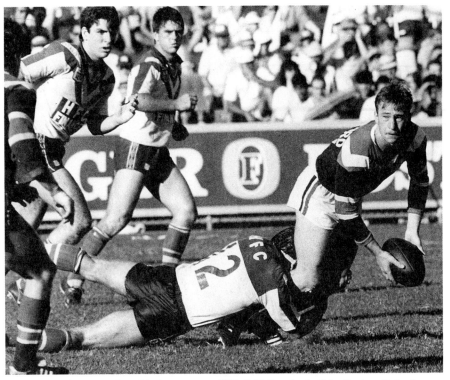

Dean Bell 1985-style in his first season of Winfield Cup football for Eastern Suburbs.
Despite being taken low, he still gets his pass away against Canterbury-Bankstown.
Dean Bell Collection

"All the same, I was determined to go to Australia no matter what happened then. I'd decided that if I was going to learn my trade properly, then I had to play there. So, Easts it was going to be and from then on the money was beginning to stack up a little better, although you still couldn't make a living out of it."

The focus at Easts was the legend himself, and a monstrous legend he was—coach Arthur Beetson. Beetson and the Easts management definitely had a policy of going Kiwi in 1985, with Bell and Hugh McGahan both signed on at the same time. And the Roosters had also taken on Balmain's Kiwi enigma Olsen Filipaina.

The side wasn't short on talent, including Dave Brown, Brad Tessman and Jeff Masterman, who had all played test football for Australia, future internationals Paul Dunn and Chicka Ferguson, plus John Tobin, Laurie Spina and Ron Gibbs.

"I worked so hard at home to be ready for Easts and, by the time we left, I was in pretty good nick," says Bell. "But when the media met Hugh and me, we made the big mistake of posing for photographers with our

*Tuning up for the Kiwis' campaign against Australia in
1985, Joe Ropati and Dean Bell.* NZ Herald

shirts off. We stood there like real dicks trying to show our muscles off
and, boy, did we get a real hard time from our new team-mates at Easts."

Light-hearted stuff was transformed to frightening fare when Dean Bell
played his first Winfield Cup match. He calls it his most memorable
moment in his debut season in Sydney—but definitely not memorable
because he enjoyed it.

"It was against South Sydney. They had Mario Fenech, David Boyle,
Craig Coleman, Neil Baker, Tony Rampling, Michael Pobjie and others,"
recalls Bell. "I just couldn't believe Winfield Cup football was going to be
like the way they played it. A lot was said about the Souths team and
really they were just lunatics that day.

"At one stage, I picked up the ball from dummy half and passed it—
and about a second later 'Whack!' Pobjie, one of their centres, came around
from marker and whacked me across the jaw, then stood over me yelling,
'Come on, get up you Kiwi so-and-so.' They were calling us Kiwi this,
Kiwi that, saying your mother's a so-and-so. All these obscenities. It was
full-on throughout the game.

"I saw the fire in their eyes and thought, 'Shit, how can I handle this all season?' As it turned out, not all the games were like that, but that first Winfield Cup game really stood out. The Souths players were just wild and I was a bit frightened."

The Kiwis' 1985 series against Australia also had its wild moments, certainly in the Lang Park opener when the three Eastern Suburbs Kiwis, Bell, McGahan and Filipaina, were New Zealand's three tryscorers in the 26–20 loss, with Filipaina kicking the other points. Of Bell's 11 test tries, his one in this match is the most celebrated.

"I was one man off the ruck, Hugh ran around me, I dummied to him— and the next thing, when I straightened up, I'd run into a big hole. And then I ran away from Garry Jack to score. It was a very memorable try.

"It was after that test that some of the Sydney scribes started ribbing me, like they had with Olsen [Filipaina] and Fred [Ah Kuoi]. They'd be writing, 'Why can't he play that way for Easts? Why does he do it only when he pulls on the black jersey?' That sort of thing."

Bell's wonderful try from around 50 metres out had the Kiwis out to a 20–14 lead in a test they were positioned to win. However, two crucial injuries conspired to ruin their plans. Mark Graham was maliciously and cynically put out of the game, while centre Gary Prohm also had to be replaced, forcing a major reshuffle, with Bell coming off the right wing into the centres, and a young Aucklander Mark Elia taking his place in his debut appearance.

When Wally Lewis hurled one of his special long passes wide on the left to find Wayne Pearce, the inexperienced Elia was sucked infield leaving John Ribot unmarked on his wing. He shrugged off Dean Bell's cover tackle close to the line to score the matchwinner.

"That test was there for us to win—and I felt responsible for us losing it in the end because I missed that tackle on Ribot," says Bell. "I had covered right across the field but, when I got there, Ribot came in and away and slipped out of my tackle.

"The business of the way they dealt with Mark Graham was also a key factor. They went out to get Mark. They knew he was our chief playmaker— and they certainly did a good job on him. He took a hammering and obviously his loss affected us. We were a lot more confident when he was on the field."

What was actually a tingling football contest and spectacle is always remembered for a far more spectacular reason—the sideline brawl between Kevin Tamati and Greg Dowling.

"That's firmly imprinted in most rugby league followers' memory banks," says Bell. "I wasn't anywhere near it when it happened—and obviously you don't want to be when two men like that explode. I suppose that marred the match, and I don't condone it, but sometimes that sort of thing happens. What we had was two props having a real bash at each other, although you have to say the system is a problem when two players who have been sin-binned after fighting then have to walk off the field together. That's just asking for trouble."

This series seemed to attract the spectacular and the dramatic. The Kiwis provided most of the former in the second test at Carlaw Park, thrilling with their attack but being awarded only a James Leuluai try when there might have been others given by the erratic French referee Julian Rascagneres. So, as the Kiwis clung to a 6–4 lead with only 90 seconds left, Australia laid on the dramatic touch.

Again a Wally Lewis pass was involved, this time to Garry Jack, who slipped past Hugh McGahan's tackle before offloading in Gary Kemble's tackle to Ribot, who again found himself unmarked. Joe Ropati, who'd replaced an injured Dean Bell on the right wing, was the culprit this time, coming off his wing and being left stranded in the middle of nowhere. The Australians escaped with a series-clinching 10–6 win which even they agreed they didn't deserve.

"It will always be the test we won everywhere but on the scoreboard," says Bell. "I was in the dressing room when Ribot scored his try. I'd had trouble with my knee before and this time when it happened, I couldn't believe how much pain there was. I was reluctant to go off on a stretcher, because I always have it in my mind what my Dad drummed into me, 'Never go off unless you're carried off.' I didn't want to go off at all until Glenn Gallagher [the physio] persuaded me to get on the stretcher. He said I'd only do more damage by walking on it.

"Under the stand, all I could hear were the roars of the crowd. It was frustrating not knowing what was going on. Someone was giving me reports and, when I was told there was only two minutes to go and we were still in front, I said, 'Yes!' Even though I was in pain, I was elated that we were going to beat them, especially after coming so close in the first test.

"I heard another softer roar and I thought we'd finished them off— only to find Ribot had scored. That was devastating. Devastating. It was like there'd been a loss in the family."

Bell was rated as having no chance of playing the final test just a week later. Even he thought so. "I was 100 per cent sure I wouldn't be playing, but it was decided we'd work on my knee all week and see what happened. For Glenn that meant treating me hour after hour, in the middle of the night and all, yet even the day before the game, I still wasn't right."

But Bell gave it one last shot, going for a run to see what he could achieve. He thought he was capable of playing, said he would and that was it. "I couldn't have done it without Glenn Gallagher's work. He was solely responsible for getting me on the field.

"While I didn't hold out much hope all week, I was still desperate to play that third test after the devastating loss. If it had been any other game maybe I wouldn't have played. I wasn't right and didn't have much of a role in the game—but I'm glad now that I did play in it."

Everyone in the squad was, because from the desolation of the previous week's series-losing experience, the Kiwis thrilled their nation and themselves, and humiliated their rivals. Australia, unsettled by an internal New South Wales vs Queensland split, couldn't answer the thrill-a-minute New Zealanders as they were dumped 18–0.

Bell's elation at exacting revenge was tempered by his knee injury which was becoming chronic, and something of a liability from then on. "For a large part of the 1985 and 1986 seasons with Easts, I went to the doctor's surgery on the Friday before a Sunday game," he says. "He'd suck the fluid out of the knee and give me a mild dose of cortisone. I did that most weeks to get me through.

"I knew cortisones were something I should avoid but, if there was something that could help me play, then I was prepared to try it. I'll probably suffer for it later as the knee is giving me more and more trouble each year now. The hard grounds were hell on it."

Bell didn't have an especially flash season with Easts, nor did the team, as they finished seventh, four points outside the top five. On one season's evidence, Bell rated Easts a bit of a good-time club, not as switched on to football as he had expected. That disappointed him.

"As a coach, Arthur Beetson was alright," he says. "You have to respect him for what he'd achieved and for his knowledge. I got on well with him, he's a great guy. If he had a problem, though, it was that he couldn't really handle the man management side of things.

"On the football side of it, I had my own problems. I had backed myself to succeed in my first year even though I knew it was going to be demanding—but it was far more demanding than I'd imagined."

Bell also made it more difficult on himself when he ran into strife in Easts' clash against Canberra on 11 August. A high tackle on Canberra forward Jon Hardy couldn't have been more costly as the New South Wales judiciary suspended him until 15 October; and that was deliberately designed to deny him early outings for the Kiwis on their tour to Britain and France.

"Jon Hardy had to be the world's biggest man, just enormous," says Bell. "I remember him coming out wide in the centres where I was playing. All I could see was that there was me and no one else—and this giant coming at me. I thought I had to take him ball and all because, if I went low, he would get the ball away.

"So, I leapt up off the ground stupidly and tried to wrap him up. But my first connection was with his neck. His feet came off the ground and, bang, he hit the deck. I was straight off—and he was carried off.

"With my sendings off, they have never been malicious. They've just been head high tackles through bad technique, not swinging arms or going for the jaw."

Kiwis Dean Bell, Kurt Sorensen, Ricky Coan, Vaun O'Callaghan, Mark Elia and Ron O'Regan (back row) plus Howie Tamati and Clayton Friend (in front) doing a spot of posing on the 1985 tour of Britain and France. Dean Bell Collection

At that time, Bell was a lightweight centre, probably no more than 82 kg, but still possessed with the ability to tackle with ruthless ferocity.

"I used to think to tackle high was the tough way to do it, that you needed to. Obviously today, you still need to wrap up the ball. What you have to watch is your technique.

"There was no doubt I deserved to be suspended. I had to be. I actually got some bad advice, though, being told I should plead guilty—and all I got was a long lecture from Jim Comans and a long suspension.

"Arthur had warned me about my tackling and told me 'they're watching you.' I paid the price for not heeding his advice because the suspension was damned tough, cutting across the Kiwis' tour."

It severely limited his preparation for the first test against Great Britain. In fact, the ban came off in time for just one match before the test—the Kiwis' clash against Cumbria, usually regarded as a low-key encounter compared to those against the glamour club sides Wigan, St Helens, Leeds, Widnes, Hull Kingston Rovers and Hull.

However, it was highly significant for Bell. This was primarily because it provided the hit-out he desperately needed, but it also added to a piece of history. When he was at Carlisle, Bell was in the Cumbria team that played the 1982 Kangaroos, making him the first and only foreigner ever selected for Cumbria. This time he played against them, helping the Kiwis to a 32–6 victory.

For Bell there was the added excitement of this being his first tour after being denied the chance in 1982. They were also awkward times as two distinct camps formed; one was the touring team, but when test week arrived the selected England-based Kiwi professionals joined the side. So, for the first test at Headingley, that meant Gary Kemble, James Leuluai, Fred Ah Kuoi and Dane O'Hara were called in from Hull, Gary Prohm from Hull Kingston Rovers and Kevin Tamati from Warrington.

"I'd be a liar to say it didn't have some effect, especially on those players who would otherwise have had some chance of making the test side," says Bell. "It made it a little bit awkward that the English-based players weren't touring themselves, although that was no fault of theirs. But naturally you still have to pick your best team."

The series was never less than dramatic as the Kiwis won a thriller 24–22 in Leeds; another piece of magic between Kurt Sorensen and James Leuluai creating the matchwinner, although there was ample bleating from the British about the validity of Sorensen's short ball to Leuluai.

The second test found the Kiwis without the inspirational Mark Graham and they were trounced 25–8 as Garry Schofield scored four tries himself. And the series decider turned into a game of attrition; a torrid encounter with the accent often on outright war before a late Lee Crooks penalty levelled the score 6–6 to leave the series squared.

Dean Bell remembers the campaign for some less than impressive officiating and for the way Great Britain put Mark Graham out of the first test.

"Sharko was again in the wars, his cheekbone smashed by a blatant Des Drummond foul," says Bell. "You expect more protection from the referee with something as blatant as that. The fact we didn't have him for the second test was a major blow to us. When you lose a player of that calibre it has to have some effect on you.

"The third test I found so frustrating. I couldn't believe how many times the English linesman Don Watson came on for little incidents. It was his report to the referee that got Great Britain the penalty from which they drew the game to deny us winning the series.

"After the game, I went off my nut at the referee [Barry Gomersall] and that linesman. I couldn't believe what I was doing because that's not really me, but I was that pissed off and wound up about what had happened. I just had to let my frustration out.

"That carried on to the after-math function. During the game, Ellery Hanley got a bit personal when Clayton niggled him, telling Clayton he'd sort him out after the game.

*Chilly tourists in Paris—Gary Kemble, Ricky Cowan, Clayton
Friend, Dane O'Hara and Dean Bell on the French leg of the Kiwis'
1985 northern hemisphere tour.* Ross Setford

"At the after-match function, the word got around about that and we
were all wound up about it. Kevin Tamati was Clayton's minder that night
and he was waiting for Ellery to turn up. Just as well for Ellery he didn't
show, because it avoided a confrontation which would have been ugly.

"I nearly got ugly anyway. I was still in an aggressive mood after the
function and got into an altercation with a taxi driver. I'd hopped in the
wrong taxi, some words were said and I put my arm around the driver's
throat—Jackie had to drag me away before the police arrived!"

There was also lingering disquiet for Bell about another aspect of the
tour—and that was Mark Graham's role. Of the 12 matches played, Graham
appeared in only four, including the first and third tests.

"Mark was reluctant to make that tour. He came on it only after Lowie
had persevered with him," says Bell. "And throughout the tour you felt
that reluctance.

"I know he had injury problems, but then we heard he'd made it clear he wasn't going to France, and the rest of us didn't believe that was right. If you come on tour, you should be there for the lot and not pick and choose when you play. As he was the captain and elder statesman no one really complained but there was some ill feeling."

The French section was a breeze as it was always likely to be, although the Kiwis—with a young Hugh McGahan as captain—didn't entirely blow France away in either of the two tests, playing solidly to win both 22–0. What was more threatening was the political volatility in France following the *Rainbow Warrior* bombing. It wasn't the best country for New Zealanders to be touring that year.

"We would turn up at hotels and be told we weren't expected, weren't booked in, or meals weren't available. It wasn't said in so many words, but we felt it was all to do with the *Rainbow Warrior*," says Bell.

"There would be rumours as well that a bomb had been planted underneath our bus and, with what had happened to the *Rainbow Warrior*, some of us were a little edgy about that. There was even talk between management and some of the players that we should consider going home at one stage."

It didn't reach such a drastic conclusion but, when Dean Bell did return to Sydney, there was time for only a limited break. The life of the league professional soon resumed for a second season under Artie Beetson.

my sort of player

Arthur Beetson

As Queensland coach in 1984, I had fair reason to take special notice of a couple of Kiwi players: one was Dean Bell, the other Hugh McGahan. That's not to say I didn't know something about them before that; I'd seen enough of Dean in his first year in test football—the 1983 series when the Kiwis beat the Australian team I coached at Lang Park. Hugh missed that series, but I'd noticed him when he toured Australia with New Zealand in 1982.

In 1984, they were both in the same New Zealand team, the Residents team Graham Lowe brought to Brisbane to play Queensland. We won that time, but Dean and Hugh were both impressive in a beaten side; they both scored tries and I had them marked down as players I'd like to have as I looked towards the new job I was going to in 1985—as first grade coach with Eastern Suburbs.

It's often been said that Dean was the only one I was after, that Hughie came to Easts as a bit of an afterthought, or on Dean's coat tails. That wasn't the case at all. I wanted both of them and I suggested to Ron Jones (Easts' general manager) that they were the two players we should buy.

Now Dean Bell was, and still is, my sort of player. He was strong and willing...mate, he had speed, a good step and he was keen on defence. Aggressive, too; I guess I like aggressive sort of players. The only trouble was, I soon found he was too aggressive for his own good! Well, too aggressive to last in the Winfield Cup at that time.

Dean stayed with us for only two seasons (1985–86), and while he played some great games for us, we didn't see the best of him. We also had Gary Prohm—another New Zealander who could play in the centres—but, had we kept Dean Bell for the 1987 season, he might have been the difference between us winning the grand final and getting knocked out the week before.

Dean's biggest problem then was his tackling technique. He was ordered off twice and suspended for high tackles. The game was going through a period of change in terms of how physical or tough it was, and Dean was flirting with danger every time because he did have a tendency to creep up in the tackle. We played him on the wing or in the centres and he was one of those players who'd come in and leave his mark on defence. There was nothing around the legs from him then. We spoke to him a fair bit about his tackling technique because you didn't have to be Einstein to see that he needed to change it, otherwise he wasn't going to survive. And, of course, he did change, in time—not then, though.

Dean could have played in any era; I know that. He was so tough. Back then, while the game was going through that transition, it was still tough going. Players were getting away with quite a few head shots, and copping them as well. Dean could handle it both ways but I know there are a lot of people in the game today who wouldn't have played in my time because they would have developed acute hearing! They'd be hearing the footsteps, mate! Not Dean, he *never* had acute hearing.

He was a great bloke around the club as well, very popular. And the fact he's survived for so long at the highest level is testimony to his ability. While he has lost that explosive speed in more recent years, he still had that great step and, along the way, his leadership abilities began to emerge.

We were bitterly disappointed to lose him after only two years because we did pay a big transfer fee for him at the time. He didn't leave on bad terms or anything like that, but I know Ron Jones wasn't too enchanted about it. Still, it was our fault for not tying him up better right from the outset. It didn't change my estimation of him though. Like I say, Dean Bell is my sort of player.

Arthur (or Artie) Beetson was an Australian international from 1966–1977 (28 tests) and also captained Australia. He played for both Queensland and New South Wales; was Queensland captain in the first State of Origin match in 1980 and coached Australia against New Zealand (1983). He has also been an Australian selector and Queensland coach. He played first grade for Redcliffe (in Brisbane), Sydney clubs Balmain, Eastern Suburbs and Parramatta, plus Hull Kingston Rovers in England and coached first grade at Eastern Suburbs, Cronulla-Sutherland and Redcliffe.

a game divided

People who never do any more than they are paid to do, are never paid for any more than they do.

The Warriors' senior pros had a sombre trip home across the Tasman after their reverse in Wollongong. So the Saturday night flight back after the horror show at North Sydney should have been even more painful. John Monie ensured it wasn't. Not because the coach was intentionally trying to distract his players from dwelling on a frightful display; it just happened that rugby league had been jolted to its foundations by the most dramatic developments since its birth.

Sydney had been buzzing since the night before the Warriors' date with Norths, as news broke about the arrival of Super League. The Auckland players had largely been insulated from it as they focused on a mission which ultimately went terribly wrong. But Monie was well aware of much of the detail which saw Super League shatter the Australian Rugby League's defences, only he wasn't ready to let on about it until the trip home.

"John started telling a few of us what had been going on and what his involvement was," says Bell. "And what he had to say suddenly took our minds off the loss more than a bit. I was quite shocked because I hadn't expected to hear about Super League after Kerry Packer had defused it in February, certainly not so soon.

"Clearly John knew better back then because, even though Packer had made a move, John said Super League wouldn't go away, that it definitely would happen. Now it had.

"He told us he was in a position where he had to start sorting out some players. He had to come up with 15 names there and then and he obviously had it in his mind who the 15 should be. Clearly he'd known a lot about it for quite some time, long before the day of the Norths game when the whole thing blew up in public.

"There was a meeting at John's place the day after the Norths game

Super League stormed into existence, and that set Hitro Okesene up for a much-improved contract. On the field, he was again among the Warriors' best in their demolition of Illawarra. Nigel Marple (Fotopress)

and it was then that most of the players were signed up. I read a newspaper story suggesting some of the Warriors' players had been at John's home for a video session! I laughed to myself because I knew there wasn't much video watching going on! It was all cloak and dagger stuff, very secretive."

While Monie had asked Bell to consider being involved, there was never much chance he would go for it. Age was one factor, commitments back in England after his Warriors' contract were another. But Bell remained part of the process in what was a frantic week between the Warriors' matches against North Sydney and Manly.

"John invited me to a meeting the following weekend, after the Manly game, to see what the Super League people had to say," says Bell. "I think he was quietly hoping I might get interested and sign up myself. But I was adamant all along that I wouldn't be getting involved. Then again, if I was five years younger...

"Whatever my own position, I still found it hugely exciting. John told me guys like Hitro [Okesene], Tony Tatupu and others, who were probably on only $20,000 or so, were looking at $120,000 by signing with Super

League. That's good for the players and I was happy for them. To be truthful, what I was a little jealous about were the loyalty payments players were receiving for doing nothing really, and they were huge sums too. It would have been nice to get part of that."

Dean Bell is no rugby league conservative. He's always welcomed change if it improves the game but, with the rapid rise of Super League, he did have some initial fears for the game's traditions and its future.

"Like a lot of people, I was deeply concerned for the game as a whole," he says. "I had a lot of questions. Obviously a lot of people had been convinced it was good because they'd received money, but I looked beyond that and was worried about what was right.

"When I analysed it, though, the Super League scheme is the way to go. While everything has looked rosy for rugby league in the '90s, there are still a lot of clubs having financial problems, especially among Sydney clubs, never mind in England.

"During the 1995 season, I watched a Friday night game on television—Souths against Illawarra—and there were only 3000 or 4000 people at the Sydney Football Stadium. You know then that rugby league needs something. While we were one of the new clubs, the addition of the four new sides in 1995 meant there were too many teams in the Winfield Cup to my way of thinking.

"The concern with this was, of course, that a split immediately developed with the Australian Rugby League and their teams on one side and the Super League and their teams on the other. That's not good, but if that's the way it must be, so be it."

It stood to reason that the Warriors' regular Monday night team meeting would have a major distraction for the second successive week. The previous week it had been the replacements issue from the Wests game, now that had been overtaken by a far more significant matter.

As the Warriors' players assembled, the realisation dawned that quite a few of the first graders now had Super League contracts, while others were talking about them or were set to sign.

"They had to sign quickly too," says Bell. "As I heard it, they often had just a few hours to sign and those who signed got a lump sum there and then.

"It was amazing how quickly everything was happening. In the week after the Norths game the New Zealand Rugby League had signed up with Super League, and I was happy with that because they did something on their own, making a move that they saw benefiting the game. While they said they hadn't been bought, they had. So what? Who cares? It was an answer to their financial problems and it was giving New Zealand league a future."

Before the week was out, top News Limited personnel made a flying visit to Auckland to watch the Warriors' Friday night clash against Manly

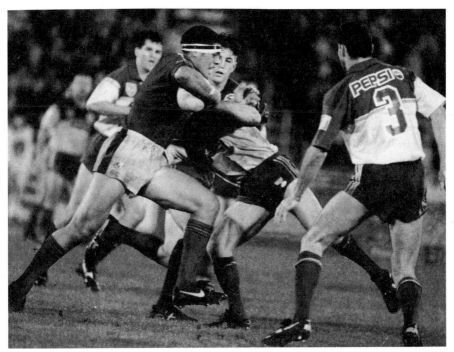

Warriors second rower Stephen Kearney crunches into Des Hasler's tackle with Mark Carroll (behind) and Danny Moore (right) poised to assist in Manly's 26–14 win at Ericsson Stadium. Ross Land (Fotopress)

and to do some more Super League business, at the same time showing the New Zealand Rugby League some solidarity now they'd signed up.

"The next day they had this meeting John had asked me to go to," says Bell. "Apart from John Monie, Ian Robson was there, plus the 15 players who had signed or were set to sign. John Ribot, Ken Cowley and Lachlan Murdoch wanted to show the players some support from Super League, to thank those who had signed and to talk to those who hadn't.

"But that Ribot was bloody cheeky. He looked at me and said, 'Oh, sorry Dean. You're just about as old as me!' And I thought to myself, 'Yeah, and you'd still go alright on the field, wouldn't you?' Too old!

"I wasn't too aware of what the Warriors were doing about Super League as a club. Obviously Ian Robson knew about things because John was keeping him in touch about what he was doing with the players.

"Just how Ian felt about it didn't really concern me too much. But we were a new club just accepted into the Winfield Cup by the Australian Rugby League and now, in our first year, there was talk about joining a new league. I'm sure it's something the Warriors could have done without so soon."

Somehow, against all of this business, the football show still had to go on. It's mind boggling now to wonder how Monie could have his players switched on for their clash against Manly. Exactly the same had to be said for Manly. They were obviously sticking with the establishment but, as they arrived in Auckland on the night before the game, change was in the wind. Kiwi fullback Matthew Ridge and prop Ian Roberts confirmed they were switching to Super League, so creating a split within their own team.

At least Manly had been winning, unlike the Warriors. Savaged by Norths and knowing the only two competition points they had were temporary, was no way to take on Manly. And to have most of the players embroiled in the Super League war was a further hurdle, or at least a distraction.

Despite that, the Warriors were impressive in a 26–14 loss on a damp night before another astonishing crowd of 29,500. With 20 minutes to go, Sean Hoppe's outstanding try of the night had levelled the score at 14–14, with anything possible after that.

"We did go fairly well but I blame myself for the try that let Manly get away from 14–all," says Bell. "They came down the short side as I was stuck on the ground. Sean had come in to marker and chased out, but I could tell what Cliff Lyons was going to do as I lay on the ground. He dummied, went down the blind and then sent Danny Moore in. I should have got off the ground faster.

"To me, it was another game like the Brisbane one where we were right in there but couldn't come up with what was needed to win it. The Super League thing wasn't an issue for me personally because I wasn't involved in it, and I don't believe it was a distraction for the players who had signed or were thinking about it. We couldn't blame that."

This was also the game when Phil Blake gave away a pair of old boots to one of Manly's support staff whom he knew from the days when he played there. Matthew Ridge had brought only a pair of boots with moulded studs, which didn't suit the surface—so he finished up using Blake's boots!

"And he never missed a shot all night as he kicked five goals—and also scored a try," says Bell. "I thought he had an outstanding game that night. Matthew is a guy I've never played alongside and, when I'd watched him on television, I still had my doubts about him. But in that game against us he came across as a really determined character. He puts himself on the line and uses what he has to the full."

The match had its controversy when referee Eddie Ward denied Auckland what proved to be a legitimate try—and what would have been the first of the match—to prop Se'e Solomona. But, without consulting his in-goal touch judge, Ward immediately disallowed it.

That deflated a Warriors side still looking for their first legal win, but Sean Hoppe twice revived them, first with a fabulous take off a Gene Ngamu cross kick, leaping high above John Hopoate and crashing over.

Dean Bell caps his sixth appearance for the Warriors—and their first genuine win—with his first try of the year in the 38–12 victory over Illawarra. Nigel Marple (Fotopress)

And another in the second half when he stood Hopoate up to score wide out.

The Warriors, though, couldn't quite match Manly's all-round quality, not when three of their most potent match-winners—Ridge, Cliff Lyons and Steve Menzies—were all in dazzling touch.

So Auckland were still effectively empty heading into round six—the return clash against Illawarra. There was scope for hope in that the Steelers were clearly a club in turmoil having hastily sacked coach Graham Murray over his Super League involvement, replacing him with the club's foundation coach Alan Fitzgibbon.

But the Warriors also knew Illawarra had players who had tormented and overrun them in Wollongong—John Simon, Brett Rodwell, John Cross, Neil Piccinelli and, most of all, Darren Fritz.

"I was also very edgy about the game because I realised if we didn't win this one, we'd basically be looking at six games without a win and that would have been a disastrous start to the year," says Bell.

"That made us an absolutely desperate team. We just couldn't come off the paddock without a win."

It was a game when very little went wrong for the Warriors, other than allowing Illawarra to strike back after an early Hoppe try to take a 6–4 lead. There was no need to fear, though, as Auckland then stacked on seven tries in all, four of them from kicks—a Stephen Kearney grubber created Hoppe's first. Tea Ropati's try came courtesy of a Phil Blake chip, Greg

Alexander scored when the Illawarra defence failed to control his chip and Gene Ngamu's deft nudge laid on the most popular try of the game—Bell's first as a Warrior.

"I enjoyed that too. It was a relief for me," he says. "I hadn't been scoring as many tries as I used to and I don't expect to. In fact, I didn't score once for Wigan in the 1993–94 season, so it was nice for my confidence to get this one."

But outside the 38–12 scoreline, the major victory of the day was the job the Auckland forwards did on the monster man Fritz. He went from brute at Steelers Stadium to nothing much at all in front of the 28,604 fans at Ericsson. He was battered out of the game by some aggressive, crunching defence and, in the end, didn't want to know, looking like a man waiting for the coach to take him off.

It was a personal victory, too, for Bell, who for the sixth match on end underlined what a wonderfully consistent performer he was proving to be for his team. And there was equally a personal thrill for John Kirwan, who, after only his third run in reserve grade, came off the interchange bench for his first appearance in first grade.

But the sweetest sight of the day was the scoreline. This time the Warriors had a real win, worth two points, and with no problems over the number of replacements used.

home away from home

There is no fun equal to the satisfaction of doing one's best. The things that are most worthwhile in life are really those within the reach of almost every normal human being who cares to seek them out.

For a New Zealander brought up to revel in the great wide open, the thought of making a town like Wigan home doesn't make a whole lot of sense. The tranquillity and natural inspiration found in a Coromandel Peninsula retreat like Sandy Bay surely offers rather more aesthetic appeal than a north of England town like Wigan. So does life in Sydney. But a rugby league player with talent has to consider sacrifices in the cause of earning a living from his game. And Dean Bell had never been afraid of making concessions and exceptions to further his career. He had to do that in 1986.

Wigan has its own appeal and charm. There is no town or city in the world which can rival its almost singular focus on one sport—and it's not soccer, rugby union, cricket or anything else. For Wigan, rugby league is everything. Brisbane can't match it; the Broncos and league might be big time but they are still not the only game in town, with rugby union competing in winter and cricket dominating in summer. Auckland became a one-team city with the Warriors in 1995, but its sporting interests and passions are diverse. Not so with Wigan—this is *the* league city of the world.

That in itself wasn't why Dean Bell went the Wigan way and became an institution there. He wasn't drawn to Wigan because of its rugby league traditions; it was the Graham Lowe magnet which he found irresistible. So irresistible, he spurned a better offer from Leeds so he could join Lowe at Central Park.

"I had to go to Wigan because Lowie was there. It was as simple as that," says Bell. "And luckily I hadn't actually signed on the dotted line with Leeds. Once I heard Graham was going to be Wigan coach, I must admit I thought to myself it would be good to go there although he never

Dean Bell battles to break free against Cronulla-Sutherland in his second season with Easts in 1986. Dean Bell Collection

talked to me about it. Things just happened quickly with Maurice Lindsay [Wigan chairman] contacting me.

"I took less money to go to Wigan just because Lowie was there. That's how much he meant to me. Leeds offered me £25,000 but I went to Wigan for £20,000. Obviously I've always been able to look back on it and say it was the best move I ever made for the sake of £5,000.

"It was good that I wasn't totally money-oriented because, apart from Graham being there, I also looked at the players they had and thought I could win more games at Wigan than I would if I went to Leeds. It wasn't that I was thinking in terms of the win bonuses that would mean, more the fact that I wanted to be with a winning team.

"I always thought then, and have ever since, that the Wigan directors weren't as confident as Lowie about signing me, and I've had Maurice on about this many times. I wasn't really a big name then. I'm just glad that the coach wanted me."

Bell needed the stimulus of a new footballing challenge because of all

The way it is after every test defeat. Hooker Wayne Wallace and Dean Bell make a forlorn sight after losing to Australia at Carlaw Park in 1986. Auckland Star

the playing years in his lengthy career at top level none was less memorable and less rewarding than 1986.

"It was a forgettable year for me," he says. "I think it was then that I thought I was better suited to the soft grounds that I'd encountered on the Kiwi tour of Britain and France. I got back to Sydney after the tour and my knee immediately started playing up again, and it never improved all year. I had a few arthroscopes to try and sort it out but I wasn't getting very far with it."

In fact a nondescript year for Bell at Easts was remembered for the wrong reasons—his second ordering off in less than a year. And again it came in a match against Canberra, with Seiffert Oval the venue once more. In 1985 it had been a tackle on Jon Hardy; in 1986 read Craig Bellamy.

"It was a technique problem again. Deja vu time. I went high in what was purely a reflex action. I thought, 'Oh no! Not again!' The judiciary knew exactly what they were doing. They knew the suspension they gave me was going to cost me the third test against Australia and then the tour to Papua New Guinea as well.

"I deserved to be sent off. But there were cases going before the judiciary then that were much worse than mine, yet they were getting lighter sentences. I felt victimised that time. It cost me Kiwi appearances when I wouldn't have been able to play much for Easts anyway with all the test football on. I really felt low at that time."

It was also a year better forgotten for the Kiwis after the heroics of 1983, 1984 and 1985. The three-test series against Australia became something of a walkover for the Aussies as they won 22–8 in the Carlaw Park mud, 29–12 in Sydney and 32–12 in Brisbane. Australia were building into an impressive side in Kangaroo tour year. It was a team oozing with talent; primarily the halves Wally Lewis and Peter Sterling, but also Garry Jack, Michael O'Connor, Brett Kenny, Gene Miles, Steve Roach, Noel Cleal and Wayne Pearce.

Bell, though, did provide another individual high point with his outstanding try—the Kiwis' only one—in the Carlaw Park encounter. He figured in the movement twice, first unloading the ball as he was tackled, then climbing up off the ground to back up and score the try.

For all his talent, Bell still had flaws as a player wanting to become a successful professional. For one, he knew his tackling technique had to be refined. Perhaps, too, the good-time nature at Eastern Suburbs was influencing him too much; that's the way it seemed when the Kiwis went into camp for the second test in Sydney.

"I learnt another harsh lesson, then," says Bell. "When we assembled, I got onto the drink with a few of the guys and I really gave it a good nudge. I was in a bad way for a couple of days afterwards and, when it came to the test on the Saturday, it just passed me by. I didn't feel right and, from that test onwards, I learnt that I would have to start looking after myself if I wanted to succeed.

"If I had a decent drink after that, it was usually straight after the game, never in the last few days before one. My performance in that Sydney test might have been nothing to do with the night I had on the drink, but it just might have been the reason. So, the best way to prevent that possibility in future was to watch my drinking. Your preparation has to be right."

His suspension saw to it that he missed the third test at Lang Park and what lay ahead in Papua New Guinea. The tour was plunged into controversy as Graham Lowe and his players suffered the shame of being the first side to lose a test to Papua New Guinea, beaten 24–22 in Port Moresby.

"That result brought a lot of shame on New Zealand," says Bell. "When I heard about it, I thought something must be wrong with the team up there. But, in saying that, when I toured Papua New Guinea for the first time in 1987, I could see how it happened that the guys had been beaten. It's a tough place to play in."

Against the backdrop of suspension and what he regarded as less than satisfactory form throughout the year, Bell was an even more distracted

The Kiwis' 1986 series against Australia was a flop—but Dean Bell beats Garry Jack on his way to a wonderful try in the Carlaw Park test. Auckland Star

footballer when Leeds began courting him. His two-year deal with Easts was about to end but there hadn't been any approach from the club about his 1987 plans. It was time to confront the gaffer.

"Ron Jones was a dictator and, of course, as history shows, he ultimately found himself in lots of trouble over his time at Easts," says Bell. "Clearly he did some bad things but I couldn't fault him for the way he treated Jackie and me.

"I recall when I first arrived at Easts I was told to always call him 'Mr Jones'. I never did. I called him Ron. I'll remember him most for what he did for Jackie when she had problems with an ectopic pregnancy. It was really serious and could have been very dangerous but Ron ensured Jackie had the best possible treatment."

But Bell's approach to Ron Jones during 1986 wasn't on humane grounds, it was straight business.

"He probably wasn't that thrilled that I was looking to leave Easts after just two years. At the same time, I had a good offer in front of me from Leeds. They were offering £25,000 for a signing on fee which, to me, was very good money then.

"I wanted to find out what Ron could offer me to stay at Easts. They couldn't match it, not with match payments and everything wrapped together. Well, Ron said they couldn't and, to be fair, I hadn't given them a lot of reasons to hold on to me with my performances in 1986.

"There was probably also the worry that I'd been suspended twice in my two seasons there, and they might have seen me as a liability. So I didn't expect them to fight too hard for my services; I was ready to move on to something new.

"I felt I'd given my best in terms of effort at Easts. I always like to think I do that. But I certainly hadn't shown my best and that did eat away at me as unfinished business. To be properly judged, you have to play in the toughest competition, which the Winfield Cup was. I don't like to belittle the English competition because it's tough in its own way, but it's definitely not as intense as the Winfield Cup."

So, goodbye Eastern Suburbs, hello Leeds. Well, not quite. Hello Wigan, who intercepted Dean Bell before he could sign a contract, so denying Leeds the test player they felt sure they'd have on their books for 1986–87 (Leeds ultimately signed a young Andrew Ettingshausen instead).

Going to Wigan was as new for Dean Bell as it was for the coach he'd grown to admire. When Graham Lowe arrived at Central Park he inherited players he knew only a little about, perhaps not even a little in many cases. Among the playing staff were three former Springbok rugby union internationals, Rob Louw, Ray Mordt and Nick du Toit. The next season they were unwanted by Lowe but Bell believes Mordt, especially, should have been persevered with.

"Ray was so strong and fast," he says. "Maybe he should have done a little better, although I don't think Graham gave him enough of a chance in many ways. He needed to be worked on because he was a rugby union winger and was very raw.

"Rob wasn't possibly suited to league in many ways, but all three of them were neat guys. Being a New Zealander, you're influenced by what people say about South Africans and apartheid. Because of the way it's all projected, it's easy to have preconceived ideas about them but they were first-class guys and became very good friends of ours."

The proof of that could be found years later in 1995 after Bell had signed on as Leeds coach and was after new players. "Rob was in touch with me then. He'd basically become an agent for us in South Africa, looking out for rugby union talent that we could sign."

Wigan were long on talent when Lowe arrived, but fairly short on trophies. Of the major ones, Wigan had never won the Premiership Trophy, were the current holders of the John Player Special Trophy (which they'd won only one other time), they'd won the Challenge Cup only once since 1965, and hadn't won the first division championship for 27 years.

Talent wasn't a problem. Apart from Bell and the South Africans, Wigan's 1986–87 squad included Brian Case, Shaun Edwards, Henderson Gill, Andy Goodway, Steve Hampson, Ellery Hanley, Joe Lydon, Ian Potter, David Stephenson and Graeme West, with South Sydney's Ian Roberts signed early in the season and Andy Gregory moving from Warrington later.

"My first game for Wigan was against Leigh, and I just knew straight away that I'd made the right decision," says Bell. "I couldn't believe the class of the players around me.

"And Ellery Hanley! I saw him score a try that day and I just thought, 'Wow!' I couldn't believe the guy. I'd never seen a player get rid of tacklers as well as he did. It was a real eye-opener.

"I'd come across a lot of good players in my time, but to me he had always stood out. That was going back to 1984 when he was in the Great Britain side we beat 3–0. Even in a struggling side he was dangerous, and earlier that year in the Oceania-Europe match in Paris he'd caught the eye the way he was pushing off Mal Meninga and everyone. A fantastic athlete, up there with the very best there has ever been in the game.

"You wouldn't say he was the best passer around in terms of setting people up but his finishing, his strength and his endurance set him apart."

In that debut appearance, Bell was virtually straight off the plane, on the wing and hungry to score a try. He did, too, as Wigan won 35–0, igniting a Wigan career which finished eight seasons later with 253 appearances in all and 96 tries.

But the feature of the 1986–87 English season wasn't Hanley, Bell or any individual player. It was the entire Wigan team and the huge impact Graham Lowe had on the English game in his debut year. Essentially it

*Dean Bell poses with the John Player Special Trophy,
just one of the prizes that came Wigan's way in a
glorious 1986–87 season.* Dean Bell Collection

meant revolutionising attitudes on defence, which had for so many years been the weak link.

"But Graham didn't concentrate just on tightening the defence at Wigan," says Bell. "He balanced things. He had a lot of good ideas on attack, with a lot of moves, a lot of them very intricate.

"He might have been a foreigner coming into the English game but Graham didn't have any special difficulty convincing the Wigan players about what he was trying to achieve. There might have been some suspicion in earlier years about an outsider. By that year, though, players had turned the corner and Lowie was well accepted, just like me. There was no sign of anyone at the club believing that the English way was best. They were all ready to flow with the changes."

And the changes were dramatic as Wigan ran through the season all but unchecked. It was in the first division championship that their superiority was most pronounced. A title they hadn't won since 1960 was secured two weeks before the end of the programme and left them 15 points clear of second-placed St Helens. The Riversiders rewrote all manner of first division records—most tries (174), most points scored (941), least points conceded (193), least tries conceded (29) and most championship points (56).

Wigan had only two first division defeats all season (both to Warrington), while they also won the Lancashire Cup, the John Player Special Trophy and the Premiership Trophy. And then there were the individual honours—Graham Lowe automatically Coach of the Year, Ellery Hanley named Man of Steel, Andy Gregory picked by fellow professionals as the First Division Player of the Year and Shaun Edwards named Young Player of the Year.

In 45 games that season, Wigan amassed 1346 points, including 246 tries. Bell himself appeared in 42 games and scored 22 tries, but that had nothing on Ellery Hanley's staggering 59 tries, made all the more remarkable because Lowe switched Hanley from the backs to loose forward during the season.

"We were winning games very easily and winning trophies," says Bell. "And there was a growing jealousy from other clubs who resented Wigan winning so much. The sort of jealousy and complaints about Wigan buying a side with a cheque book.

"It's easy to sit back and say you can buy a team but it doesn't always win trophies—and Leeds have been an example. You need to get it right with the coaching as well as buying the right players. Graham Lowe brought a lot of new ideas in what was at least a mini-revolution if not a total one.

"We just blew so many sides out and it was never like that again until Wigan won fairly easily in 1994–95. In the other years we had to work much harder for our success."

But for all the silverware won in 1986–87, there was one famous blot on an otherwise glittering season—failing to win the Challenge Cup, the most prized jewel of all. What's more, Wigan didn't even advance beyond the first round proper.

"It was the result which made Oldham famous, and especially Paddy Kirwan, who scored the try that levelled the scores [with Mick Burke] converting for a 10–8 win," Bell remembers ruefully. "My Mum and Aunty Marilyn were holidaying in England at the time, so I've always blamed them for being bad luck charms! We really thought, and everyone did, that was our year to get to Wembley and win it. So to get knocked over at the first hurdle was a hell of a shock. We never thought that would happen.

"The players can say the first division championship is the hardest and therefore the most important to win, but then again most players, including myself, would rather play at Wembley. The fans want that too. So do the club's directors. That's the big one of the season.

"I can still see myself standing in the Oldham clubhouse afterwards. As each one of the Oldham players entered the room, the fans would erupt and we could only stand there and endure it all. I made a pledge right then that I didn't want to experience that again, and I believe that day has a lot to do with why Wigan have since been to Wembley so many times.

"A lot of people go to Wembley for the trip and some of the players did that season. I told them I wouldn't. I didn't want to go to Wembley until I was playing there."

If the Wembley thrill was missing, Dean and Jackie Bell had an even bigger one during that first season at Wigan—the arrival of their son Kurtis in November. A cause for joy for them, but not a time when Dean covered himself in glory.

"Jackie was well into her pregnancy when she had a regular check-up and it was found her blood pressure was high," he says. "It was decided she should be kept in hospital to monitor things. Standard procedure, I thought, so I went to training and afterwards went around to Rob Louw's to have dinner.

"In the meantime, the hospital was trying to contact me because Jackie's blood pressure had gone way up and, when I got home, our neighbour ran over and told me I'd better rush to the hospital.

"By the time I got there, Jackie had had Kurtis by emergency Caesarean. She'd been terrified and there I was having dinner and a few wines with Rob Louw! She never lets me forget it either.

"It was a traumatic time because Kurtis had to be looked after in the special care unit, which meant a lot of trips to hospital for us. He was seven weeks early and they were anxious times worrying about how he was getting on. He was a battler, though, coming through it after five weeks in the unit."

As a true professional, Dean Bell wasn't about to the let the birth of his son disrupt his football schedule. He never missed a training session during that time. "I'm sure Jackie wishes I had sometimes, just for the sake of saying I'd done something for them rather than being totally dedicated. But that's the way I am."

Bell's original deal was only a one-year arrangement. Needless to say, a vastly improved deal was quickly put together three months before the end of the season to secure Bell at Wigan for another three years. He'd confirmed Lowe's faith in him and he'd proved to club bosses why the coach had wanted him so much.

Graham Lowe had intended to continue as Kiwi coach after the 1986 season and also fulfil his new job as Wigan coach. It was a dual role the New Zealand Rugby League had initially agreed to only to renege in the end—for Lowe it had to be one or the other. He believed the signs were clear. He was being shown the door, only he had to open it himself.

"I believed it would be a bit difficult for Graham to do both coaching jobs," says Bell. "So, I took it in my stride that I was going to have a new Kiwi coach in 1987. It wasn't such a big issue for me, although I obviously loved playing for Lowie."

He also wanted to give something to the game at home. So, rather than warm up for his Kiwi commitments by playing for Auckland, Dean Bell thought a little laterally.

"I looked at the Auckland side and thought they had some English-based players returning—and they were strong enough as it was," he says. "I thought it wouldn't hurt to play for someone else."

That someone else was the South Island, ironically for a match against Auckland in the national interdistricts competition. And this was genuine old-fashioned league territory, too—Wingham Park in Greymouth on the West Coast.

"I'd started hearing a lot about this guy called Kevin Iro when I got home," says Bell. "And the first time he got the ball he swatted off about half a dozen guys and I thought, 'Gee, this guy's quite impressive.'

"Auckland got quite a lead (18–0 at one stage) and then we started coming back at them. It was quite funny watching the clock too. Every time we scored, the clock would start going backwards a couple of minutes. We must have played about 50 minutes in the second half! But it was not quite long enough to enable us to win [Auckland just made it 26–24]."

It was in that game that Dean Bell the leader began to emerge, as he organised the South Island's backline defence and inspired the revival against Auckland. When the Kiwi team was named for the short tour to Australia and Papua New Guinea he was naturally in it, with Ron O'Regan named as tour captain. O'Regan, however, was forced out with injury and suddenly Bell had become his replacement.

"It was quite a shock, because I hadn't been a captain since my early teenage years," he says.

After a 44–12 warm-up win over Northern Rivers at Lismore—Bell with two tries—the Kiwis faced Queensland at Lang Park. A few weeks earlier a New Zealand Residents XIII had been beaten 18–14 by Queensland in Auckland, and it was a fair Maroons side, too, including Wally Lewis, Gene Miles, Colin Scott, Greg Dowling, Greg Conescu and a young Allan Langer. Miles was missing for the return clash, but the Kiwis triumphed impressively 22–16, a result which proved to hold real significance for the test to come.

But before that there was a one-off test against Papua New Guinea that saw Dean Bell advancing from tour captain to test captain as Hugh McGahan was battling a shoulder injury. The Kiwis survived 36–22: Bell provided two tries and Kevin Iro was astounding with a world record 20 points on debut from three tries and four goals.

"It didn't take long for me to appreciate why the Kiwis had been beaten there the previous year," says Bell. "We were really struggling in the heat. If you're not totally focused it can get you. Then after the game, the security people were throwing locals down the stairs and clubbing them over the head. It was so uncivilised."

But the big event of the tour was obviously the Lang Park test against Australia. Hugh McGahan was recalled as captain, although his injury meant he couldn't be totally effective. Otherwise it was a vastly reshaped line-up, with Bell and Clayton Friend the only other survivors from the Kiwis' 18–0 win over the Aussies just two years earlier.

McGahan, Bell and Friend were the only players whose number of test appearances was above the single figure range. Darrell Williams, Shane Cooper, Mark Elia and Wayne Wallace had some test experience, but Kevin Iro, Gary Mercer, Ross Taylor, Adrian Shelford, Sam Stewart and Mark Horo had next to none.

Bell was delighted McGahan was back for this test, although at the same time slightly miffed. "I was a bit pissed off actually that I wasn't still captain for that test," he says. "Perhaps it wasn't right that I should have been, but I'm only being honest about it. I'd been the tour captain and I'd been captain against Papua New Guinea. Everything had gone well and I believed perhaps I could have kept the job, without it being anything personal against Hugh at all."

The match, whatever the captaincy issue, was quite sensational. Australia had all the names and experience but the tyros rocked them. After Peter Sterling had given the Aussies the early edge, the Kiwis then controlled the first half, first through Ross Taylor with a try off a Sam Stewart pass.

Soon after, Hugh McGahan's long pass set Bell free on a carving run through the Australian defence before he flipped the ball back over his shoulder, Gary Mercer coming inside from his wing to collect it and dive over for a spectacular try. With two Kevin Iro goals and a Shane Cooper dropped goal, the Kiwis led 13–6 at halftime and then defended it outstandingly in a scoreless second half for another New Zealand win against all odds.

And for Bell an achievement no other New Zealand player could boast. The Kiwis, 12 years without a test win over the Aussies, had suddenly won three in the space of four years in the 1980s, and Bell was the only New Zealander involved in each of the triumphs.

"I'm proud of that record," he says. "To look at it and say you were involved in three winning Kiwi sides against Australia doesn't seem a big deal. But it is because Australia are so strong and because we beat them so rarely [and it's worth noting the Kiwis have beaten them only once since that 1987 success—in Melbourne in 1991].

"I was emotional after that win too. So emotional I donated my Man of the Match money—$A1,000—to the team. I didn't think I really deserved it and believed it was right to do it then. But later that night I was trying to get some of it back! Jackie couldn't believe I'd given it all away. They caught me in a weak moment!"

Whatever Bell's assessment, he was a standout performer that night. But for a hero, it was difficult to go past captain Hugh McGahan, who played the test with a painful shoulder injury, one he aggravated during the match. He really couldn't compete to the level he was used to.

"But he was vital for us that night, just to have him there for his influence. It was the Mark Graham thing coming through with Hughie being his successor. The team needed that sort of player, especially in the forwards where we had so little experience," says Bell.

Bell had filled in for McGahan for one test and lost the job the next when his former Eastern Suburbs team-mate returned; but there would be nothing temporary about the captaincy when the Kiwis next appeared on the international stage in 1988 without McGahan.

the skinny bloke from manukau

Hugh McGahan

Dean Bell. It was a name you always heard about if you were playing rugby league at junior level in my era. One of the stars of the future, it was said. But when I first saw him, I couldn't believe it. Who was this skinny bloke from Manukau? He was skinnier than I was—and I was *really* skinny. You had to ask, "How could that kid make it?" Still, if he was going places, then I thought I must be able to as well.

By the time I progressed to premier or first grade for Otahuhu in the Auckland first division, Dean had already been there for a year or two for Manukau. It wasn't until 1982, when we were both in the Auckland team together under Tom Newton—with Dean's uncle Ian as captain—that we got to know each other.

I knew Clayton Friend, Dean's cousin, fairly well before that and it was after the 1982 national interdistricts tournament that Clayton, Dean and I were being touted as newcomers to the Kiwi team to tour Australia. It was a real surprise when Dean missed that side.

We all knew him as a centre, although it took time for him to establish himself in that position for the Kiwis. He wasn't what you'd regard as a classic centre, in the sense of one who created play for his wingers. Dean was primarily a runner, and an explosive one who created chances for himself by busting through or being thrown into a hole. He was a devastating finisher because he was so quick and strong, deceptively strong.

That strength could be traced directly to his passion for weight-training, something which started to become evident when we were both signed by Eastern Suburbs late in 1984. Easts gave us training schedules and Dean was that fanatical about it, and trying to acclimatise to Sydney conditions, that he trained in wet-weather track suits in the gym.

His appetite for training at Easts had to be seen. He'd always be up near the front in anything that was being done and, after training, he'd always head into the gym and do 100, maybe 200, sit-ups on his own. If he could drag some others in with him he would, and I used to hate him for it. I was too slow getting away from him; he'd headlock me and say, "Come on, let's go!"

From what I gathered from Joe Lydon, Phil Clarke, Denis Betts and others, it was never any different with Dean when he was at Wigan. He was always at the gym. Sometimes I would ring him in England and Jackie would say, "Oh, no. He's down at the gym." What a surprise.

That's the way it had to be with him. He looked upon his football career as his job, so he had to work at it all the time. To me it was still a sport. I dedicated myself to my sport but I also dedicated myself to a career outside sport. With Dean, rugby league was both his sport and his job...his life. He told me he had to treat rugby league that way. He had no trade and no education; when you look at it that way, he's learnt a heck of a lot. With his ability in the public relations area and his people skills you'd think he'd had a very good education. In fact, he's learnt it all through his football career. It's an example of what a sporting life can do for some people.

On the football side, I readily recall our years with Easts. And that usually means recalling the two suspensions he earned there, both after games against Canberra. The first time there was this monster Jon Hardy with Popeye-like arms and Belly said to me, "I'm not scared of this bloke!" Well, he just dropped him, dead-set necked him. The next year he came out of nowhere and dropped Craig Bellamy—high again. I don't know whether those stints on the sideline made him look at himself. I suspect they did. But, in 1995, for a guy to still be playing with the aggression he showed for the Warriors, said an awful lot about his character and the inspiration he provides for those around him.

As a player, what I liked about him was that you knew exactly what you'd get from him on the paddock. You knew where you stood with him, too. If the ball was heading his way you had no concerns about what would happen. If there was trouble, he'd always be right beside you. If he was ever beaten or pushed off—which didn't happen too often—you knew he'd be up off the deck to chase his opposite down. Most times he'd get him, too.

We developed a very strong bond in our Easts year; Julia and I and Dean and Jackie, we had lots to do with each other. And there it was again in 1995 when Dean landed the job as Leeds coach and asked me to be his assistant. The old partnership was back in force.

Hugh McGahan was a Kiwi test player from 1982–90 (32 tests), and captain in 17 tests. He has the New Zealand test try-scoring record (16) and played 53 matches in all for the Kiwis. He scored a world record six tries in the 1983 test against Papua New Guinea and was co-winner of the Golden Boot Award in 1988. He played for Otahuhu in Auckland before joining Eastern Suburbs in 1985, captaining the side and making 116 first grade appearances until his retirement in 1991. He was an Australian-based Kiwi selector in 1994–95.

staying alive

Fame is a vapour, popularity is an accident, money takes wings. Those who cheer you today may curse you tomorrow. The only thing that endures is character.

When John Monie left Parramatta to lengthen and strengthen his coaching career at Wigan in 1989, the once-mighty Eels had already become a memory. The side he'd coached to grand final glory in 1986 had broken up and not surprisingly Parramatta had slipped from champions to simply being competitive.

But if the Eels had subsided as a real force then—although still eighth in the minor premiership in 1989 and not a world away from the top five—the Parramatta Monie returned to as enemy coach in 1995 was worse than a pale imitation of the side he'd known for so many years.

This was arguably the softest game of the year for the Aucklanders, given Parramatta's dreadful state. So there was never a question that Monie and his players should leave Parramatta Stadium with two competition points from the seventh-round visit.

The Warriors now knew they could win, knew how to win and also knew they had two legitimate competition points on the Winfield Cup ladder. Now they had to learn how to put some victories together and their third away game promised easy points.

"Ours was a good performance against Illawarra," says Bell. "Sometimes you can win and that's all. We did much more than that, and what was also great about it was that a lot of the Illawarra forwards were sore after the game. That's always a good sign. You then have the satisfaction of knowing you got right over the top of them.

"But the Parramatta match never promised to be anything like that. There was the away from home factor and the travel to consider again—but if we failed to come away with two points from that game we would have been more than disappointed. Our season would have shaped up as a real struggle.

Even the biggest players have trouble coping with Dean Bell's legendary defence. Parramatta's massive second rower Brett Plowman finds out for himself in the Warriors' seventh-round Winfield Cup clash. Andrew Cornaga (Photosport)

"They were struggling and a lot of their best players were also out injured. Complacency was never a factor, even though Parramatta were a long way removed from the side of the '80s when they had Kenny, Sterling, Cronin, Price, Grothe, Ella and company. Some of them were there that day—but in the crowd, thankfully."

Bell's season also took a change in direction, as John Monie had always hinted it would. At Wigan, he'd often been inclined to use Bell at loose forward: in fact, it was in the No 13 jersey that he won the Lance Todd Trophy in the 1993 Challenge Cup final against Widnes.

With Stephen Kearney out injured, and Tony Tatupu's form not as hot as it had been in earlier games, Monie reshuffled his forwards by moving Logan Edwards into the second row with Tony Tuimavave.

"If the coach tells me he wants to play me at loose forward, that's his choice," says Bell. "It doesn't worry me, although it did for that game. I told John my only concern was my hand and that in the forwards I obviously stood more chance of knocking it, where in the centres I could probably survive.

"He agreed, but couldn't come up with any other options because he didn't have any confidence in any of the other back-row forwards in the club at the time. He kept coming back to me for his No 13, so that was the way it stayed."

What the positional change for Bell did was to create the opening for John Kirwan to make the first grade starting line-up for the first time, Whetu Taewa moving in one from the left wing to Bell's spot.

That seemed totally logical, for Kirwan had settled in quickly, including a try against Manly among his three reserve grade appearances and performing efficiently when he was used as a first grade interchange against Illawarra.

His promotion certainly proved justified, for the big former All Black winger had the dominant role in two of Auckland's eight tries, although he did embarrass himself once in the first half. After Tea Ropati had made a bust, he fed an unmarked Kirwan with the tryline 40 metres away; but with his first try in first grade on offer, the new boy made a meal of collecting the pass.

And that was indicative of the way the Warriors went for the entire first half. Mercifully, Bell's stint at loose forward proved abbreviated because with him missing from the centres, Auckland were bumbling through the first half and looking directionless. Monie moved to rectify that as he'd always planned by switching Bell back to the centres and bringing Tatupu on.

"The truth was I felt a bit lost being back at loose forward," says Bell. "When you play there you have to fill in wherever and whenever. I ran around a fair bit but I didn't feel right, as I hadn't played in the forwards for so long.

"It didn't make any difference to John's plans though. Even if we'd been going well, he would have taken me out of the forwards when he did, as he has a record of sticking fairly closely to his pre-match plan."

Certainly the Warriors were a changed unit once the Bell-Tatupu switch was made later in the first half. From only 10–4 ahead at the break they exploded with a 30-point second half spree to coast to a 40–4 win. Phil Blake maintained his astonishing strike rate, lifting his try tally to 10 in only seven matches, while Hoppe wasn't far behind on eight. And there was also a sign of times ahead when the brilliant youngster Stacey Jones made his top grade debut off the bench, and didn't half have an impact with a try and conversion as well.

Bell claimed lethargy had again affected the display, although he was no wiser about why it was happening. The players simply felt flat, and it looked so obvious in the first half when they let the Eels score first. At the other end of the field, they were lacking finish and polish, although there was still enough class to score a couple of fair tries, especially Tea Ropati's effort after Kirwan had danced down the touchline and fed a nice pass inside.

"It was a big winning margin, but certainly not a flash display," says Bell. "Then again, it was a win away, our first at that, and we collected two competition points for the second week running. You can't dwell on the quality of the performance too much."

That's the pragmatic Dean Bell. The match is over, history. Learn from what went right and what went wrong but soon switch on to the next one. And the next one promised a much sterner test—the Sydney City Roosters, Bell's old Eastern Suburbs side travelling under a new name in 1995.

With Hugh McGahan's lengthy ties with the Roosters, it set up a bit of a grudge match for the two former Kiwi captains. And they had a side bet on it, the loser owing a night at a restaurant. It meant much more than that for some of the Roosters' players and for coach Phil Gould.

In Gould, Sydney City had one of the outstanding coaches of the modern era, a man who'd won premierships coaching Canterbury-Bankstown and Penrith as well as guiding New South Wales to State of Origin success. His departure from Penrith late in 1994 triggered a buying spree for the Roosters as they signed a number of players, including Kiwi prop Terry Hermansson from South Sydney, Wigan's Great Britain international Phil Clarke, ex-Penrith winger Graham Mackay, Manly hooker David O'Donnell and St George stand-off Andrew Walker, plus rugby union backs Darren Junee and Peter Jorgensen.

The match was again a basic race for two Winfield Cup points, but there was battle within the war, especially in the front row, where Roosters props Hermansson and Jason Lowrie plus the Warriors' props Hitro Okesene and young Joe Vagana were giving Kiwi coach Frank Endacott something to follow. And there was also born-again Tony Iro to consider in the second row.

Joe Vagana's promotion to the starting line-up backfired. He'd been outstanding off the interchange bench in recent outings but, rather than stay with that formula, Monie wanted to throw him in against some tough opposition from the start.

"John wanted to find out for himself what Joe was made of," says Bell. "It was a fairly rugged opening to the game and perhaps it didn't work so well. But John was quick to take him off when he realised it wasn't a success. Joe still had a bit to learn then."

If it didn't run so smoothly for Vagana—who was on the end of a furious assault from Hermansson and Lowrie—it was much worse for the Warriors on the scoreboard. And crucial to the Roosters' start was the highly impressive Iro.

He busted the Warriors' left-handside midfield defence to put Shane Whereat across and then figured on the other flank midway through the half, fading across from the open side of the ruck to the short side to give Junee a superb try-scoring pass. In between, Hermansson's rhino charge scattered Auckland tacklers for another try, none of them converted and the Roosters had an ominous 12–0 lead with plenty of the half to go, and a powerful breeze behind them.

They didn't respect it, though, and a Bell try close to halftime proved to be the lifeline the Warriors needed, trailing only 12–4 at the break and knowing the wind would be theirs in the second half.

"I made hard work of that try," says Bell. "All I had to do was catch the pass and I was over. But I started staggering, almost falling over. The ground in that part of the field had been resown or regrassed and it was all loose. The turf was coming away from under me and it was all I could do in the end to stay up long enough to get the ball over the line."

That proved the bonus because, straight after the break, the Warriors struck twice. Just two minutes in, a big Gene Ngamu kick freakishly hit the crossbar, a fast following Tony Tuimavave collected it expertly and put Duane Mann in. And a few minutes later the Warriors were 16–12 up after a Tony Tatupu try. Suddenly the complexion of the contest changed.

Vagana, back in the game, was taken high by Iro and referee Paul McBlane almost instantly pointed the former Kiwi off the field permanently. While the Warriors had already turned the game against a 13-man Sydney City line-up, one man less gave them a decided edge and almost instantly they went further ahead, 20–12, with a Ropati try.

Their tendency to go soft on defence was evident again as Junee's second try had the Roosters trailing only 20–18, but Bell's second clinched the match despite a late Mackay try trimming the margin to 26–22, and that was more than enough to satisfy another monster home crowd of 28,650.

But the winning outing was blighted by more serious problems with Bell's thumb injury; and this time painkilling injections weren't going to be enough to keep him on the field in future games.

"I had my usual injection before the game but then knocked the thumb in a tackle in the first half. I thought then it felt more painful than normal so I had another injection at halftime," says Bell. "This time I'd fractured it completely. Displaced it as it turned out."

Even with the thumb shattered, Bell played on and, the day after his 33rd birthday, he'd found cause for a triple celebration—the victory and two tries, his second hinting at vintage Bell when he shook off the defence and had a lot more work to do than he did for his first.

It was three wins on end for the Warriors, but x-rays the next day confirmed Bell's worst fears that his thumb wouldn't allow him to play for a few weeks. His team would have to survive without him for three matches, and, critically, the next two were the demanding back-to-back away assignments against Newcastle and Cronulla-Sutherland.

Born to lead. Dean Bell takes his troops onto Eden Park for the ill-fated 1988 World Cup final against Australia. Ross Land (Fotopacific)

Above: *Trying to break free in the 1988 World Cup final.*

Bruce Jarvis (Fotopacific)

Left: *New Zealand Rugby League president George Rainey does the introductions as Dean Bell meets Prime Minister David Lange.*

Ross Land (Fotopacific)

Right: *Mark's Monsters, a crew not to be messed with on the Kiwis' 1985 tour of Britain and France – captain Mark Graham (left), Ricky Cowan, Mark Elia, Mark Bourneville, Joe Ropati, James Goulding, Wayne Wallace and Dean Bell.* Dean Bell Collection

Right: *Dean Bell savours the Wembley winning feeling for the first time, part of the 1988 Wigan team which also included Kiwi coach Graham Lowe and New Zealanders Kevin Iro, Adrian Shelford and Tony Iro.* Wigan Observer

Below: *Coach and captain revelling in another Wembley triumph. John Monie and Dean Bell after the 1992 Challenge Cup win.* Dean Bell Collection

Above: *Memories are made of this . . . Dean Bell and the Challenge Cup in company with British Prime Minister John Major after the 1992 final.* Right: *The ultimate moment in British rugby league – hoisting the Challenge Cup at Wembley.*
Dean Bell Collection

Top left: *Feeling totally at home doing the Wembley walk before yet another Challenge Cup final appearance.*
Dean Bell Collection

Top right: *Wigan captain on the rampage. Dean Bell stretches Widnes' Jonathan Davies on defence in the 1993 Challenge Cup final.*
Dean Bell Collection

Middle left: *Once more with feeling, Dean Bell gives a throng of photographers the sort of shot they can never stop snapping at a Wembley final.*
Dean Bell Collection

Bottom right: *Dean Bell checked by Warrington's defence in the 1991 Challenge Cup final.*
Bob Thomas (Fotopacific)

Bottom left: *Could it be those are tears of joy? Quite probably, as Dean Bell joins the fans after Wigan had won the 1992 Premiership Trophy final.* Dean Bell Collection

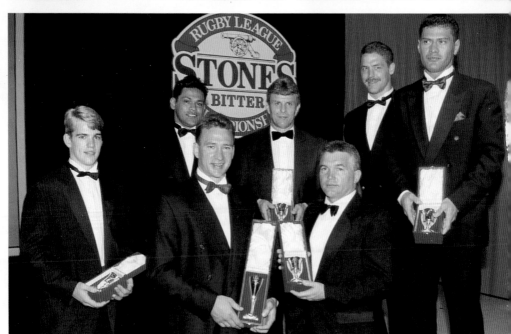

Few captains have handled as much silverware as Dean Bell and, in 1992, he lifted not only the Challenge Cup but also the First Division Championship Trophy (top left) and the Premiership Trophy (top right). What's more, he capped the season by claiming the supreme accolade as Man of Steel (above).

Rugby Leaguer & Varley Picture Agency

wigan's wembley wonders

The greater the obstacle, the more glory
in overcoming it.

Inanimate they are, but the world's great sporting stadiums and venues evoke the most astonishing emotional responses from competitors and fans alike. Augusta, Lord's, St Andrews, Wimbledon, the Melbourne Cricket Ground, Twickenham, Old Trafford...they all have an instant appeal for the sports connoisseur. And partnered with famed events, sports or teams, they make the ultimate cocktail—Augusta and the US Masters, St Andrews and the British Open, Lord's and an Ashes test, Twickenham and a rugby test, Old Trafford and Manchester United. They are all special...always.

And there's Wembley Stadium, out on its own as a sporting shrine, staging two of the great annual sporting contests in different codes—soccer's FA Cup final and rugby league's Challenge Cup final. Usually spaced just a couple of weeks apart, maybe three, they feed off and depend on the Wembley stage.

The setting has been known to generate an obsessive desire, at least for rugby league players who live for Wembley. It tantalises them with what they view as the ultimate rugby league ritual. That's why Dean Bell and his Wigan team-mates were so shattered when they didn't come even close to the Challenge Cup dream in 1986–87.

The significance of the event had always been imprinted in Bell's mind; even back when he started playing first grade football for Manukau in Auckland, when winning the Fox Memorial was the pinnacle of the club season. In those times, Wembley's Challenge Cup final was something that generally happened in the early hours of the last Sunday morning each April, and it was usually given only delayed coverage on television.

For the aficionado, it has always been an annual high point but, significantly, New Zealand interest only intensified once the 1980s began. That's because until then there had been fairly minimal involvement for New Zealanders in the biggest league occasion of them all.

Ces Mountford, Tom Lynch, Brian Nordgren and Peter Henderson were some of the fortunate few before 1980, but between the 1956 and 1982 finals not one New Zealand player featured in a Challenge Cup final at Wembley. Unwittingly, Gary Kemble and Dane O'Hara started a Kiwi explosion when they played for Hull in the 1982 final against Widnes. Six New Zealanders were on the Wembley stage in 1985, up to eight for the Wigan-Leeds clash in the 1995 and there hasn't been a final since that 1982 one without the Kiwi factor, right down to coaches in Graham Lowe and Mike McClennan.

"When I was just into the Kiwis, playing alongside Gary Kemble, Dane O'Hara, Fred Ah Kuoi and James Leuluai, it was always in my mind how lucky they'd been to play at Wembley," says Bell. "They were the inspiration for everyone. They made it to Wembley back then with Hull and, in the case of Gary and Dane, they went there a few times. So I was always envious of them."

By the end of the 1987–88 season he no longer had to envy anyone about Wembley, nor had he wanted for Kiwi helpers to rectify the one notable wrong of the previous season when Wigan had failed. The New Zealand influence had ballooned to the point, where apart from Bell and Lowe, Wigan could also list Kiwi prop Adrian Shelford, plus the dazzling young Kiwi test centre Kevin Iro and his older brother Tony.

Together they all made the Wembley trip as Wigan earned a showdown with champions Halifax for the title. But that, and Wigan's subsequent commanding display in the final, rather disguised some of the early drama. Once again, the first round proper very nearly snared Wigan—and Dean Bell was powerless to do anything about it.

"It was our tie against Bradford Northern," says Bell. "I wasn't even there. I was watching it from my hospital bed because I'd only just had an operation on my groin.

"I was in a sweat watching it, knowing I would be right to play in the later games—provided we went through. And the only thing that got us through was a Joe Lydon penalty, the only points in the game. I was that relieved."

Progress was more assured in the next two rounds, as Leeds were comfortably outpointed 30–14 and then Widnes 10–1, Wigan benefiting from the home draw for all three matches.

Defending champions Halifax initially advanced in a far more authoritative manner, expectedly so over amateur side Heworth (60–4), followed by another soft draw and an easy 30–4 win over lowly second division Rochdale Hornets. Hull Kingston Rovers weren't too demanding in the third round either, beaten 26–4, but Halifax's semifinal was something else. After a 0–0 draw with Hull it went to a replay four days later, Halifax barely surviving 4–3.

For Wigan, the gateway to Wembley Stadium was opened via a trip to neutral territory at Bolton for their 34–4 semifinal cruise against Salford, so forcing Wigan to institute routines which would become part of their system for seven straight seasons in Bell's time with the club—and then an eighth in the season immediately after his departure.

"That first one set the scene for all the others to follow," says Bell. "On the Thursday morning, we trained at Central Park before the bus trip to London with a few games of cards on the go. Once in London, it was something to eat and that night a show was booked for us; some players didn't go, others sneaked out to play pinball or do something else instead.

"On Friday morning, a short, sharp training run was followed by the Wembley walk. And that's when it really hit me that first year. Even though it was empty, you could see and feel what a special place it was going to be.

"We were lucky that year that so many of our players had been to Wembley before—Andy Gregory, Joe Lydon, Henderson Gill, Shaun Edwards, Brian Case, Nicky Kiss and Ian Potter. They all knew something about the place and that was invaluable for guys like me, as well as Kevin, Tony, Adrian and even Ellery and Andy Goodway, who were also new to it.

"Each year we went there after that, there would usually be someone in the squad who hadn't been to a Wembley final before, so the walk around the stadium was the chance for the rest of us to give them some tips.

"Then on Saturday morning, it was all on. We were up early for a bit of a run around the car park to loosen up, stretch, throw the ball around, and then get ready for the game."

What really counts for players new to Wembley isn't the lead-up, though. It's the drive to the stadium, to the famous Twin Towers. It's getting ready there. But, above all—before the game itself, of course—it's the measured walk out onto the ground.

"The first time walking out in front of that crowd was just spine tingling. It was...wow! Once we were on the ground, we tried to do exactly what the guys who'd been there before had told us—and that was just to focus on what we were there for and stay cool. Not to get overwhelmed by the atmosphere.

"When the Halifax players came out, they were waving to their wives and friends in the stands. It was strange really because Halifax had been there the year before so you would have expected them to know what was required.

"It's easy to get carried away, but we were cold about it. You're there to do one job alone and the more experienced guys had prepared us very well in that sense. For we four Kiwis in the side it was all new, as it was for Lowie, so we needed all the help possible."

Wigan were unstoppable; they were ahead 16–0 at halftime as Kevin Iro revelled in the setting with two excellent tries. In the second spell, Tony Iro scored early as Wigan stretched to 26–0 before Halifax managed to

First time at Wembley and, for Dean Bell, the perfect debut as he lunges over for his try ahead of Halifax winger Martin Meredith. Dean Bell Collection

concoct something themselves. Bell provided the sixth of Wigan's seven tries on a day when the champions' most glaring deficiency protected Halifax from even greater embarrassment. Their goalkicking was awful. Only two tries were converted in a huge Challenge Cup final winning score of 32–12.

The result secured, the celebration mood could at last take over: the walk up the steps for the players to receive their winners' medals, and for 21-year-old captain Shaun Edwards, the youngest captain in Challenge Cup final history, that most magical moment of all (some might even say bordering on orgasmic)—hoisting the Challenge Cup proudly, aggressively, jubilantly. Utter ecstasy captured in a few seconds.

It's a day when the lap of honour goes on and on. Fans shout out, wave, cheer. They hand over scarves and hats, and the players are drunk on the atmosphere alone. They stop and pose for team photos. They walk around, taking turns to parade with the prized silverware. Dean Bell had yearned for this moment and he didn't let it go quickly on 30 April 1988.

"After the match we went to the function room at Wembley for a few drinks with the wives and girlfriends, all of them done up to the nines in new outfits and hats. It's a big weekend for them, too," says Bell.

Wigan's Kiwi connection laps up the 1988 win at Wembley—winger Tony Iro (left), centre Dean Bell, coach Graham Lowe, centre Kevin Iro and prop Adrian Shelford.
Dean Bell Collection

"The next stop was a function put on by the club and sponsors at the hotel where the wives and girlfriends were staying. It was wild and you made it to bed any time from two to six in the morning, or not at all.

"After a late breakfast, there was the bus trip back to Wigan. We stopped off at the side of the motorway just before Wigan to transfer to an open-topped bus, those of us who were still standing that is. Others had to be carried on after the antics on the way up. It was a drinkathon.

"Then it was the drive through Wigan and, from the moment you hit the town, it's just a huge sea of red and white wherever you look. The most amazing scenes you could hope to see.

"I was at the front of the bus and I was moved to tears seeing little kids of only two or three all dressed up in Wigan colours. Dogs, too! I was milking the day for all it was worth because I reasoned I might never be able to do it again. Not until the later years, did I move to the back of the bus and let some of the newer players move forward and take it all in. You have to be made of steel not to be moved by it.

"Back at Central Park, 30,000 people were waiting and that first year we—Kevin, Tony, Adrian, Graham and I—had to get up on the stage and do a Maori song.

"And to think, after all of that, you could have to front up for the

Driving through the streets of Wigan with the great prize. For Dean Bell, it was an emotional experience, especially after the first Challenge Cup success in 1988. Dean Bell Collection

Premiership Trophy the next week, if you were still in it. It really is a huge anti-climax, the wrong way to end the season. Fortunately we didn't have to worry about it that first time. The season was able to end the perfect way for us."

The Wigan directors certainly make it worthwhile for the players too. By his seventh and last Challenge Cup final, Bell was looking at a win bonus of something like £7,000, while, in that first year, it was probably around £2,500. Put it together with the improved bonuses in the earlier rounds and Challenge Cup time is a healthy earner for the players involved, perhaps around £8,000 all up per player in 1987–88 and considerably more by 1993–94.

The Challenge Cup final alone underlined Kevin Iro's value. He had to be contracted by a major club after his astounding start to international football in 1987; the fact his older brother Tony joined him at Central Park was virtually an accident, yet he too made a try-scoring Wembley debut.

The Iros weren't immediately on the scene as Kevin was first forced to see out the New Zealand season and then the Auckland tour to Britain which followed. It was not until mid-November that they began to figure at Central Park.

It was an even more protracted business before Adrian Shelford made it onto the field for Wigan. Ruben Wiki earned notoriety for signing with both the Auckland Warriors and Canberra before his case was settled in court in 1995. In late 1987, Shelford was also in a sticky contracts predicament, wanting to link with Wigan when he already had a contract with St Helens. After much legal debate, the court ruled in Wigan's favour.

"Adrian just mucked up, but that happens," says Bell. "I was involved in that case as a character witness for him. Lowie was in London for it, as well as the directors and the club's solicitor, Tom Fishwick.

"We would be up late at night talking to Tom about the case, how it was going, and what Tom thought our next move should be. That was interesting for me because I'd never been in court before."

Footballers, though, have some difficulty maintaining a serious and formal outlook for too long.

"One day, while we were in London, Adie and I went into a joke shop," says Bell. "We thought we'd hit the directors and Tom with a few stink bombs.

"Tom Rathbone, one of the club's directors, took us to dinner at this really posh restaurant and afterwards we caught taxis back to the hotel. Maurice Lindsay, Tom Rathbone, Jack Hilton and Tom Fishwick climbed into a cab and I made out to join them, all the time knowing I was going to catch another one with Adie. I carefully dropped one of these bombs while I was at it, stood on it and told them I'd be fine to catch another taxi.

"I told our cab driver, 'Follow that cab!' And around 20 seconds later Adie and I could see all the heads turning, looking at each other. As we found out later, they were all wondering who was responsible for the stink. By the time they got further down Oxford Street the four of them were all trying to get their heads out of the windows to get some air. We were just cracking up, but we did give ourselves up in the end."

The Shelford contracts case smacked just a little of Dean Bell's own plight in 1986 when he was set to go to Leeds only to sign with Wigan at the last moment. Shelford, through his actions, had further fuelled the already fierce feeling between Wigan and St Helens.

And Bell had done the same to the Wigan v Leeds rivalry a year earlier when he was given a rather warm reception at Headingley. The crowd began chanting: 'Judas! Judas!' Their discontent was aimed at Bell, not that he appreciated it fully until told about it later.

"I said to the guys, 'That was nice of the crowd, wasn't it? Chanting "Genius! Genius!"' Then someone told me they'd been saying 'Judas'. Even then it didn't hit me because, not being a religious type at all, I didn't know who Judas was. Someone had to educate me."

While he had survived the acid test of a volatile Headingley crowd in his debut season, Dean Bell's 1987–88 season seemed destined for some months to have anything but a glittering finale at Wembley. There were genuine fears about his long-term future —and his short-term one as well—after Wigan played Leigh in a first division match in late September.

It had been business as usual in most respects. Wigan were too strong, with a 36–8 win. But the naked statistics disguised the reality.

"I felt a bit of a groin strain but had played on," he says. "After the game, I sensed there was something wrong in my lower abdominal area around my groin and overnight it really got bad. There was that much pain the next morning I couldn't lift my head off the pillow without the pain shooting right through that area.

"I knew then that there was something seriously wrong. That was the start of a fairly horrendous time for me. I saw specialist after specialist and no one could diagnose what the problem was. I had so much physiotherapy, I tried acupuncture, I tried manipulation. Everything. I'd be at the local hospital at eight every morning, being treated and doing exercises trying to get it right. After a couple of weeks, I thought it had improved and I played again only to feel a real tearing sensation in my groin.

"Weeks became months and I went to Lilleshall Hall National Sports Centre in Shropshire, which is the Football Association's centre of excellence. It's more a place you go to recover and I went through this tortuous week of training. I came back and played and it still wasn't right.

"While I was a Lilleshall I was talking to a guy about the problem I had and he believed it sounded just like what he'd had, an inguinal hernia. He said he knew a specialist in Harley Street, Mr Gilmore, who would be worth seeing and I did. Within about 15 seconds he said, 'Right, I know what's wrong. I'll have you right in about six weeks.' He asked when I could have an operation. 'What about tomorrow?' I replied. It was the most fantastic news I'd had in months.

"And that was it. I was in the Princess Grace Hospital and it was unbelievable, like the best hotel you could ever see. Wigan were great about ensuring this kind of thing was done for their players; after all, you're their investment so they need to look after you.

"I had that operation in late January and, within five weeks, I was back playing. After all those months out of action—about four in all—and it was that easy basically. If I'd seen Mr Gilmore straight way, I would have missed little more than a month. This way, half the season had gone for me. And, of course, that meant no match payments coming in for us to live off."

Bell was back at the most important time of the year, that time when the major titles were being decided. He finished with just 20 appearances and 10 tries, unable to do much to help the cause in the first division championship. Wigan had dropped far too many matches in that competition. After starting the season with 11 straight wins in a variety of competitions, they stumbled against Hull and then Bob Bailey's touring Auckland team (when Kevin Iro played against his new club). Other first division lapses against Castleford, St Helens, Bradford Northern and then three on end to Warrington, Hull and Hull Kingston Rovers, left them out of contention, finishing third, four points behind champions Widnes.

There was a black mark in the John Player Special Trophy, as Wigan lost their semifinal to Leeds and the end-of-season Premiership Trophy knockout competition never got out of first gear.

Bell's long-term injury also denied him another experience—playing in the World Club Challenge against Winfield Cup champions Manly-Warringah. A crowd of 36,895 jammed into Central Park on a night Bell was confined to the role of a spectator as Wigan won 8–2 in an engrossing if tryless match.

Manly had second rower Ron Gibbs sent off for use of the elbow on Joe Lydon, while fighting led to two sin binnings in a white-hot contest.

"That atmosphere was among the most electric I've ever encountered. And it also gave the British game a huge boost as Wigan's line-up that night was all-British. It was a night to remember, that's for sure."

Bell rued missing that game, and there was only limited success in other competitions—the Charity Shield and Lancashire Cup were both won—but he had helped in what really mattered. After all, Wigan would have been pleased enough to fail in all competitions, as long as they won the Challenge Cup. If Bell didn't fully appreciate how much that one trophy meant in England, he definitely did now.

"Just seeing people queue for Challenge Cup final tickets each year at Central Park is a great sight," he says. "To think they were going to watch me play and would get so much enjoyment out of it was a thrill for me," says Bell.

Two Wigan legends—indeed two league legends—had felt the Wembley thrill for the first time at last. For Ellery Hanley there would be another three experiences like it with Wigan. For Dean Bell there would be six more winning ones, and they'd all still be a thrill.

the ultimate pro

Ellery Hanley

It was Great Britain against New Zealand in 1984, and I remember this explosive package of a player. I thought to myself, 'Christ Almighty, this guy's one tough cookie—I hope I don't have to face him again!' But I did have to, twice more in that test series. It was Dean Bell.

I was a young kid then, and obviously Dean was as well, but he had such aggression and passion that it was obvious it meant everything to him playing in a test match. I thought to myself that I had never come across a player like him before; I knew immediately that Dean Bell was going to be a success story.

Now I look back and I class him up there with the immortals. Even now if I had to pick a team, he'd be one of my first players, not just for his aggression, but for his total commitment and his professionalism as a player.

He's a winner in all respects. Even if you were losing on the pitch it didn't show with Dean. You could be down 20 or 25 points and he would *never* give in. If you were a close mate of his playing in the opposition, you better forget about being a mate while the game was on because he didn't care who he faced. He's both one of the most feared and most respected players in the world.

Off the field, he's a really nice bloke. But that's something the players who faced him probably never saw. All they would be thinking was, 'Jesus Christ! We've got him to face—that step and maybe that swinging arm as well!'

He and I were at Wigan together for five seasons, and we certainly related to each other. I know there was one little thing we used to do before a game which I'm sure none of the other players knew about. I don't think *anyone* knew about it actually.

We'd be in the changing room and, before every match, we'd look at each other and raise our eyebrows three times each. It wasn't a nervous gesture. It was just something we did. Some players slap hands together before they go out onto the field, or they bump shoulders or nod heads together. Not us. We'd raise our eyebrows and smile! It was our way of saying we were ready.

As a captain, you couldn't look any further than Dean. He was a natural successor to me when I moved to Leeds. And, even though I was the captain at Wigan, the motivation I got from his example kept me going. He was a captain as well, even when I was on the field; he guided the side as much as I did. He's not a captain who talks constantly during a game but, if you were down, Dean would have something to say. Heads would roll, and not always the opposition's heads.

He did step over the line sometimes, and found himself suspended; which you had to expect with such an explosive player. But he was still a real professional in the sense that he generally knew how to stay within the limit of the laws, while stretching the limit as far as he could.

When it came to the tough stuff, he could dish it out and take it. Many guys have squared up with Dean and he'd take it. You get some players who'll come in as second man and third man in a tackle, but Dean would be right in the front line.

It's unfortunate as far as the Kiwis are concerned that Dean didn't play a lot longer at test level—he had so much to offer. New Zealand's loss was definitely Wigan's gain. It meant he was able to stay fresh for Wigan and wasn't burned out from playing too many matches. We at Wigan, and in England as a whole, saw the best of him. There's no doubt about it that New Zealand lost out on all the quality he had to offer.

So when he finally did go back home to Auckland as a player, it was to captain the Warriors. That didn't surprise me at all, because he was always keen to take on a challenge. It's what he looked for.

Now he's taken on another one by moving to Leeds as coach. That was perfectly natural too. There are certain players and people in the game who are instantly regarded as great leaders or coaches. If there's a problem, people have said let's stick Ellery there, or Dean, or Graeme West there, or Graham Lowe or John Monie. Those within the game—the players and directors—know the players to respect. That's why Dean Bell had to take over at Leeds. I knew he would. He was the man for the job and there was no shock about that.

He sets a great example. He wears his jersey like a badge—and you can't say more than that about the man.

Ellery Hanley began his Great Britain test career in 1984, finishing it in 1993 after 36 appearances, scoring 20 tries. He captained Great Britain and replaced Malcolm Reilly as Great Britain coach for the 1994 Ashes series against Australia. He started his career with Bradford Northern in 1978–79, scoring 55 tries in the 1984–85 season. He played for Wigan from 1985 to 1991, scoring 63 tries in all games in 1986–87, including a record 44 in first division matches. He played for Leeds from 1991 to 1995, when he took his career total past 400 tries. He signed with the Australian Rugby League in 1995.

nightmare in newcastle

To try and fail is at least to learn. To fail to try is to suffer the inestimable loss of what might have been.

John Monie always maintained the Warriors' draw for their first year in the Winfield Cup did them no favours. History will say he wasn't wrong. The newcomers were provided with an acid test from the outset, the first six rounds providing home games against Brisbane, Manly and Illawarra and away tasks against Illawarra and North Sydney, the only anticipated relief offered by a home match against Western Suburbs. Nothing comfortable about that, and so it proved.

At the other end of the year there was the month from hell, when the Warriors had to tackle St George, the Sydney Bulldogs, Canberra and Brisbane. And of those 10 rounds in the competition, Monie's team managed to collect just the two legitimate wins—against Illawarra at Ericsson and the Bulldogs in Sydney. Only four points from a maximum 20 points.

Yet the segment of the draw which always concerned Monie involved rounds 9 and 10. A brain surgeon's intellect wasn't required to deduce why. One week had the Warriors going to Marathon Stadium to confront Newcastle and, whatever happened there, they had to cross the Tasman again a week later for another difficult mission, Cronulla at Caltex Field.

Monie rightly reckoned those were two of the toughest venues to travel to and come away with a win. At the start of the season, he might well have welcomed one win from the two games as a major success. In the event, the Warriors managed that ratio; only it was more than a major success, it was more like exceptional.

As the Warriors had put together three successive wins, there was a reasonable glow of optimism heading to Newcastle. Dean Bell shared it. He could feel the confidence all week and convinced himself the omens were even more promising, because a number of Newcastle players would be backing up after the City Origin v Country Origin match around 38 hours earlier; the Knights had Paul Harragon, Adam Muir, Darren Treacy, Ashley Gordon, Andrew Johns and Jamie Ainscough involved in the Wollongong game.

The Warriors now had a fairly settled unit, although Monie had altered the balance by dropping the tackling machine Tony Tuimavave to reserve grade, claiming his second rower had missed too many tackles against the Roosters.

Monie was keen to make another change as well, wanting to bring in the highly-valued British import Andy Platt to start the match in the front row, almost certainly instead of Se'e Solomona.

"But Andy said he wasn't ready yet," says Bell. "John was desperate for a hardened campaigner like him against a tough set of forwards like Newcastle's. Platty wasn't fit then but he had to make the jump back some time soon. It was a case of knowing when.

"He had been on in reserve grade, and came off the bench against Parramatta in first grade, but he was still a sad sight at training and in games. He was limping every time he ran.

"I felt so sorry for him. He'd travelled halfway around the world and had an injury he shouldn't have had. A simple operation on his knee wasn't done properly, had to be re-done and he was still having trouble with it.

"He was getting a hard time, too, with people saying he was a dud buy. That was hard for him to take and I was disappointed about it because I'd been through a lot with Andy and knew what he could offer. John did as well, of course. That's why he bought him."

But the fact that couldn't be over-emphasised wasn't so much Platt's continued absence but the effect the loss of the inspirational Dean Bell would have on the side.

The doubters had long since stopped questioning his signing, acknowledging how vital his sheer passion and intensity was to the Warriors' cause, but now, for the first time, they had to find a way to survive without the rock of the backline. And there couldn't be many more intimidating prospects than going to Marathon Stadium without your most committed performer, the man who pulled all the strands together.

Bell himself was totally dejected about it because, against the Roosters, he'd felt the happiest with his own form since he'd returned to Auckland.

"I had the thumb broken just when I felt so encouraged with the way I was going," he says. "In fact, I was so pleased with it that I believed I could play for another year or two and was starting to think about that possibility.

"I had originally wanted to retire after 1995, mainly because I was expecting to have some problems with my groin, and I didn't know how my knee and my shoulder were going to come up either. The fact was, they were fine at that stage."

His right thumb broken and in plaster, Dean Bell was limited to the sideline with Warriors national sales manager Callum McNair (centre) and his former Kiwi team-mate Brent Todd for the Newcastle match. A good game to miss, too. Andrew Cornaga (Photosport)

And, while out of action, Bell wasn't about to forget his team. That's not the way he intended to operate anyway.

"John wanted me to travel with the team to Newcastle, which I always like to do when I'm injured. I used to do that in England; that way I felt I was still part of the team and would make a point of being on the team bus. A lot of players in England, if they're injured, don't even go to the game at all and I think that's bad."

Travel precautions were taken, arriving in Australia a day earlier than for the three previous away games. What benefit that provided was, in the end, impossible to detect. First the reserve grade were blown away 30–10 and then the 'nightmare in Newcastle' gained its ugliest chapter in a performance which was even worse than the one against Norths, and that had seemed impossible to match, let alone 'better', at the time.

Within 14 minutes, Newcastle had hit the Warriors with two tries to lead 12–0 yet, five minutes from the break, that was still the score. Despite being extended, the Aucklanders had regrouped and were battling bravely to stay in the contest. A 12–0 halftime deficit wouldn't have been a bad result in the circumstances, not a whole lot different than what had happened against the Roosters the previous week.

But in the 35th minute, Newcastle rediscovered their scoring touch to make it 18–0 and in the opening seconds of the second half they were in again. The game was out of reach at 24–0. In a flash it became 48–0, before finishing 48–6 through the merciful intervention of Phil Blake's 11th try of the season.

For the second time in a few weeks, the players had to cope with an increasingly futile situation where they were so far behind it didn't matter. Always there's the question of how players react in those times . Do they consciously or subconsciously surrender? Do they still try to a degree? Or is it a complete waste of time and effort?

"From the sideline, it looks like the players aren't trying any more when they're down by 25 to 30 points or more, and it probably happens as well. I would never think a game was a total lost cause unless we were 25 to 30 points down with less than 10 minutes to go. Then there is no hope.

"All you can do when you're trailing by a lot, as we were against Norths and then against Newcastle, is to call on your pride. What else is there? It's all about damage control, but we couldn't even manage that against Norths or against Newcastle. When teams get on a roll, especially with the 10-metre rule, they keep coming and coming at you unless you really put your body on the line.

"What also happened with those big losses was that they played havoc with our points for and against and, in the end, that's what hurt us during the season.

"I never say it to players in so many words, but my personal attitude is the old one of, 'If you go down, you go down fighting.' I wouldn't say that to the players because, if I did, it would be a sign to them that I'd given in and, as a captain, you can't let your players know that.

"There were other games when we fought well in losing situations, like the ones against Manly and Canberra later in the season. Even against Illawarra there was no sign we'd given it away. We kept coming back with tries when we lost that day and, when the Penrith game was beyond us, we saved a little face with late tries.

"As a club we were totally unlike Wigan or one of those other clubs where there is so much tradition. In the first year we were trying to build that character and tradition from scratch. It wasn't the same as playing for the pride of a long-established club."

Bell, forced to watch the horror afternoon from the sideline, was appalled about a defensive effort which was leaky all over the park. And he wasn't amused by some of the players' attitudes after the debacle.

"It was disappointing to me that some of the players didn't seem to be bothered about the loss, more so some of the younger ones in reserve grade," says Bell. "They were living it up in the bus on the way back to Sydney and I thought, 'You just got your arses kicked—why are you doing that?' It wasn't right.

"It seemed like some of the young guys thought making the Warriors was enough. They've got to learn that you don't dwell on your losses but you don't carry on like it's a party either. If I'd been playing, I would have been sulking all the way home.

"Instead I had a quiet game of cards at the front of the bus, which was obviously something I shouldn't have been doing either—as I found out at the team meeting on Tuesday. John had a few gripes and made a point of referring to guys 'playing bloody cards'.

"I didn't have to say anything at the meeting because it all came from Laurie [Stubbing] who addressed us about attitudes and behaviour. He really gave it to us in no uncertain terms. It was what we needed. We were going to get a dressing down about our on the field performance in any case but it was good to hit us about general attitudes as well.

"What was worse was that we'd been told we were a chance to have the Friday night game against Cronulla the following week so, when we drove back to Sydney, the point had been made to take it easy. That message didn't seem to have much of an effect on a lot of the guys."

None of this was encouraging for the second leg of the draw from hell—back across the Tasman the next weekend to take on Cronulla-Sutherland, who in recent weeks had let their guard slip a little. During the first part of the 1995 season, they were in fact beaten at home by expansion side the Western Reds.

The Warriors, though, had gone from settled before the Newcastle trip to a team in serious danger of finding the season an exceptionally long one. Monie had, for the opening nine rounds, adopted an evenhanded selection approach but, for this game, he took a major detour.

"He'd been patient with everyone, but now it had gone too far," says Bell. "He made a huge number of changes, the most he'd ever made for one game in his coaching career—and I certainly couldn't recall him being so radical at Wigan."

It was almost like starting all over again. Of the starting line-up used against Newcastle, Phil Blake, Se'e Solomona, Whetu Taewa, Duane Mann and Tony Tatupu were out for various reasons. Tony Tuimavave, who had surprisingly lost his place against Newcastle, replaced Tatupu, Platt came in for Solomona, Syd Eru for Mann, Greg Alexander moved to fullback, Ngamu came in to scrumhalf and Stacey Jones was given his first start in the run-on side at stand-off, while Mike Dorreen had his first start in first grade as well, in for Taewa.

There was also a significant change in the support staff on hand in Newcastle—the captain stayed home. "After the dressing down over what happened on the way back from Newcastle, I decided not to travel for the Cronulla match," says Bell. "I thought I was the last distraction they needed.

"John had been in a shitty all week and when I mentioned to him that I might not go over, he said something sarcastic like, 'Will you be in the squad?' I think he regretted it later and said I was welcome to be with them, but I thought the players might be better sorting themselves out without me there to complicate things."

Dean Bell, rising 31, in his second to last season with Wigan, but still too hot for the Leeds defence. Dean Bell Collection

Above: *Stay at Wigan as long as Dean Bell and the trophies are bound to mount up; this all in a season's work in 1991–92.*
Wigan Observer

Right: *Something Dean Bell and John Monie did plenty of during their time together at Wigan – winning trophies. This one the 1993 Challenge Cup success.* Dean Bell Collection

The Kiwi connection was ever-present during Dean Bell's eight seasons with Wigan. Above: Adrian Shelford (left) and Kevin Iro were with him as Challenge Cup winners. Dean Bell Collection

Below: And when Wigan won the first division title in 1993–94, Bell (left) was joined by Shaun Edwards and Barrie-Jon Mather plus New Zealanders Va'aiga Tuigamala, Sam Panapa and Frano Botica. Fotopacific

Top left: *Dean Bell, husband and father, with wife Jackie and their children, Kurtis and Chloe.*
Dean Bell Collection

Bottom left: *Dean Bell's link with Wigan is set to be broken as he's united with an Auckland Warriors jersey for the first time, a year before he would leave England to prepare for the Warriors' 1995 Winfield Cup campaign.*
Dean Bell Collection

Right: *Break on through to the other side! Rugby league history created as Dean Bell leads the Warriors into their first battle – against Canterbury in Christchurch in January, 1995.*
Andrew Cornaga (Photosport)

Left: *In one of the best performances of his season with the Warriors, Dean Bell is set to give Illawarra second rower Neil Piccinelli a defensive examination.*

Andrew Cornaga (Photosport)

Top right: *Taken low by his opposite Brandon Pearson in the ill-fated Ericsson Stadium clash against Western Suburbs. The Warriors lost their championship points for using too many replacements.* Fotopress

Middle right: *Warriors in arms – Dean Bell with Kiwi team-mates Duane Mann (left) and Sean Hoppe.*

Fotopress

Bottom right: *The captain giving his players their riding instructions before going into battle.*

Andrew Cornaga (Photosport)

The searing pace and raw aggression of the mid-1980s had gone but, at 33, Dean Bell proved to the New Zealand sporting public, and especially the Warriors' faithful, that he remained a rugby league player of uncommon quality – either in the centres or at loose forward. Andrew Cornaga (Photosport)

It wasn't until the 10th round clash against Cronulla that Andy Platt finally started a first grade match for the Warriors—instantly providing the steel the forwards had often lacked.
Nigel Marple (Fotopress)

Inspiration wasn't lacking on the day. Earlier that morning Peter Blake, Russell Coutts and crew had lifted the America's Cup by completing a trouncing of Dennis Conner (and it was Mother's Day as well!). It was, the Warriors admitted afterwards, a more than useful motivational aid for them.

With Dean Bell watching the game nervously on television with his father Cameron, the Warriors made a scorching start when a Gene Ngamu break provided a try for Dorreen, few relishing it more than the usual No 3 watching back in Auckland.

"Mike Dorreen is one of those players every club needs," says Bell. "It's good to see guys like him get a run—and get a try as well. He's one of those perfect back-up players you need in your squad, a guy I likened to Ged Byrne and Sam Panapa when I was at Wigan."

While Cronulla edged to an 8–6 halftime lead, a two-try blitz early in the second half vaulted Auckland to a 14–8 lead and there seemed to be a strong hint of authority about their play, helped no end by the direct approach Platt had brought to the forwards.

John Kirwan was one of the try-scorers—his first in first grade—although the transplanted left winger was still showing his in-bred right winger's habits by running with the ball in his right arm as he squeezed in at the corner.

The goalkicking was poor—thankfully Frano Botica was just a few days away from showing up—as Ngamu managed only one out of six attempts. What grated more, however, was the way the Warriors went soft again just when they were in position to dictate the outcome.

Two Cronulla tries in three minutes, one to Andrew Ettingshausen, suddenly had the Sharks in front 18–14 and almost everyone imagined the Warriors were headed for another defeat.

"I was so frustrated watching what they were doing," says Bell. "They did enough to win the game in the end, but they also did enough to lose it. At least there was some character shown this time."

Crucial to the comeback was Richie Blackmore, the first of the three late starters to the season after finishing up with Castleford. He'd come home and gone straight on the interchange before Monie put him on for Dorreen. He instantly impressed, too, especially with a wonderful piece of skill late in the game with the score still 18–14 to the home side. In a tight position, a superb reverse flick pass freed up Sean Hoppe who tip-toed down the sideline, staying in by just centimetres, to score his second try.

The Warriors played smart football minutes later to set up Stacey Jones for a dropped goal, and the 19-year-old showed what a cool player he is to make it 19–18. Right on fulltime, Hitro Okesene finished it off properly with the Warriors' fifth try and a 23–18 win.

It was scarcely in the America's Cup class on such an historic day in New Zealand sport. But this was still an outstanding victory, although not an outstanding all-round performance. It went deeper than that, though. It proved to the Warriors that they had the mettle to rebound from misery one week to create ecstasy the next week, and they'd have to do that again before the season ended.

stagefright and scandal

Contrary to the opinion of many people, leaders are not born. Leaders are made, and they are made by effort and hard work.

New Zealand rugby league's ability to self-destruct on the big stage has never been a myth. It has been painfully real, and familiar...legendary even. A swift scan of the memory cells can throw up numerous contenders for any collection of embarrassing moments.

Even in 1995, between their glorious performances—and there were many of those—the Warriors shamed themselves in their at-times rough Winfield Cup baptism, the most excruciating being what was the season finale.

The Warriors ran onto ANZ Stadium with everything to play for in front of the biggest crowd of the season, up towards 55,000. There were various possibilities, but the equation that mattered the most was so basic—beat Brisbane and they were in the top eight play-offs.

Not a chance. New Zealand league's fatalistic streak struck again, with a little outside help from a couple of British players and an Australian. But the nature of the 44–6 failure had the all-too-familiar New Zealand-made collapse quality about it.

For the 1995 Kiwis, read much the same. With Australian league in disarray, there couldn't have been a better chance for New Zealand's first series win over the Aussies since 1953. Super League-signed players were ruled ineligible for the Australian team, while the Kiwis could field all of their best players; and there was also the added benefit of so many more New Zealand players being exposed to Winfield Cup football now the Warriors were a going concern.

But, despite facing a vastly under-powered Australian side (with the exception of the freakish Brad Fittler), the Kiwis were left embarrassingly empty-handed, beaten 26–8, 20–10 and then, woefully, 48–10.

In 1991, it was also humiliating. One moment the Kiwis were good enough to stun Australia 24–8 in the first test, the next they were beaten 44–0 and 40–12, when in a position, mathematically at least, to win the series.

Even psychologists might have some difficulty understanding a New Zealand league psyche that allows so many chances to be passed up. But not just to lose...to lose with shame. It's something Dean Bell still had to grapple with as he finished his playing career, not in the accepted winning manner, but amid the debris of the shocking display against the Broncos.

Yet neither that performance, nor the others mentioned, rates as New Zealand's most ignominious league moment in recent memory. That will, for some years yet, surround events at Auckland's Eden Park in the 90 or so minutes after 4.00 p.m. on 9 October 1988. Rugby league's World Cup final against Australia at New Zealand rugby union's most celebrated ground represents a horror story the game can't forget.

No one knows that better than Dean Bell, the Kiwi captain on a day which went from being the most eagerly awaited to the most unwanted. Even when he was counting down to the Warriors' Winfield Cup debut against Brisbane, he found himself recalling the 25–12 Eden Park defeat, and the way the game's biggest day in this country had flopped. He was desperate to avoid a repeat in the Warriors' opener at Ericsson Stadium, and luckily he wasn't let down.

By 1995, Dean Bell was unquestionably one of the rugby league world's most respected and experienced captains. Also experienced enough to admit, in hindsight, that he shouldn't have been captain in the 1988 World Cup final.

The Kiwis' plans that year were significantly boosted when outstanding back row forward Mark Graham ended his self-imposed exile from international football. Stunned by the New Zealand Rugby League's decision to replace Graham Lowe as coach in 1986, Mark Graham—and Olsen Filipaina—voiced their protest by declaring themselves unavailable for the Kiwis.

"I never felt inclined to follow Mark and Olsen by protesting about Lowie's sacking in that way," says Bell. "Obviously Graham introduced me to the international ranks and was the catalyst for my career. I really got used to him with the Kiwis and then at Wigan, but I never felt the need to do anything drastic.

"I was level-headed about it. I knew coaches would come and go and that I would just go with the flow. I wanted to play for New Zealand and who was coach was not the issue for me. I was disappointed in the way Lowie was put out of the job, I'd be lying if I said I wasn't. At the same time, I was just prepared to play under whoever the coach was."

In 1988, that meant continuing an association he started the previous season with Tony Gordon; and obviously Mark Graham's return for the entire World Cup programme significantly strengthened New Zealand's

In just his fourth test as captain, Dean Bell leads the Kiwis into the biggest match in New Zealand rugby league history, the 1988 World Cup final.
Ross Setford (Fotopacific)

forward pack. However, with Graham back, there was also the matter of who the captain should be.

Dean Bell stood in for appointed captain Hugh McGahan in Papua New Guinea in 1987, then stepped aside when McGahan was fit for the following test against Australia. McGahan was a non-starter for the 1988 World Cup campaign and, even if he had been fit, Mark Graham was still the most experienced captain of the trio, having led New Zealand 18 times.

"It didn't work well with me being the captain once Mark was back in the side," says Bell. "And ultimately that was a huge problem for us in the World Cup final.

"I would have been as sour as anything if they [the selectors] had overlooked me as captain because I believed I'd done a good job the previous year. But even though I would have been dirty, Mark's return to the side put a different slant on it. With him there it would have been the right decision to make him captain. He had more experience, he had the mana and influence. You can be a little pig-headed and blind about these things, but now I believe they made the wrong decision.

"It did annoy me that Mark was picking and choosing when he would play, and that probably went in my favour when the decision was made about the captain. You could have asked, 'Why should he [Mark] have been captain when he's just come back into the side?' Really, though, we would have been better off with Mark as captain.

"There wasn't a problem between us on the field with calling or over calling. And we didn't have a problem about if off the field either. Because I'd been made captain, I think Mark probably felt he shouldn't step into that area. He didn't make it uncomfortable for me at all, but I know I felt awkward being captain with him in the team. And that didn't allow me to carry out my job properly.

"I didn't have the knowledge that I do now and, I must be honest about it, I wasn't ready for such a big job in such a big game. At the time, I thought I deserved being given the job but sometimes you have to look a little deeper than that."

The final was a vital mission for the Kiwis. In past years, the World Cup had followed a tournament format. When last held in 1977, it was called the international championship and Mark Graham had, in fact, made his test debut then. This time, though, it had been run over a four-year period with specified tests since 1985 carrying World Cup points (eight tests for each country).

The Australians sealed their spot, despite stunning upset losses to the Kiwis in 1985 and Great Britain in 1988. But New Zealand and Great Britain faced a ticklish fight to join them.

The same July weekend the Brits overturned Australia 26–12, Dean Bell's second test as Kiwi captain produced a 66–14 trouncing of Papua New Guinea in Auckland to set up a decider against Great Britain in Christchurch a week later. If New Zealand won, they would play Australia in the final at home, while a Great Britain win would have taken the final to England.

"In that first match against Papua New Guinea, the captaincy wasn't such an issue, which was to be expected," says Bell. "I felt things were running okay then.

"Leading up to the clash against Great Britain, I remember trying to think of different methods of motivating the players. I felt it was my responsibility to do that sort of thing and I thought I came up with something that was really quite moving.

"The night before the clash against Great Britain, Tank had brought in Lowie to talk to us. That was very moving in itself. He told all of us that we weren't going out to win just for ourselves. He told us we had to win for all the others before us, for players like Kevin Tamati, Dane Sorensen, Fred Ah Kuoi, James Leuluai, Gary Kemble, Olsen Filipaina, Gary Prohm, Dane O'Hara and Howie Tamati.

"They had all played a lot of tests for the Kiwis, and had been there at the start of this World Cup campaign but had now finished playing. Likewise, Hugh, who was injured and couldn't play, was with us that night. Of the original team in 1985, there were only a few of us left—Mark, Kurt

Sorensen, Clayton and me.

"So Lowie's effort started us off. There were plenty of tears after he'd finished. He's so good at that sort of thing. Then I asked the guys to stand up one by one and explain why they thought we should win, and say what it meant to them. Well, boy, the tears really flowed.

"I remember Clayton saying he owed the game plenty because the game had done so much for him, which certainly moved me. It was difficult for a lot of them who weren't used to speaking from the heart, and especially doing it in front of team-mates. It had the desired effect, though. Guys got up and broke down, or said a few words and couldn't continue. They really opened up."

It meant the Kiwis didn't lack the mood for the encounter, but the showdown at the Showgrounds was blighted by outrageous weather. "Even though I've played in some really cold conditions, in snow and ice in England, that day in Christchurch was the coldest I've ever been," says Bell. "And then to have cold showers afterwards!"

Somehow the Kiwis contrived to win the match 12–10, after leading only 12–8 playing with the considerable advantage of the weather. With so little possession—the scrums favoured Britain 18–9, the penalties 7–3—the New Zealanders defended so outstandingly they conceded just two points in the second half.

The Kiwis were rich on heroes, but the man who made all the difference in the end was replacement Gary Freeman, who'd been thrown into the test early after loose forward Mark Horo had been injured. Two tries later the decision to use Freeman had proved a masterstroke.

"Just as Clayton had come on in test matches and had an impact for us in 1984, this was the match when Gary Freeman did the same. This was the test when he really emerged," says Bell. "Shane Cooper was switched to loose forward and Gary went to stand-off. It was Tank's doing, a smart move. He obviously had a lot of confidence in Gary and that was well-placed.

"But all we could do in that test was survive, not just because our lead was only 12–10 but because it was so bloody cold. We just couldn't wait to get off the pitch. It was a very important game, I know, but stupid as it sounds I found myself thinking that all I needed to do was to get off the ground to get into the showers. And yet I should have been thinking only of fighting to win a test that was so close.

"To win it meant everything, but it's not a test Andy Platt, Andy Gregory and Joe Lydon let me forget. They always remind me about Andy Gregory's disallowed try when he ran around Kevin Ward. They always say they were robbed. I thought it was a forward pass myself. So did the referee."

The final wouldn't be played till almost three months later but, in no time, New Zealanders were generating an almost fanatical interest in it, essentially because it would be the ultimate trans-Tasman battle. And the fact Eden Park was secured as the venue intensified the anticipation, as it opened the way for rugby union diehards to be in on the occasion.

In the countdown to the final, Dean Bell was reunited with Graham Lowe when he coached the Rest of the World side to play Australia in a Bicentenary match in Sydney. And in a team including eight New Zealand players, Mark Graham was captain that night.

Bell also resumed an off-season contract with Eastern Suburbs. In his third season with the Roosters, Arthur Beetson was still the coach, before being sacked and replaced by Russell Fairfax in what was another all-too-familiar year of disappointment for the club.

While Hugh McGahan was still out of action, there was a new Kiwi flavour in the side with former All Black Kurt Sherlock in his second season and young Aucklander Dean Clark also there on the New Zealand Rugby League's rookie scheme.

"The worst part about this stint with Easts was that we had yet another trip to Seiffert Oval. Yes, Seiffert Oval where I'd been ordered off in 1985 and 1986," says Bell. "I was that nervous about it.

"As we went out onto the field, a guy in the crowd yelled out, 'See how long you can last today, Bell!' I had a wry smile on my face, but he wouldn't have known how anxious I was.

"I was actually still on the field at half-time and as we came off the field, he piped up again, 'Ah well. You've lasted half a game, Bell!'

"By fulltime I was still on the field. We'd lost but I was so relieved I'd lasted the game. I tried to find the wag afterwards but couldn't spot him. One of those times when a spectator was clever."

The Kiwi selectors also seemed to be fairly clever going about selecting their side for the World Cup final, boosted still further by Kurt Sorensen's return from Widnes to join Mark Graham in the second row. There were two obvious debits with fullback Darrell Williams and Hugh McGahan both out of contention.

But when it came to the big event in front of a remarkable crowd of 47,363, the Kiwis were absolutely awful, allowing the Australians to surge to a 21–0 halftime lead—even with Wally Lewis playing with a broken arm!—and then 25–0 soon after the break. League supporters were demoralised; rugby union people wondered why they had bothered.

"We lost the plot. We were too intent on the rough stuff, thinking that's the way we had to play it to compete in such a big game," says Bell. "We were so ill-disciplined and unprofessional. We didn't handle the occasion at all.

"I thought the Aussies did a good professional job on us, on and off the field. They'd played down the game, saying the Kiwis had to be favourites and all that sort of thing. We were just riding along with all of that.

"Our biggest blunder was playing Gary Mercer at fullback. He had a rib injury and shouldn't have played, although it was his call. Only the

The Kiwi captain looks for support, with the man he thinks should have been captain—Mark Graham—looming in the background.
Ross Land (Fotopacific)

player himself knows whether he can play and I suppose he was so keen to play, not wanting to miss out on such a big game. But it backfired."

That's the short version, but Bell also offers the long version of the disaster, one which he again turns back on himself and the captaincy aspect, as well as coaching problems.

"You wouldn't say it was a smooth build-up with all the hype and everything that went with the occasion," says Bell. "We spent more time practising the haka and doing other things than worrying about the game itself. I'm part Maori but to me that all went way over the top.

"With my knowledge now, I would know to eliminate distractions like that, but I didn't have that knowledge and experience then so I didn't speak out about it, or change things. Again I think that showed up the fault of me being captain.

"In the big game itself, when things weren't working out, I didn't know what to say. That was the time I really felt alone and exposed. It was such a huge game and I found myself thinking, 'What do I do?' I had no experience for it.

"The training sessions weren't right either, nor were the team meetings. The players didn't have confidence in Tank, which wasn't allowing training runs to flow.

The end of a tragic day for New Zealand league, and for captain Dean Bell, as he collects his loser's medal from the Prime Minister, David Lange. Ross Setford (Fotopacific)

"As senior pros, guys like Mark, Kurt and I couldn't get a say in how training runs should be run. They were so stop-start and we couldn't get moving. The trouble was, we didn't want to undermine the coach by causing too much trouble. On reflection we could have, and probably should have, got in there and demanded some changes ourselves. It's a lesson learnt, and one I would prove I'd learnt from in my last year at Wigan when I had similar problems with John Dorahy."

It was a very costly lesson for New Zealand league, though. There was also the issue of why so little was done to try to arrest the slide at half-time. Down 21–0, the Kiwis began the second half with an unchanged line-up.

"There should have been changes," says Bell. "We had Shane Cooper on the bench and I thought at halftime that we needed him on soon. He was a playmaker and we needed points, he was wasted sitting on the bench. Once again, though, because I was in this awkward position as an inexperienced captain I didn't say anything to Tank about it at halftime. I felt it was his call and my job was to carry out his instructions, not that there were too many at halftime.

"Mark and Kurt didn't say anything either, probably not wanting to cut across me again. Mark was probably pissed off that he wasn't captain, but he still didn't want to intervene. That's the way we all felt."

It was ugly, hellishly ugly, on the field for the Kiwis. Second half tries for Kevin and Tony Iro did absolutely nothing to soften the impact of a disgraceful defeat, other than making the scoreline seem a little respectable.

But even uglier was the aftermath, when New Zealand Rugby League president George Rainey launched a very public inquiry.

"While a whole lot of things had gone wrong, most of them on the field in the final, I had to stand beside my players as captain," says Bell. "And the New Zealand Rugby League should have been doing the same, which they most definitely didn't.

"I wasn't asking for the blame to be pointed at anyone at all, not the coach, the players or anyone. And definitely not in public. They were pointing the blame at the players, though, and as captain I naturally felt it was my duty to defend them.

"I was never asked for my thoughts about what went on. If an investigation of any sort was being conducted you would have thought it would be logical to ask the captain. The fact that I wasn't approached really irked me.

"Any witch hunt should have been done behind closed doors and should have involved the captain, the coach, the manager and perhaps a couple of senior players. With this one it was Gary [Freeman] and Clayton [Friend] who had to endure the worst criticism. They shouldn't have been slated in public. No one should have been. It gives you no confidence in the people you're working for.

"George [Rainey] has always been very friendly towards me ever since. In any case, I don't hold a grudge against him or anyone else. It happened and it wasn't a good chapter in the game's history.

"I think they [the New Zealand Rugby League] realised they were wrong and I made it very clear from England at the time what I thought about their actions. I said, 'If I'm going to be working for people who react like this, then I'll have to seriously consider my playing future for New Zealand.' In the end, that meant not coming home for the series against Australia in 1989."

At the same time, Wigan sweetened the pot more than a little to encourage Bell to become purely their property; and the grind of a full English season followed by off-season campaigns back in New Zealand was another consideration.

"Wigan had realised that, with me going back in the off-seasons—as I had in 1987 and again in 1988—it was year-round football for me, given that the English off-season is very short. So they offered me a lump sum of money over and above my contract to consider retiring from international rugby league.

"It wasn't just the money factor that weighed in. I was definitely looking for a rest after playing so much football. I'd been saturated and wanted to freshen up, so the idea of going home in 1989 was never really likely no matter what Wigan did.

"Certainly the witch hunt over the World Cup final was a factor as well. I could have worked with Tank again that year if I had wanted to go home; I would have been a lot wiser, that's for sure."

It meant Dean Bell never played another test at home, returning to the Kiwis only for the internationals on New Zealand's 1989 tour of Britain and France before quitting test football altogether. And time and again he's asked whether he regrets his decision; after all, he was only 27 when he played his 26th and last test.

"Probably I could have played a lot more tests looking at the way my career has gone," he says. "Then again, if I had played for the Kiwis, my career mightn't have panned out the way it has. By sticking with Wigan only, I've been able to freshen up in the off-season. I wouldn't have been able to do that by continuing to play for the Kiwis.

"To finish my test career was never easy. I agonised over that decision. But regrets? No, I don't have any."

a perfect signing

Maurice Lindsay

When Dean Bell spent the 1982–83 season with Carlisle, he actually played for them against Wigan in a Lancashire Cup match. He was an outstanding young player then. We could see that. After a season with Leeds (1983–84) and then two with Eastern Suburbs in Sydney, he was set to return to Leeds for the 1986–87 season. But, just before Dean signed on the dotted line with them, Graham Lowe agreed to join Wigan as coach. We asked Graham, if he was to sign players, who would be his number one choice—and he said, "Dean Bell—right age, right attitude, very competitive and a man I've seen perform brilliantly in the New Zealand shirt." Now Graham had the pick of the world's best and richest players. We told him we'd back him on whoever he chose, so it was a bit of a surprise to us when, without hesitation, he said Dean Bell was his jewel in the crown. He was right, though.

Obviously, as it turned out, we managed to get Dean at just about the perfect moment. We were able to sign a player who, at that time, was the best three-quarter in the world, and from that year onwards we had eight years of the most tremendous service from Dean Bell.

The fact that Graham went for him had as much to do with Dean's character as his ability; Graham knew that when he got Dean he would be getting a never-say-die character. Dean had tremendous pace, a tremendous sidestep, quality and athleticism, yet I'm sure it was his all-round competitiveness that Graham went for.

That was all added to by Dean's absolutely genuine character. I used to negotiate the contracts with the players at Wigan and I would have to spend weeks with some of them. Not Dean. With him it was a 10-minute discussion and handshake. We knew Dean's worth, so he had to be well-rewarded, but they were always comfortable negotiations. He never used an agent. He just came in, looked you in the eye, did the deal and was very fair. He didn't ask for too little, certainly didn't ask for too much, shook hands and got on with his business.

Like Denis Betts, Dean gave us incredible commitment. He rose to become captain; a totally natural event because he had those qualities. He's the sort of bloke that, if you were in the trenches, you'd want to have alongside you. And, equally, when you were on top, he'd win with style, win with dignity.

Constantly, people who have been associated with him will talk of his toughness. It's unavoidable. I remember one game when he was hurt and had to leave the field to have 17 stitches inserted in a cut in his face—and then he went back on the field. There was another occasion, when Wigan played at Hull, where he had an accidental head clash with Denis Betts. His whole bottom lip was severed from his mouth—bloodthirsty stuff this. He didn't know how bad it was because he was semi-concussed, but the wound required 33 stitches. The following day, the doctor said having 33 stitches inside your mouth would be one of the greatest discomforts imaginable, that it would be like having a whole lot of razor blades inside your mouth. Dean never complained about it, though. He wanted to play in the next game, but the doctor wouldn't let him—but he did return for the game after that. I've never known a player as mentally tough in my life.

If he ever missed a tackle, we used to feel sorry for the guy he missed because Dean would chase back and get that player come what may. That didn't happen very often, but when it did, he would chase, and catch the player and smash him to the ground.

No tribute is too high for Dean, and the highest I could pay is that he is one of three or four people who were solely responsible for turning Wigan around from the mid 1980s. I'd put him alongside Ellery Hanley, Graham Lowe and John Monie for having the most dramatic effect on Wigan's development. Without Dean Bell, Wigan would not be what they are today.

He'll be absolutely tremendous for Leeds as a coach. They don't know how lucky they are. I had it in my mind that one day he would be Wigan's coach and, indeed, that may still happen, but for now I wish him the very best at Leeds.

Maurice Lindsay has been the chief executive of the Rugby Football League in England since 1992. He was tournament director for the 1995 Rugby League World Cup. His career in rugby league administration began in 1979 when he became Wigan chairman, staying in the job until 1992.

tigers, panthers—and loiners

A failure is not always a mistake: it may be the best one can do under the circumstances. The real mistake is to stop trying.

A non-playing captain's life is an exercise in frustration. And in June 1995 it became that much more frustrating for Dean Bell—but with relief in sight, and with some unexpected attractions as well.

For Warriors coach John Monie this was a more confounding time of the season than any other, and not strictly because of results. Injury had denied him his captain when he needed him most, with international commitments beginning to eat into his players' resources and disrupt his regime.

At the same time, there were compensations. The Warriors' Castleford signing, Richie Blackmore, was now on board and had instantly appealed as the centre Monie was looking for after his display against Cronulla. And, soon after, the British invasion was complete, as the two other "Bs" the Warriors had been waiting for—Botica and Betts—showed up after their last, and all-conquering, season with Wigan.

For nine rounds, Monie had been forced to survive without all three and for 10 he'd been without Denis Betts and Frano Botica. That was always going to happen, but by the time Betts and Botica hit town the team was still spluttering, sitting mid-table with eight points from four wins. And that was less than everyone had hoped for.

There was also the issue of split round football. Across the Tasman, the State of Origin series meant the annual practice of spreading three rounds of football over six weekends before heading into a compact test series against New Zealand. The split rounds can be both a help and a hindrance; the positive side is that it allows players to freshen up and it eases the load —slightly—on those with representative commitments. In Monie's case, it also gave him more time to work his new arrivals into the Warriors' routine.

But the down side is that a team on a winning roll is held up. It was

Try time for Denis Betts in his outstanding Warriors debut against the Sydney Tigers. This was the second of his two tries in a 36–12 win. Ross Land (Fotopress)

possible to argue that this was the case for the Warriors; after their victory over Cronulla on 14 May and their away clash against Western Suburbs on 25 June, they had just two matches—against the Sydney Tigers and Penrith—during the break.

Bell had planned to play in both and obviously the clash against the Tigers had special appeal as it promised to be something of a Wigan reunion. Bell was looking forward to being on the field with Betts and Botica as well as Platt. It was also a homecoming for the Warriors, their first game at Ericsson Stadium since beating the Roosters five weeks earlier.

But an already frustrated Bell had those plans scuttled, and not by his thumb injury. That was healing satisfactorily enough and Bell believed he could have played without too much trouble from that—but he wouldn't have been able to play anyway. He'd pulled a hamstring. A fact kept quiet at the time.

Also kept quiet were developments for Bell's football career which started to brew the week before the Tigers match, and it was the arrival of Betts in Auckland which contributed to that. He had his agent David McKnight with him and, while Bell had never bothered with agents himself in the past, he asked McKnight about the possibility of finding a club to play for in England.

"I'd heard all about these loyalty payments players were getting and

David asked me whether I'd received one," says Bell. "I explained I hadn't because I had indicated I was going to retire so it hadn't been a possibility.

"David told me if things were to work in my favour for a Super League deal—and a loyalty payment—I needed an offer from the Australian Rugby League. That was the way the dealing was being done then and he thought I could get an ARL offer to help.

"The effect of that was that it set Jackie and I thinking about having another year with the Warriors. If I was holding up, why not? I didn't know whether the Warriors would want me for a second year but we rang our [business] partners to tell them what we were considering. They told us we'd be silly to turn down big sums of money for the sake of one more year away from the business [a boutique in Wigan]."

Action began to happen from all directions, because around the same time Bradford Northern contacted the Warriors' captain to sound out his interest in being a player-coach for them. Bell's answer was a definite yes, although not in a dual capacity; it could only be as a coach or as a player. He never heard back, and in due course St George coach Brian Smith was signed instead.

The machinations of clubs chasing an attractive prospect wound into top gear as one of the league world's most famous clubs also joined the race for Bell, in whatever capacity.

Leeds, or the Loiners as they're known in the north of England, have for years been the underachievers of the English game: heaps of money, heaps of talent, but no trophies. In fact, not one major success since Dean Bell's season with them in 1983–84, when they won the John Player Special Trophy.

They had ex-Widnes coach Doug Laughton in charge, but there'd always been a lot of criticism about his methods and his lack of success since guiding Widnes to trophy wins in the mid 1980s. Leeds obviously had concerns, because chairman Alf Davies rang Bell.

"He wanted to know my plans. He also told me they'd talked to Graham Lowe and wanted him as coach, only they were concerned about his health problems," says Bell. "After that, I phoned Lowie and wondered whether I could fill an assistant's role for him if he went to Leeds. Perhaps I could play and assist him and, in that way, it would be a good stepping stone to the coach's job. That's how I thought it would work best and he liked the idea.

"Lowie said he was really interested in the Leeds job, although only if it was worth his while. What he did, though, was to put in a good word for me to the Leeds people.

"In the end, Lowie didn't come to an agreement because Leeds came back to me with an offer as a player/assistant coach, playing in the shortened English season and working as Doug Laughton's assistant. When Super League started I would go 'up the coaching structure' in their words."

The Headingley proposal had natural appeal, but still Bell, because he'd been so thrilled with his form, fancied another season in Auckland, and arranged a meeting with Warriors chief executive Ian Robson and John Monie.

"I imagine they probably thought I was just trying to get an offer on the table to help me get a better deal somewhere in England, playing one off against the other," says Bell. "That wasn't my plan at all. I was serious about staying in Auckland, but also wanted to check through all my options.

"Jackie probably would have preferred to go back to England but she could see the value in staying if that was the way it worked out. And the offer Ian and John made was very attractive, it was very good money. I'd been on a good deal in any case and John once said to me, 'Ian reckons you're already on a Super League contract anyway.'

"The truth was that Super League had put the stakes up even more. The money they were talking would have given me the biggest pay day of my career in my last year of playing. Better than anything I ever received at Wigan. It was good for the ego to know they thought that at 34 I could still play a role for them.

"Things had turned around so much. A couple of weeks earlier it had looked like I was going to retire but here I was being given a damned good offer to stay.

"After that meeting, I was in the gym and John sidled up to me and whispered, 'And you still will be captain.' It wasn't worrying me, but he probably felt he needed to say it to me."

All factors were considered and discussed in the Warriors' meeting, right down to moving Bell out of the centres permanently because they had some big plans for his spot there.

"John told me that if they got Jonah Lomu—and at that stage they were confident they would—they wanted to play him in the centres with Richie [Blackmore]," says Bell. "It meant I would have had to play loose forward and the way he said it, or the implication to me, was that he was saying he couldn't always guarantee me a spot in the team.

"I came straight out and said, 'John, I don't expect to be guaranteed a position in the team. I never have and I never will and I'll prove I'm worthy of a position like I always do.' I probably misread things a little."

Knowing there was a safe haven for him at the Warriors, the temptation for Bell was to stick with that alone, but he was still concerned about his long-term involvement in the game, and the Leeds approach had more than curiosity value.

"When Ray Shuttleworth from Leeds contacted me soon after that meeting, I told him what the Warriors were offering and that I was seriously thinking of staying," says Bell. "I thought that might scare them off and, when I told David McKnight about the Warriors, his immediate reaction was that I should take it, that I wouldn't get money like it in England.

"It was certainly different for me to be using an agent. But because a lot of the dealings were being done on the other side of the world, I needed someone to look after things for me.

"In the past I've done the dealing myself, knowing in my mind what I want. I asked for it and once I got that amount that was it. I never started bargaining and looking for a bit more. That wasn't my way. Even if I heard rumours about so and so getting that much more than me, it didn't concern me. I've always signed my contract and been happy with it. That's the way it should be."

So, amid all this frantic activity, Bell's primary focus for 1995 hadn't changed. It was still on the Warriors and, after a three-week break from action, they didn't disappoint the Ericsson Stadium faithful, all 28,713 of them.

"Before the Tigers game, I felt I needed to talk to the players," says Bell. "I don't usually do that when I'm not playing, and I'm not usually into setting goals or targets too far ahead. But I told the guys that, looking at our next eight or nine matches, there was a fair chance of going through unbeaten. I wanted them to make that our objective and start the right way against the Tigers."

They did precisely that in another carnival atmosphere as the fans lapped up more of the Warriors' attacking qualities. They won as they liked to, 36–12, on the back of two tries each from debutante Denis Betts and try-scoring machine Sean Hoppe, plus six goals from Frano Botica.

"It was a great start for Denis and Frano, especially Denis coming straight into the side and winning the man of the match," says Bell. "To be honest, though, the Tigers were no test. They didn't stretch us. If we couldn't beat them by plenty we would have known we weren't making any progress at all."

The split rounds created another break for the Warriors and time for Bell to organise his return after missing the last three games, but, on a grim Sunday afternoon, the visit from Penrith gave the Warriors' their only poor home performance of the season so far.

Admittedly, they had players backing up from the Kiwis' ordinary display in their second test draw against France in Palmerston North. And they were also missing Betts, out with a hip injury after being the side's best against the Tigers, as well as Greg Alexander. He failed a late fitness test, a mortifying experience because it prevented him playing against his old club.

"Everyone was saying we should beat Penrith easily, the public that is," says Bell. "They hadn't seen us play for quite a while until the Tigers' game and I think they got a bit carried away with that performance. Penrith were a much better side. I knew they'd be tough—and wasn't I proven right about that one! Decisions went against us, but they played with so much enthusiasm; they definitely deserved the victory.

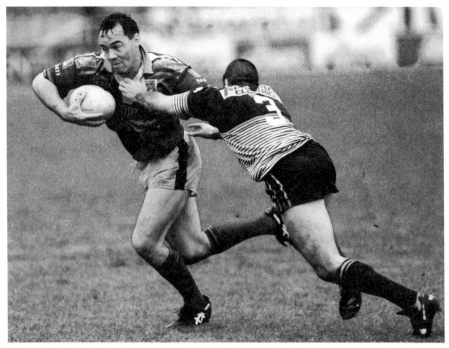

Few Warriors had any joy against Penrith, but centre Richie Blackmore, fending off his Panthers opposite Ryan Girdler, scored twice in the heavy defeat. Ross Land (Fotopress)

"They were hyped up. They were yahooing and yelling. We didn't respond to it and they were fired up. When we had games of this type at Wigan, we would pick up a gear and respond. We could handle teams that were fired up, if you like. But against Penrith, we were unable to do that."

Dean Bell was plain Dean Bell in his first game back. Nothing different, just supreme effort in a losing cause as the Warriors found themselves trailing by an embarrassing 34–8 in the second half. There was more pluck than in the defeats by Norths and Newcastle, though, as they trimmed the final margin to 34–16 with two late tries. At the same time, they lost Botica early and not one of the four tries—Blackmore with two of them—was converted, reminding everyone once more just why Botica had been signed.

"I was surprised how my fitness held up," says Bell. "I hadn't been able to do as much training as I would have liked with my hamstring the way it was, but I got the man of the match. I was embarrassed about that because it was such a lousy result. Mind you, I wasn't going to give it back either. They were giving us a stereo and a watch for the award—that gave me three of each for the year!"

Bell didn't buy the argument that the Warriors' displays were unduly affected by players backing up from test duty for the Kiwis during the international season.

*Exciting scrumhalf Stacey Jones holds off Penrith winger
Scott Pethybridge in the Warriors' Ericsson Stadium loss
to the Panthers.* Ross Land (Fotopress)

"We coped with that during the games themselves because our test players were coming off poor performances and so they usually had something to prove," says Bell. "How it did affect us was in our preparation for games, because we wouldn't have a full squad together all week.

"I was looking forward to when the test commitments were all over because we could then get back to having a settled operation and a settled team. It was a bit selfish, but I was getting frustrated about it. We'd run with reserve graders in the line-up at training but you knew they weren't going to be there when it came to the game. You still had to train with them in case they did have to play. To their credit, all of our Kiwi players did back up. We couldn't use the tests as an excuse though."

Penrith's Gary Freeman certainly wasn't using them as an excuse. He bounced back from the second test against France with a display which turned the Warriors upside down. He scored two tries, showed tons of cheek and did a real job on the Warriors' bright new hope for New Zealand league, Stacey Jones.

"Gary was just feeding off his forwards," says Bell. "He was under pressure after the test match and he was facing Stacey who was the next in line. He's a good competitor. He carried on heaps after that performance and good luck to him. He's that sort of guy. That's his nature."

The result left the Warriors' play-off hopes delicately balanced with Penrith climbing to 12 points with the win, the Warriors still on 10 after 12 rounds. And Bell was still doing a balancing act with his career, until it took a sudden turn as developments at Leeds moved on.

"When they first came to me with their offer I was a bit disappointed because I was expecting it to be close to the Warriors' offer," says Bell. "Then I weighed it up properly and, while I'd be getting less money than I would with the Warriors, I realised it was a good offer. It gave me some security and future prospects; a deal to do the truncated 1995–96 season and then the two Super League seasons to follow.

"I also knew Leeds would buy good players. They were the sleeping giants of English league and I figured if I could get in there and help out the sky was the limit.

"At the end of the day, I had to be honest with myself. I'd done alright as a player with the Warriors but I knew I couldn't do the things I used to do. I'd lost quite a bit of speed in the past couple of years. That was disappointing to me personally. I wanted to be able to do more. I thought I could handle a Super League year, but here was this coaching opportunity with one of the biggest clubs around.

"I had asked David McKnight to sew up the deal and Leeds had also called me to say Doug had approved my appointment. I wasn't sure about him. I'd heard so many stories about Doug. But I decided I'd make that judgement, that I have to take people the way I find them not through hearsay."

Player discussions with Leeds had already become part of Bell's operation and he soon discovered a lot of rugby union talent was being chased.

"Leeds were then showing an interest in the South African halfback Joost van der Westhuizen, but Junior Tonu'u was also being pushed around by Premier Crew. Leeds said they were interested in Jonah as well...and who wasn't?

"Another name that cropped up was Tawera Nikau, if Castleford were prepared to let him go. I thought if we could get him, he could be the difference between us winning something, even though he'd be taking my loose forward's position, and there'd also be Craig Innes and Kevin Iro in the centres."

Just why the Leeds deal then took such a dramatic turn wasn't clear to Bell. All he knew was that overnight he was no longer the assistant coach but the top man.

"There was no indication or suggestion that Leeds were going to get rid of Doug. I don't think they were in a position where they thought they could," he says.

"After I had informed Ray Shuttleworth that I'd accept their offer he indicated Doug would ring to congratulate me. But the phone call I got was to tell me Doug had resigned, and no one seemed to know why. I suppose it might have been a good thing, as it meant I could go in not having to look over my shoulder.

"I was worried, though, because I don't really have a lot of self-confidence. However, Jackie told me if I didn't take the job then somebody with less experience would take it because he believed in himself.

"Leeds didn't ask me directly, but they hinted as to whether there was any way I could get out of my Warriors' contract to be in Leeds straight away. I told them in no uncertain terms that I wouldn't do that. I signed for a year and I would fulfil that contract. A contract is a contract to me. You don't change in midstream."

Bell immediately realised he needed an assistant to take on some of the responsibility so he could concentrate on the rest of his year in Auckland. In a short time he'd offered the job to his old Kiwi team-mate Hugh McGahan, so revitalising an association which had run through days in New Zealand teams and at Eastern Suburbs.

Now, the idea of another year with the Warriors had gone. So had the thought of playing at all.

"Leeds wanted me to keep an open mind about playing, at least for the shortened season before Super League starts. But I couldn't see any point in it. I'd rather see some youngster in there. There's no future in me playing."

But he still had a playing future, limited as it was, with the Warriors. Making the play-offs was his next mission. Being the Loiners' coach had to wait.

farewell lowie

Many receive advice, only the wise profit by it.

When Dean Bell talks about his coaches, he's never backward in giving two of them special credit for shaping his career and his life. It's not that surprising really, because the pair rather dominated his playing years in the game.

Tracking through from his 1983 test debut to his farewell in 1995, the evidence shows only one calendar year—1994—when Bell played without direct coaching input from Graham Lowe or John Monie. For four years Lowe was his Kiwi coach, and then for three English seasons his coach at Wigan. From 1989–93, Monie provided the Wigan coaching association, and then again in 1995 at the Warriors, leaving Bell to survive without one of his two mentors only in the 1993–94 English season.

Understandably, then, it was an upheaval for Bell to lose coaching contact with Graham Lowe after six years together in all. One moment Lowe was leaving Wigan to be closer to his daughters Sarah and Amy in Brisbane, the next Ken Arthurson had him signed to coach Manly-Warringah in the Winfield Cup. That series of events didn't concern Bell, but seeing Lowe go did.

"I think he believed he'd taken Wigan as far as he could," says Bell. "But it was a sad time for me because he'd been the catalyst for my career really taking off. He'd introduced me to the international scene and made me look at things differently, at the game and why I played it, and at my life."

Combining the Kiwi and Wigan years, Bell had been under Lowe's coaching for what amounted to seven seasons. For many players that could be far too long playing for the same coach. Not for Bell.

"Even after all that time, Lowie still kept me interested," says Bell. "The message in his coaching was still new and fresh to me. I've got nothing but the greatest praise and thanks for what he did for me.

Lowe's last stand. Master coach Graham Lowe revels in another magic moment at Wembley after Wigan had beaten St Helens to win the Challenge Cup final for the second successive year. Wigan Evening Post

"He left one heck of a legacy at Wigan. In many ways, he had created a monster. At first, he might have been a bit deep for some of the English players with his coaching methods, but they soon warmed to him."

So did the directors, for Lowe had rejuvenated the club as he and the players helped fulfil chairman Maurice Lindsay's vision for Wigan. The former Kiwi coach was able to leave the Central Park faithful the perfect end-of-season and, in the event, parting gift—the Challenge Cup delivered for the second straight season, again in bewildering fashion.

There were also a couple of other prizes which weren't unwelcome, the Lancashire Cup and the John Player Special Trophy, but Lowe and his players were unable to prevent Widnes winning the first division title for the second successive season, and they also tumbled early again in the Premiership Trophy competition.

For Bell, shaking off the spectre of the Kiwis' shocking World Cup final display was a hefty task on its own; and that final also seriously affected Wigan's season. After all, Graham Lowe had to function without a vital slice of his preferred combination—centre Bell, winger Tony Iro and prop Adrian Shelford returned home to join Kevin Iro for the final; the younger Iro couldn't join Wigan until after the World Cup decider.

And around the time of that final in Auckland, Wigan were doing it tough with back-to-back first division losses to Castleford and Leeds; they would prove to be costly in the final analysis.

The Kiwi quartet returned with blistering effect in the Lancashire Cup final encounter with Salford, as they scored all of Wigan's points—Tony Iro with two tries, Shelford and Bell one each and Kevin Iro with the extras—in a 22–17 victory.

It was a key match in a solid season's work for Bell—33 appearances and 15 tries—but it should have been even busier. While this was another impressive season for the team, with Lowe again named coach of the year, there was an unwanted blemish for the New Zealand skipper.

After the Lancashire Cup victory, he played a support role in a bizarre match in the first round of the John Player Special Trophy. Wigan faced an already struggling Runcorn Highfield, who had been even further handicapped by their players going on strike. So they fielded a side made up of amateur players plus their then coach, the 1971–72 Great Britain international—and former Wigan player—Bill Ashurst. Ashurst was obviously a little past his prime by 1988 and lasted just a few minutes before being ordered off for fighting.

In a farce, Wigan won 92–2 as Kevin and Tony Iro scored seven tries between them, and Kevin finished with 34 points himself. But from that freewheeling effort Wigan plunged a week later; and Dean Bell found his year had become even gloomier.

It was an away trip to The Willows for a first division date with Salford. Wigan were beaten 24–16 and finished the match with only 10 men, two ordered off and Andy Gregory in the sin bin at fulltime. And one of the players marched was Bell.

He was binned in the 13th minute for a high tackle which put Salford centre Ian Bragger out of the game, needing stitches for a cut mouth. And, early in the second half, he was sent off for a high tackle which saw former England rugby union international Peter Williams taken off on a stretcher. Bell paid for it heavily with a six-match ban and often finds himself wondering what happened that day.

"When I think about it now, I feel so ashamed and disappointed with myself," he says. "Things will happen on the field, something snaps and you do something you shouldn't. That's what would happen then, but now I can snap on the field and control it."

The suspension finished just in time for him to play in the John Player Special Trophy final in early January. In the meantime, he'd missed Wigan's second-round 16–16 draw with Hull Kingston Rovers, their 30–0 replay victory and then a semifinal win over Bradford Northern.

"So when I came back I couldn't get into the centres," he says. "Joe Lydon had been going really well there so Lowie put me on the wing. The only trouble was we were playing Widnes, and who should I be marking but Martin Offiah.

"It was a big call, because Martin was killing a lot of defences that season, so I just kept following him all around the park, using my experience, and

138

Like father, like...four of Wigan's best show they're more than just professional rugby league players. Andy Goodway, Dean Bell, Ian Potter and Andy Gregory at Central Park with their smallest fans, their kids. John Leatherbarrow

not letting him get away from me." It worked. Offiah didn't score a try—and he managed 58 that season!—as Wigan won.

Maintaining the title-winning run might have seemed easy enough for Graham Lowe, but his three seasons at Wigan weren't without stresses, especially with some of his high-priced footballing talent.

It was almost a weekly occurrence at times that someone would ask to be put on the transfer list. Ellery Hanley did so after a massive bust-up with Lowe, so did Shaun Edwards and, during this 1988–89 season, scrumhalf Andy Gregory caused Lowe any amount of grief.

Said to be unsettled, he was on offer late in the year only to ask to come off the transfer list in January. Disenchanted when Lowe named him as a substitute for the Challenge Cup encounter with Bradford Northern, he went on strike, threatened to quit and then made up in a matter of days. There were times when Lowe was attacked and abused, even at his home, for his treatment of Gregory. And he had his moments, too, over the odd run-in with Hanley.

"One of the most difficult things for Lowie, and then for John after him, was incorporating all the different personalities into the side," says Bell. "There were a lot of guys with big egos who happened to also be very good footballers.

"They didn't try to dominate or make it difficult at training. While many would have egos off the field, they were genuinely professional on it. None of this stuff got in the way. They worked for one another as players.

"When they want to be, Ellery and Andy [Gregory] can be quite difficult and we had some fairly sticky moments at times. They were issues I stayed out of, though. When you've got a couple of big egos like that, you're better off keeping your distance. Graham was always going to have trouble with some players and all he could do was confront it and deal with it if it arose. When it did, he sorted it out."

Apart from Gregory's discontent about being put on the bench, there were ructions over the captaincy when Shaun Edwards was given the job, later to be replaced by Hanley. When Wigan moved to sign Wally Lewis—a deal which ultimately fell through—it also had some side effects and Lowe's at-the-time radical decision to switch Hanley from stand-off to loose forward in the 1986–87 season generated an edge too.

"There were plenty of doubters, but moving Ellery was a masterstroke," says Bell. "He used to score a lot of tries anyway, but at loose forward that first season he was even more prolific.

"Even I thought it was a strange move at the time, but now you look at it and realise it's the perfect position for him. He's strong enough and has all the right attributes for a loose forward. To change him showed Graham's vision in the game."

While Bell says Wigan's multitude of egos didn't unsettle the team or disrupt the game plan, there have been telltale signs on the field sometimes.

"You would see it with Shaun and Ellery," he says. "With both of them being so good at backing up, there were times when I saw them trying to bump each other out of the way, fighting to back up a break and score another try. Andy Goodway also fancied himself as a bit of a poacher and, in some of our easier games, it could be quite funny watching those three trying to get to the tryline."

With Dean Bell it's more a case of what you get is what you see. More intriguing are his insights into how some of his super star Wigan team-mates operated.

Ever since he became the youngest man to play in a Challenge Cup final at Wembley—he was 17 years 6 months and 19 days when he played in the 1984 final—Edwards has epitomised the angry little man of league; fiercely competitive, but not easily humoured.

"Shaun's very much misunderstood," says Bell. "He's had rugby league rammed down his throat since a very young age from his father. Then again, if he hadn't, I don't think he would have turned into the player he has. He's one of the best competitors I've encountered.

"He had one major fault in my earliest years at Wigan. While no one really likes criticism, Shaun just couldn't take it at all. When criticised, he reacted terribly.

"But as a footballer, his anticipation and try-scoring ability—the way he backs up—puts him right up there with the Ellery Hanleys of this world. I've seen him score 10 tries in a game—which I also saw Martin Offiah do—and only very special players can do that. I do remember making one fairly easy for him that day, passing the ball to him when I was already over the line. He was always there supporting.

"Again, his was a case where Wigan were on his doorstep with his professional forms the very moment he was eligible. That guy was just brought up to be a rugby league professional. You either love him or hate him.

"He always threatens to move to another club but he's never going to. He's a homebody. He knows how to play the directors off and get the best deal. He's clever and I think he'll make a damned good coach because he was born into the game and he's studied it."

Andy Gregory fits the same category of the temperamental, but brilliant, scrumhalf.

"Greg is a real cock of the roost type of guy," says Bell. "He really added so much to us when he came across from Warrington. At the time Greg was signed, we had Mike Ford and Shaun Edwards as our scrumhalf options.

"But it goes to show how Wigan think. Even though they had two quality halfbacks, they would still be looking for someone better and would have a good go at getting him. In the case of Andy, they got their man. It was unfortunate for Mike Ford, because Greg pushed him out. That's football, though. Only the strong survive and Andy was a better player than Mike.

"Greg made things happen. He could find you gaps, he'd throw out great balls and he had great vision. Of course, he was helped by the players he had around him, but they complemented him perfectly with the way they ran onto his passes; it all worked exceptionally well."

Wigan make it their business to chase and sign the best talent available. Andy Gregory was signed during Lowe's first season, as Bell was at the start of it. Adrian Shelford and the Iros were bought for the 1987–88 season and Andy Platt for 1988–89.

"It never stops," says Bell. "And I always liked it when new players came into the side. I welcomed them because they made the team stronger, and even when it was a player coming in who would be aiming for my position, I wasn't phased.

"It's not everyone's mentality to be like that. When I first signed for Wigan, they had David Stephenson in the centres. He'd been at the club for a few years but he sort of gave up when I arrived. He didn't fight for his spot and ended up transferring to Leeds. He was never dedicated enough.

"The club could have gone out and bought two or three centres and I would have been happy. I would have backed myself to secure one of the centre positions, but I'd also know buying other centres would make the team stronger.

"We knew we were getting a quality player with Andy Platt. Shane Cooper was moaning about us signing Platty, complaining that we'd taken St Helens' best player. He was probably right."

Platt's arrival meant a major cut in action for dependable forwards like Brian Case and Ian Potter, Wigan's pack being built around the power up front of Platt and Shelford, who was the most used Wigan player that season with 40 appearances.

"When people talk to me about Wigan, I'm always quick to mention the likes of Brian Case and Ian Potter because they did such a great job for us, more than playing their part," says Bell. "They weren't the big flashy type of players, but Ian Potter would give you a million tackles in a game and Brian would take the ball up and always make you yards. They were very good pros.

"We also had a bloke like Ged Byrne who would play just about anywhere. A local product from the St Patricks amateur club, Graham bought him from Salford and there were an awful lot of people who questioned it because he wasn't a high profile player. But Ged had everyone taking notice in the end because he was so versatile, able to play at stand-off, in the centres or on the wing."

And that's where Wigan always seemed to have it through the most glorious phase of their history from the mid 1980s and on into the 1990s—that was their back-up strength and versatility.

Ged Byrne provided it time and again in 1988–89. So, too, did Bell when he was required to revert to the wing. Joe Lydon also mixed up the backline positions as well as providing the most exceptional and invaluable individual feat of the season.

Wigan had to tangle with Warrington in a Challenge Cup semifinal at Manchester City's Maine Road. Wigan against Warrington—yet another of the classic derbies in Lancashire, and Warrington weren't short on muscle and mongrel that season with Kevin Tamati, Steve Roach and Les Boyd in their pack.

They put the squeeze right on Wigan, too, with the score locked at 6–6 just seven minutes from fulltime. Then, from 60 metres out, Lydon launched into the most astonishing dropped goal imaginable; it cleared the bar without any difficulty to give Wigan a 7–6 lead, which they improved to 13–6 by the end. Once again, Wigan were on the road to Wembley.

All the time, Wigan's challenge for their second first division title in three years was ticking over, even though the usual end of season backlog was a factor. The Riversiders had to play their last five championship matches in the space of 14 days, with wins over Castleford, Featherstone Rovers, Salford and St Helens stretching their winning run to 16 matches including Challenge Cup matches. It set up the perfect clash in the last match—Widnes at home to Wigan—to decide the title race.

"And when Platty scored in the first few minutes it gave us a lot of hope," says Bell. "But Martin Offiah scored three against us, and one of them came from an absolute knock-on which John Holdsworth let go. After that controversial try, that was the end of us. They won 32–18.

"We'd lost our way in the first division two seasons in a row. For some reason, we were stumbling against sides we simply should have beaten. If you're going to win a championship you have to beat sides like Wakefield and Salford away. We didn't that season."

The forerunner to the Challenge Cup final was again the first round of the Premiership Trophy and, as fate would have it, Wigan were drawn to meet their Wembley opponents St Helens. In fact, the two sides clashed three times in the space of 17 days. St Helens won this one but that hardly mattered to Wigan, not after what happened at Wembley on 29 April.

After pounding Halifax 32–12 in the 1988 final, Wigan were even more ruthless this time, walloping St Helens 27–0. Saints brought back Australian internationals Michael O'Connor and Paul Vautin, but the error-stricken Alex Murphy-coached side contributed little quality to the match at all. Their 17-year-old fullback Gary Connolly had a frightening time knocking on a kick early in the match and being forced to cope with a rampant Kevin Iro. Once again the giant centre scored twice and might have gone very, very close to beating Ellery Hanley for the Lance Todd Trophy.

There was also a perfect touch to the match for Wigan fullback Steve Hampson; scoring a try as he finally appeared in a Wembley final after three previous attempts had been foiled by injury.

"To nil them was great," says Bell. "There aren't many better results for Wigan than to beat St Helens in a Challenge Cup final, and to do so by keeping them scoreless is the ultimate."

Very soon, though, Wigan's designs on the ultimate had been upgraded. They'd lifted the cup twice in successive years, now they could set themselves the target of becoming the first club to make it three in a row.

For Graham Lowe, there wouldn't be another Wembley final, but he left knowing Wigan was in much better shape than when he arrived. The proof was in the 10 titles he'd delivered in three seasons—and better still was in store for the Central Park juggernaut.

my mentor–and mate
Andy Platt

Graham Lowe is responsible: he's the one who brought me into contact with a man who changed my whole outlook on the game. Someone who basically blew me away—Dean Bell.

It was Graham who signed me from St Helens to play for Wigan in the 1988–89 season. Until then, I'd only played against Dean and didn't know him, although he had once done his best to let me know who he was.

Our first encounter was as long ago as the 1982–83 season when he was with Carlisle, only we didn't really come into contact that time. It was different in a Lancashire Cup semifinal the season before I moved to Wigan. We were on top when the lights went out; when they came back on, we lost our concentration and Wigan ran away with it.

What I recall about Dean in that match is making a tackle on him which he didn't particularly like. I marked up against him at the play the ball and, after the ball was cleared and as I was walking off, he didn't half crack me on the side of the head! I have him on about it now and he maintains he doesn't remember the incident. I'm sure he doesn't!

Whether it's his defence, hitting the ball up or having a shot at you, Dean Bell hits you with everything he has. Everything he does is like that, especially his approach to training. It's maximum effort.

I'm now known as a player who likes to train in the gym, who likes working on the weights and, in that regard, I'm often compared to Dean. But when I first arrived at Wigan I wasn't as dedicated as I am now. I thought I knew a lot—until I worked with Dean and realised how little I knew.

We fell into the same training schedule because we both had children and found the morning was the best time to train. He put me on the straight and narrow and it was all such a huge shock to me because, even in training, he was so focused, committed and dedicated. We might have had a good result on a Sunday but even on the Monday morning Dean would be very keen to get the most he could out of his training sessions. That professional side of him struck me, especially after coming from St Helens, where it was just so casual compared to Dean's approach.

Within the Wigan environment he was also the most enthusiastic about what he wanted to do, and also very sure of what he could achieve. I remember saying to my wife Angela early on that this guy Dean was something else. Angela calls him my mentor, which is exactly what he was. He's only a couple of years older, but when we first came into contact it was obvious he was so much more mature than me in his attitude to the game and training.

From day one he obviously possessed something different, a quality you don't find in people every day. You can't put your finger on what it is. We all saw it from him as a leader, although there was one instance when his passion for the job went wrong on him.

We were playing Bradford Northern in a Challenge Cup semifinal and John Monie, in his laid-back way, had told us what he expected. Dean was more emotive and said to all the guys, 'You can't die out there! You might hurt your leg or spill some blood, but you're not going to die out there!'

About five minutes into the game, Dean tried to clean this guy out on defence and Dean's head collided with the guy's knee. He was unconscious and he swallowed his tongue; in fact, only the intervention of the physio probably saved him. In the space of a few minutes Dean had gone from saying no one was going to die to almost killing himself.

It shook me up at the time and still does to think about it. Anything could have happened if the physio hadn't been on so quickly. And yet, even after that, it was so typical of Dean that he wanted to get back on the field. Luckily commonsense prevented that happening.

Over the years he's slowed down a bit, but that doesn't affect the 100 per cent commitment and enthusiasm you get from Dean Bell. You'll never find him giving up, and we always saw that with the Warriors in 1995; even in the games when we were soundly beaten, he kept at it.

It would have been nice if the Warriors were around five years ago and Dean had been signed by them, because we saw the best of him at Wigan. New Zealanders missed out on that, but at least they were able to see him in the last year of his playing career. Like Mal Meninga, he's one of those players with an aura about him.

Andy Platt started his Great Britain career in 1985 and, up till the 1995 World Cup, had made 25 test appearances plus another six in tour games. He played 188 games for St Helens from 1983–88, scoring 68 tries. Transferred to Wigan in 1988, he made 199 appearances (24 tries) to the end of the 1993–94 season, when he took up a two-year contract to play for the Warriors.

making winning a habit

The dictionary is the only place where success comes before work.

Winning is supposed to be habit-forming, but the Warriors seemed to have a different formula for achieving it. The habit they were beginning to perfect, even patent, was losing in a big way, then instantly rebounding with a vital victory, or at least a vastly improved effort.

Survey the season and it showed how the pattern had developed. In the second round the Warriors were 40–28 losers to Illawarra, the next round 46–12 winners over Western Suburbs. They went from the misery of a 48–10 fourth-round setback against Norths to a highly respectable 26–14 loss to Manly the following round and a 38–12 swamping of Illawarra the next. And the shocking 48–6 ninth-round defeat by Newcastle was rectified with the 23–18 triumph against Cronulla a week later.

If you put these players in an adventure park, they'd never get off the roller coaster; all season they followed the up-and-down, hot-and-cold pattern, even when they were winning in the middle stretch of it.

It was fair to assume then that this sometimes woeful and sometimes wonderful side would deliver an up-tempo performance against Western Suburbs, who were proving to be the quiet achievers of the season, running sixth with eight wins and 16 points as they prepared to host the Warriors. Clearly they were transformed from the outfit Auckland had pounded earlier in the season and had some sort of score to settle.

It has to be said that the Warriors' display wasn't at all up-tempo, but it most assuredly was an up-tempo result as they eked out a 16–12 win in a grim contest which provided an untidy spectacle.

The players were genuine combatants rather than players much of the game. Battles raged at different stages, with Denis Betts and Wests' former Kiwi forward Mark Horo both doing time in the sin bin. Other players had to go to the blood bin, in fact four times during the game for Andy Platt alone.

He started the season in the centres, but by the time the Warriors met Gold Coast, Dean Bell was on his way into the forwards on a near-permanent basis. Ross Setford (Fotopress)

"He was split open," says Bell. "It was a fairly bad head cut and the first time he returned to the field he had enough grease on to last a mechanic for a month."

By halftime, nothing separated the teams as they were locked together at 12–12 and, until the 77th minute, it stayed the same. Then second rower Tony Tatupu found a way across for yet another comeback win from a heavy defeat.

"Maybe we were lucky to win, then again Wests were just as bad as us, or worse, on the day," says Bell. "It was still a good win, though, because Wests had been going well since we'd first met them."

The injury toll gained a permanent victim from the game too. Joe Vagana, who had started in the front row, had his arm broken and wouldn't make it back before the end of the season.

Whatever the quality of the display, the Warriors needed to keep chipping away to sneak up the table and, in that regard, the visit to Campbelltown Sports Ground had the desired effect. More of the same was needed, because, for the second of three times in the season, the Warriors were on a back-to-back away assignment.

Fortunately for them, the return to Sydney for a Saturday night date at

With second rower Denis Betts in support, Warriors captain Dean Bell bursts past Gold Coast captain and scrumhalf Craig Coleman.
Andrew Cornaga (Photosport)

the Sydney Football Stadium wasn't a testing one. Well, against Souths it shouldn't have been.

The side had been revived by Frano Botica's return from injury, meaning John Kirwan's revolving door life at the Warriors put him back in reserve grade, while injury still kept Richie Blackmore out and allowed Bell to stay in the centres.

Less than 7000 fans were at the stadium but they saw the rank outsiders conspire to make the Warriors look exceedingly vulnerable by putting on two tries inside the first 13 minutes.

"Lee Jackson scored a freak try when a penalty kick hit the post, rebounded and he followed through to catch it on the full," says Bell. "I could relate to that from a game I played for Wigan against Salford. I always try to follow up kicks at goal and I must have chased hundreds of them without a result. That one time made all of them worth it. In fact, when I'm asked for my most memorable try, that one is right up there because it's the only one of that type I scored."

The Warriors' better side was on show in time; three tries putting them 18–12 ahead at halftime, including an effort from 40 metres out for Betts when he was put into space by Tony Tatupu.

After the vitality of Ericsson Stadium, the limp atmosphere must have had an effect on the Warriors because, rather than winding it up and blowing Souths out, they let them take over the contest. A penalty and a converted try actually had the so-called no hopers leading 20–18 and Souths still held that lead with only 12 minutes to go.

Finally, the Warriors flicked on the turbocharger. Tatupu planted the ball for the go-ahead try and made another one for Greg Alexander. But the most dazzling of a four-try blitz within 10 minutes were the second and fourth in the sequence, especially the second.

It came directly from a kick-off, Alexander drifting across and releasing Frano Botica no more than 10 metres from his goal-line. Botica beat three defenders, including an outrageous dummy to fox Craig Field, on a 90-metre run for a stunning try.

And Eru's second of the match wasn't too ordinary either. Showing exceptional pace, he arced around the Souths defence on a 20-metre dash to the corner. From 20–18 down, the Warriors had come back to win 38–20, causing as much consternation as celebration with their effort.

"I'd always known it, but with his try Frano underlined the fact that he is much more than a kicker," says Bell. "And Syd's second try was just unbelievable. The speed he has for a hooker is quite incredible."

There couldn't be complaints about winning. That was the aim of the game. But Monie was by now wanting a little more quality to go with it and a return to Ericsson Stadium to face Gold Coast provided much more of what he demanded.

A major contributing factor to the improved showing lay in a key positional switch for the skipper. "John called me into his office the week of the game," says Bell. "And he said, 'You know that No 3 jersey you've been wearing? Well, now you'll have to get used to putting the number 1 in front of the 3.' I always knew I'd be making the transition to loose forward on a more permanent basis once Richie Blackmore had arrived.

"Having Richie and Tea together in the centres was going to give us more strike power and more options and variation."

That's the way he saw it, although the Warriors' centres, with the attacking edge from Ropati and the foil of Bell's strong defence and all-round solidity, had worked perfectly well.

Another positional development was also evolving in a side now stacked with halves—Greg Alexander, Gene Ngamu, Stacey Jones and Frano Botica, not forgetting Phil Blake who was in reserve grade by now.

"John felt Gene needed to have less of a workload while the test series was on," says Bell. "So he swapped things around with Gene running at fullback when we had the ball, which allowed us to have Greg up from fullback in the front line. John knew we functioned best when Greg was more heavily involved; he makes so much difference when he gets in to first receiver and calls the shots.

"The trouble was John didn't have confidence in anyone else to play at

No forward was better for the Warriors against Gold Coast than former Wigan prop Andy Platt, at last shaking off problems with his knee. Nigel Marple (Fotopress)

fullback, so Greg had to play there. Later it became more permanent, with Greg being named at stand-off and Gene at fullback, but for the time being it was a flexible arrangement during games."

The match fully exposed the talents of the Warriors' playmaking halves, all of them making a contribution at some time and all involved close in on both sides of the ruck to give the attack real variation.

"The first 40 against Gold Coast was, despite the standard of the opposition, the best half of football we'd put together all season," says Bell. "We controlled the ball to lead 26–0, instead of scoring off-the-cuff tries, which we tended to do. We were playing in a much more structured way and creating tries by using the ball well."

They weren't as authoritative in the second half—conceding three tries on defence—but there wasn't too much to grumble about with eight tries and a 44–16 win. The chief benefactor was Tea Ropati, with three tries, while John Kirwan snared his first first grade try at Ericsson Stadium.

But the individual performance that had most people taking note came from prop Andy Platt, now showing everyone who didn't know already why the coach was so keen to sign him. With his fitness on the improve, he was the man most responsible for giving Auckland their go forward with the ball. And giving them the satisfaction of three straight wins, more like the strike rate John Monie was used to at Wigan.

on the monie trail

Courage is the first of human qualities because it is
the quality which guarantees all the others.

Wigan's pursuit of excellence always means that they chase only the best
of the best, and nearly always succeed in getting their man...or men,
actually. The long-term super star signings have just rolled on and on since
the mid 1980s: Ellery Hanley, Andy Gregory, Andy Goodway, Joe Lydon,
Dean Bell, Kevin Iro, Andy Platt, Kevin Iro, Kelvin Skerrett, Martin Offiah,
Gary Connolly and Henry Paul. They represent a sensational strike rate of
top quality and proven rugby league talent.

Of course, Wigan can boast a rather useful record in snaring the best
and most expensive rugby union buys as well. Frano Botica and Va'aiga
Tuigamala aren't too ordinary. And Wigan's ability to spot and secure the
most exciting talent from the local amateur rugby league ranks also throws
up the likes of Shaun Edwards, Denis Betts, Phil Clarke, Andy Farrell and
Jason Robinson.

It's a recruitment operation which engenders ample jealousy in English
rugby league, although the production rate from the amateur clubs makes
a lie of those who claim Wigan's success has been entirely bought. Not
quite true.

The same can't be said for Wigan's ability—or the English game's for
that matter—to produce the perfect men to drive a team of stars. The pursuit
for the best in coaches hasn't, since 1986, included one homegrown product,
but still the search for excellence has been the driving force. And, after
jackpotting with Graham Lowe, Wigan chairman Maurice Lindsay was
desperate to find the right man to replace him. John Monie was his name.
Another Antipodean at Central Park.

It didn't take Dean Bell long to find out he'd like the new gaffer. "In
fact, I've never warmed to a bloke as fast as I did to John Monie," he says.

"I'd been out of the game a bit the previous season and, while I'd been off Joe [Lydon] was moved into the centres and went very well. When I came back, Lowie sometimes had me on the wing; I didn't enjoy it that much. I saw myself as a centre by then.

"So, the first time John came to training, I remember him coming down the tunnel and saying, 'Hi, Dean, John. What the hell are you doing on the wing?' And I thought I could get to like this bloke very quickly."

It was the icebreaker in a player-coach-friend association which became as dominant in Dean Bell's life as the link with Graham Lowe had been.

"And, like Lowie, John had no problem fitting in with the players at Central Park," says Bell of the early times. "He was obviously a very professional coach.

"For the first few months, he simply observed the team to see who did what and how we played before he slowly started putting things into place. A lot of upheaval all at once would have been detrimental. We'd been winning before then so there was no need to tip everything upside down.

"Obviously he still had his own ideas, and primarily he wanted to tighten the defence up even more. That taught me something and it was an approach I decided I would try to follow in my coaching career; the idea that you don't try to make changes to a side too quickly."

Wigan didn't initially give Monie too much to be excited about as they opened the 1989–90 season by losing the Charity Shield to Widnes and then their next match to Warrington in the opening round of the first division championship. They also dipped out to Oldham in their Lancashire Cup semifinal. After that, though, there were enough signs of Wigan's now accustomed ruthlessness to suggest another title-laden year was brewing.

Bell had more on his mind than just Wigan and his new coach. A variety of factors convinced him to again make himself available for the Kiwis after missing the 1989 home series against Australia. Not the least of the reasons for his change of mind was the matter of convenience; after all, the Kiwis were to make their four-yearly tour of Britain and France.

"It was going to be happening around me, it was in-season for me and my form was fine so I thought, why not?"

His initial sighting of the 1989 Kiwis was as opponents, for Bell was in Wigan's centres as they inflicted a 24–14 defeat on the tourists. After their tour-opening loss to St Helens, that result had the Kiwis at very long odds to win the first test at Old Trafford, home of the Manchester United Football Club.

One year out of the Kiwi atmosphere, Bell was reunited with his countrymen in the week leading up to the first test and was effectively in camp for two weeks as the first two tests were played back to back. "I felt strange going back in," he says. "With all the tests I'd played previously I had felt part and parcel of the set-up. But this time I felt like an outsider. I wasn't made to feel like that, it was just the way I felt myself.

The Kiwis' 1989 test series against Great Britain and France were the last on the international stage for Dean Bell. Andrew Varley

"It was strange, too, I guess, thinking about playing against guys who were my Wigan team-mates. Obviously I'd faced a few of them in Christchurch in 1988, like Ellery Hanley, Andy Gregory, Henderson Gill and former Wigan player David Stephenson.

"In the first test, Andy Gregory was there again, along with Andy Goodway, Andy Platt and Shaun Edwards, while Ellery was injured. I know I thought beforehand that it would be awkward playing against guys I had so much to do with at Wigan, but once I was on the field, they were just the opposition like any other game.

"Because they were team-mates, perhaps I might have given them a little extra in the tackle, nothing over the top, just something to let them know I was there. And they'd do the same to me."

The Old Trafford test had Bell linked in the centres with former All Black Kurt Sherlock, not an unfamiliar combination, as they had played together in Bell's off-season with Eastern Suburbs in 1988. With his Wigan team-mate Kevin Iro providing the match clincher—he was on the wing—the Kiwis shocked by rolling Great Britain 24–16.

The second test was an unmitigated disaster for New Zealand, when it ought to have been one for Great Britain. They had fullback Steve Hampson ordered off for head butting Gary Freeman in the opening minutes yet, despite playing with 12 men for almost the entire match, they won 26–6.

Great Britain survived a tense series-decider at Central Park, to beat the Kiwis 10–6 in a home test series for the first time since 1965. And the Kiwis' downcast mood wasn't helped at the test dinner either when Great Britain captain Mike Gregory had his say. "He got up and said to us, 'Tough shit.' Which obviously didn't go down well with anyone, least of all us. After a tight series, which might have gone either way, it wasn't the thing to say."

Of more concern to the former Kiwi captain was what he saw as a major deterioration in off-field standards in a New Zealand touring team.

"I'd seen the signs," he says. "The team manager Ian Jenkins was a problem, if you ever saw him. There simply wasn't any discipline. Lowie expected discipline, although he was also casual to a degree; you respected that and never abused it. But on this tour, the guys were doing what they wanted and it was like a party for them."

This was the tour which earned notoriety for replacement player David Ewe's antics in his short time with the team. After what became little more than a drinking binge, he was sent home in disgrace and with all manner of stories about some outrageous behaviour.

"David Ewe got totally carried away when he arrived," says Bell. "And, when we had our wind-up party after the third test, he was obviously out of it. Out of control. I didn't see the things he was supposed to have done but nothing would have surprised me. And that all blew up the next day when we were on the bus ready to leave the hotel on our way to France.

"David reacted badly and didn't make matters any easier for himself. As for sending him home, I suppose the management had to make a stand because there wasn't much discipline there anyway. To have let it go unpunished would have made things even worse.

"You had to blame the management for what happened. I'd come through with all those pros who knew how to have a good time, but they knew how to handle themselves, where these guys had a bad attitude.

"I wasn't in France when the trouble blew up on the Spanish border, but, of course, that was likely to happen. [Three players spent a night in police custody after chasing the driver of a car they believed had nearly hit them in the street outside a nightclub.] Anything was likely to happen on that tour."

Bell was still committed to his reappearance in the Kiwi jersey. Despite what was going on, he wanted to play for New Zealand again, and that also meant the two tests in France. He didn't see them as any less important than the ones in England and, having made himself available, he wasn't about to opt out halfway through. Mind you, not everyone agreed with his stance.

"I was rooming with Kurt [Sorensen] in Carcassonne before the first test and his coach Doug Laughton rang up to give him a hard time about being with the Kiwis in France when he wanted him back at Widnes," says Bell. "I couldn't believe Dougie. He then wanted to speak to me and he started giving it to me, telling me why Kurt should be back in England and why I should be as well.

"He went on that it meant nothing to play against the French, that the Kiwis could win without us and that we were being paid by our clubs. I was flabbergasted. Every time Great Britain play France, they pick their best team possible. I was shocked the way Doug went on, especially for someone I didn't even know."

This time it was final. In a series which had also seen the end of Kurt Sorensen's test career, Dean Bell played his 26th and last international, scoring his 11th try in the 34–0 win. The tragedy now is that Bell hadn't necessarily planned on that being his final test. He had been in the mood to consider continuing his test career into the 1990s, but the negative experiences on the 1989 tour had put a dampener on such thoughts.

"John Monie never put any pressure on me not to play test football," says Bell. "He always wants his players to be involved in representative football. He's a big supporter of it and, to this day, probably believes I should have played at test level for longer. It was the directors who were keen to see me concentrating on my Wigan career alone."

For the rest of the 1989–90 season that's precisely what he did, as John Monie took Wigan to what was now becoming habitual success. If Graham Lowe was supposed to be a hard act to follow, Monie was making it look dead easy.

The Riversiders beat Halifax to take the Regal Trophy, collected the first division championship and then fixed on a now ritualistic Wembley visit. Nothing changed about it either. There was different opposition, this time in the shape of Warrington, but they weren't going to alter the impact. It was emphatic at 36–14, as Wigan won the Challenge Cup for a record third straight time.

There were anxieties over lifting the Regal Trophy, not in the final but in the third round when Wigan held on to draw 10–10 with Leeds at Headingley. This was despite having Steve Hampson ordered off (the third time of the season, including his head butting on Gary Freeman).

Wigan negotiated the replay 8–0 but the final, won 24–12, provided a slight hint of days to come. Captaining Halifax was former Australian test player John Dorahy, who had a tangle with Joe Lydon, and with Dean Bell too. Bell was penalised for a high tackle on the Halifax stand-off while Lydon was penalised for treading on Dorahy. If there was friction between them then, much worse lay ahead when Dorahy took over as Wigan's coach for the 1993–94 season.

"It was a very, very rough game that one," says Bell. "But I always remember that incident Joe was involved in. We gave Joe a hard time about it when Dorahy was announced as coach, teasing him that Dorahy would bring up the incident and leave him out of the side."

There was also great anxiety putting the Wigan machine on course for the trip to Wembley, and again it came in the opening round at Hull Kingston Rovers when Dave Marshall's try was the saviour in a 6–4 win.

There was anxiety as well, which came close to turning to tragedy, for Dean Bell in the next round against Dewsbury; Wigan won 30–6 but Bell again ran into strife over an incident which had him sent off.

"There was an Australian player who'd been niggling all day and mouthing off as well," says Bell. "Everyone was losing their temper with him. At one stage, the ball went over the dead ball line and this guy threw Joe Lydon into the advertising hoardings. I'd had enough of him and went over to him. I held my elbow up a little too high and he made out that I had caught him with it. I didn't, he milked it and I was ordered off.

"I must admit it didn't look good on video, although he still overdid it. John Monie represented me at the judicial hearing but said he'd never do it again. He told the judiciary that he knew me and that I was of good character. They came straight back and said, 'We know all about Mr Bell's character! We've been watching him! They'd been waiting to hit me and gave me a 10-match suspension, so it's easy to understand why John never wanted to front the judiciary again."

The ban couldn't have come at a worse time for Bell or for Wigan, eliminating him from the next two rounds of the Challenge Cup and also the demanding business end of the first division title race. Three times Wigan were beaten in the last stage—by Widnes, Castleford and St Helens—but victory over Leigh in the final match assured them of the trophy.

Bell's suspension finished just in time for the Challenge Cup final against a Warrington side, including 1989 Kiwi tourists Gary Mercer and Duane Mann. Warrington hung in at 16–8 at halftime, but Wigan's onslaught was remorseless in the second half as they raced to a 32–8 lead in a final again notable for Kevin Iro's try-scoring touch. For the third successive final, he powered over for two tries to lift his own Wembley final record to six, twice as many as anyone else had ever scored. It still wasn't quite enough, however, to swing him the Lance Todd Trophy ahead of Andy Gregory.

Bell's first four seasons at Central Park had brought unbelievable success on the back of two outstanding coaches and some of the most exceptional talent any player could hope to have as team-mates. One who really continued his development after being groomed in the Lowe years was second rower Denis Betts.

"Initially I didn't see Denis as something too special, not when Lowie first brought him into the side," says Bell. "And Denis took a bit of offence to that when I mentioned it in my newspaper column in 1995 just after he'd arrived in Auckland to play for the Warriors.

"Phil Clarke was a year or so behind Denis in coming through but I thought, at the same age, that Phil was a better player. He seemed to have more. I used to think Denis was a steady kid when he started, but he's made me eat my words.

"A lot of people compare Phil and Denis and the difference between the two to me now is the mental toughness side of it—Denis is much tougher in that sense. He'll keep fronting up where Phil seems to pick and choose his games, which is a bit annoying to a person like me.

"Neither of them is like a Mark Graham in terms of being able to get the ball away. They're good work rate players but on the skills level Denis is really developing. It takes time for that to happen and I've seen him over the years improving to the stage where he's a top-class player now."

In Bell's time, Wigan always had, and needed, their bread-and-butter players around the flashy stars, grafters like the two Ians they had on the books in 1989–90.

"Ian Gildart was an unfashionable player, just like Brian Case and Ian Potter who did a similar job for Wigan," says Bell. "When you had injuries to a player as good as Andy Platt you could bring in someone like Ian [Gildart], and that's why we did so well. We had quality back-ups who would never let you down. Ian Lucas was the same. Reliable."

Reliable wasn't a word always so readily associated with the enigmatic Andy Goodway. An outstanding forward at his best, there were times when Goodway didn't always endear himself to people at Wigan. He wasn't the sort to do the right thing at functions: where most other players knew how to thank the sponsors and the like, Goodway would do his best to be a nonconformist.

"We called him BA, standing for Bad Attitude," says Bell. "That summed up Andy. He was a bit rebellious, a guy who could be an unsettling influence in the team environment. He was very single-minded and he would always go around saying, 'I'll f... do this, or I'll f... do that.'

"But on the field, he was so explosive running onto the ball, up there with the top try-scorers. He was the guy who really fed off Andy Gregory's passes. To his credit, he took Denis [Betts] under his wing and showed him the ropes.

"Andy always held one thing against me. He never let me forget the tackle I put on him at Carlaw Park in 1984. He made a break, stepped me and I threw my arm out. I should have been sent off for it, without a doubt. But because it was test, the referee [Kevin Roberts] must have taken a different view of it. I was lucky."

A then-Wigan player—since then Leeds, Widnes and St Helens—who managed to infuriate New Zealanders, and many who've had anything to do with him, was Bobby Goulding. His behaviour on tour in New Zealand in 1990 endeared him to no one. He was then just a boy, and an angry one at that.

"Loads and loads of talent, another Andy Gregory in the making as far as skills went," says Bell. "With skilful players like him, the coach has to try and harness their temperament to get the most out of their ability. Bobby's problem was his attitude and aggression. He got into quite a bit of strife, which I think was very much a reflection of the fact he was brought up the hard way.

"He wasn't mad or anything but he did get carried away, which was a bit of a shame because he had so much talent. He was a kid in the team who I thought could be anything. I imagine he was just like Andy Gregory would have been at a similar age. Brash, confident, but also liable to run into strife on the field with referees and the opposition."

One New Zealander Bell learnt loads more about at Wigan was former Kiwi captain Graeme West. Until he arrived at Central Park, his only involvement with the big fellow had been the 1983 test series against Australia, particularly the Lang Park win.

"A real legend, especially now he's Wigan's coach. He's Mr Rugby League in Wigan," says Bell. "He's a guy you can't help but like, and he's not trying to be anyone but himself. He's the same old Westy. He'll do anything, go around to schools, open up fairs, attend fun days or whatever.

"He helped me with my introduction to Wigan. I'd played with him before with the Kiwis, albeit in just one series, so I was familiar with some of his skills and scored a few tries off 'Big Tex'. Those long arms would pop the ball up from behind defenders.

"A Wigan player I had a lot of fun with was Shaun Wane. In my second year, after the hernia operation, I needed some money. None was coming in in the way of match payments as I wasn't playing, so Shaun and I were involved going around the schools on a scheme the club set up with the council. It was good fun. We didn't work too hard—the hardest part was figuring out which pub we'd go to for lunch."

He had even more to do with Wigan's big buy for the 1990–91 season, only this was much more football-related. It was All Black first five-eighth Frano Botica who'd been courted by Wigan for some time and, in mid 1990, was part of the exodus of New Zealand rugby union players to the league code.

It wasn't a popular signing with coach Monie, though. "That's because Frano was chased and signed by the directors without consulting John," says Bell. "That definitely didn't please him.

"I can remember Jack Robinson ringing me up so many times asking what I knew about Frano—after he'd signed him, and after John had made it quite clear he wasn't happy about the signing.

"John didn't like signing rugby union players. He's got a thing about it which I think is a little bit unfair. So when John was blowing up about Frano, Jack was having some doubts whether he'd done the right thing.

"I spoke to Dad and he said Frano was very good, that he would make the transition easily; with the reservation that he seemed to have a knee

Battle scars for Dean Bell. An accidental clash in a match against Widnes
left him with this ugly gash above the eye, and another on his left cheek.
Jon Snape

The day after, all stitched up—17 stitches
in all—but the damage wasn't as severe as a
shredded bottom lip in 1990 which needed
33 stitches. Peter Hill (Wigan Observer)

injury. Frano was a class act anyway. He just had to do what he was capable of and he'd make it. I could see that straight away. I had quite a bit to do with him because he was on the wing outside me. And I also adopted him as my training partner.

"I would tell Frano a lot of things on the field. He didn't know our game and I helped him as much as I could. There's no better feeling for me than helping a young player or a new one like Frano. With him it was mainly telling him about positional play, when to drop back for the kicks and all those things. The finer points of the game.

"Of course, there was his kicking. Just awesome. It wasn't the big reason why Wigan bought him. He was wanted first and foremost as a player. But there was so much competition for places at Wigan and Frano could see that if he concentrated on his kicking he could ensure he was picked."

Year two under Monie still brought title success, not as much of it though, nor the same degree of assurance and authority from a side which had dictated trends for the previous four seasons.

Momentarily, too, Dean Bell had the authority knocked out of his game after a freak accident in Wigan's championship encounter against Hull, just a week out from playing the 1990 Kangaroo tourists.

"There was another time when I got one cut on the cheek and another one above one eye," says Bell. "But I was able to go back on the field after having 17 stitches put in.

"This one against Hull was a bit different, though. I went in to tackle Noel Cleal, he ducked, Denis Betts was on the other side and my mouth smashed into his head. It knocked Denis out but, at that instant, I didn't feel that much until I felt a bit of warmth going down my chin. I thought I must have split my lip but, when I went to touch it, I couldn't find my lip at all. It had all split into jagged parts and the guys around me didn't give me much confidence. They were looking at me and saying, 'Aah, no!"

"Luckily for me the club doctor Ansar Zaman specialises in plastic surgery and he was there that day to stitch me up. I'd had two arteries severed and there was just so much blood. If the doctor hadn't been there I might have lost the lip and, even after he'd finished stitching, he said we had to be sure blood kept pumping through the lip if it was to heal. It was gory.

"For that to happen the week before the match against the Kangaroos didn't please me—to miss that game just because of a cut lip! I was on the training paddock all week hoping for a miracle cure but commonsense prevailed.

"I needed 33 stitches in all and couldn't eat anything all week. I was dying for some chicken or something so I made myself a chicken sandwich—and the lip split open again.

"Dr Zaman tried to inject the lip but the anaesthetic was going straight down my throat because there wasn't enough flesh in the lip. So, he had to

The Challenge Cup is back where it belongs again, or so say Wigan. Bobby Goulding (left),
Denis Betts, Dean Bell, David Myers and Steve Hampson show it off around the streets of
Wigan after beating St Helens in the 1991 final. Wigan Observer

re-stitch me without an anaesthetic! Unbelievably painful. When you get stitched during a game, with the adrenalin running, it's not so bad having it done without an injection—but not when you're cold."

As it happened, the Australian match was a good one to miss, the only match he did miss through that injury. Wigan were savaged 34–6. In fact, it wasn't proving such a flash season all round.

Of their first nine games, Wigan beat only Barrow in the first round of the Lancashire Cup plus Castleford and Rochdale Hornets in the first division championship. They lost the Charity Shield season opener to Widnes, and then lost to the same team again in the second round of the Lancashire Cup. They managed only a home draw with Sheffield Eagles and then three losses on end—to Bradford Northern and Hull in the first division plus the Kangaroos. Further championship losses to Wakefield Trinity and Warrington, plus a third-round exit in the Regal Trophy, suggested the season might not produce too much.

So much for those theories. In an incredible feat of endurance, Wigan put together an 18-match unbeaten sequence to vault them into the Challenge Cup final against St Helens and to clinch the first division crown when they beat Leeds 20–8 in their last match. It was that close once more.

Really, though, the fixture load on Wigan was absurd as they had to play their last eight championship matches in 19 days, the final four of them in a week. It was hell—what Monie had called 'Mission Impossible'—yet the impossible became possible.

"We'd built a great reputation for being a team that came right at the business end of the season and the best illustration of that was in the 1990–91 season when we were under so much strain," says Bell.

Wigan were anything but fresh for their fourth straight Wembley appearance, having had their first loss in 19 matches when beaten by Featherstone Rovers in the first round of the Premiership Trophy. The players were physically battered, mentally exhausted and more than half the team needed painkilling injections to play.

"But going to Wembley was still no less exciting," says Bell. "It had become routine for us, but that didn't mean it was becoming boring. It's never boring. We simply followed the same schedule each year because we were used to doing it that way.

"This final was a really tough game for us, our toughest. Ellery had loads of injections in his hamstring so he could play. We needed him knowing Saints would want revenge after the 27–0 drubbing two years earlier. They were a far better prepared team under Mike McClennan.

"We were a battered team, totally exhausted going into the final. We'd played so many games and we were really beaten up. It wasn't one of our best performances but, after what we'd been through, it was a major achievement for us to win that time. It was sheer willpower that got us through.

"Saints couldn't have had a better chance to topple Wigan at Wembley, given the shape we were in, but that's where that Wigan team was just so good."

It was Botica's Wembley debut, and an extraordinary one. Inside 12 minutes he'd played a major role in effectively settling the outcome of the game. An early penalty started it and 12 minutes in a superb short ball from Bell had Betts spearing through a hole in the St Helens defence out wide before giving Botica a sideline run for a dazzling try. And he converted it from the sideline as well.

St Helens, featuring Kiwis Shane Cooper, George Mann and Tea Ropati, failed to respect the football as they continually surrendered possession and paid by losing 13–8 in easily the tightest final for Wigan during their reign.

"There was a fear factor emerging for us, the fear of becoming the first Wigan team to lose after the run we'd had," says Bell. "That made it four, but some day it would have to end and no one wanted to be involved in the Wigan team that lost the cup."

nearly as good as buck

Frano Botica

I lived to regret it, but as a new arrival at Wigan in 1990 I didn't know any better, and when Dean Bell offered to take me under his wing, I wasn't about to turn him down. I needed all the help I could get. That "help" involved Dean taking me down to a gym—which was very foreign to me—and in that month of pre-season training, I found out the worst man you could be with was Dean Bell, because of the training schedule he followed and how hard he pushed himself in the gym. I was walking around like there was something wrong with me, I was in so much pain. Dean has a reputation for ensuring you go past your limit at training and he pushed me all the way. It would always be, "Come on! One more! And another one!" When he left to join the Warriors it was almost a relief!

Dean's legendary for his appetite for weight training, only I didn't know that when I first arrived, so all the boys laughed at me for going with him. At the end of the day it helped, of course; where Dean pushes himself to the limit and more at training, he plays the same way on the field. As a leader, that rubbed off and it reminded me of Wayne Shelford. When he was captain of any side, he did the same thing. He led by example and, when he had something to say, he never said too much. You followed him because he was always leading from the front, which is the way it should be most of the time. And that was exactly the same with Dean.

I always used to go on to Dean about Buck and how good he was. So, sometimes when we were having a drink or three, Dean would ask me, "So, am I as good as Buck yet?" And I'd tell him, "You're getting there. Nearly." But I had to tell him he could never be as good as Buck. Hell, Buck would have given me a hiding if I'd ever said that! Dean was in the same mould, but there'll only ever be one Wayne Shelford.

Maybe the Maori thing came through a little, Buck and Dean both having Maori blood, although Dean doesn't look it. I suppose that's why he was so competitive and ruthless when he played. Just the same as Buck. There were never any half measures with either of them. Dean could have been almost dying and he'd still play on. I couldn't believe the number of times he went off the field to be stitched up, and then ran back on with tape all over the place holding him together. He kept going. He was always an inspiration.

Buck and Dean are way up there at the top, ahead of other captains I have played under. Some captains are good at the job because they talk a good game but, for me, a captain gains far more respect by showing his players, not by telling them. For them it's, "I'll show you the way, not tell you the way." At Wigan, if the forwards weren't doing their job properly, Dean would come in and call out, "Give me that friggin' ball." And he'd go and do it himself to show them.

Dean had more than a fair quota of serious injuries as well as bad cuts and so on, most of which you could put down to his total commitment on the field. He would put on some enormous hits and keep going back for more. Just mad, basically.

I wasn't prepared to be that mad about defence, but I had some work to do on it when I arrived at Wigan, and Dean was the ideal one to teach me some tricks. Obviously I had to get used to doing much more tackling. One problem I had was that I was going too low basically, and players were stepping out of my tackles or unloading the ball. I had to learn to go a little higher, which is what Dean taught me to do. I mean, at the end of the day, I'm a stand-off from Rugby Union—and we just don't like tackling!

He's also very good at helping new players through a game and showing them where they should be positionally, and what they should be trying to do. He did that with me, and then with Inga (Va'aiga Tuigamala) when he came to Wigan.

Everyone at Wigan knew and respected Dean for the same reasons I did. Mainly his toughness. He used to be fiery, too—until the captaincy quietened him down a bit, which was probably a good thing! He's not a bad card player either, and a useful golfer. A bit of a burglar, I'd say. As a footballer, one heck of a player and one heck of a captain. Almost as good as Buck.

Frano Botica was an All Black from 1986–89 (27 appearances including 7 tests), scoring 123 points. He played 14 times for New Zealand Maori (168 points) and totalled 540 points in 51 appearances for North Harbour (1985–89). After turning to league in 1990, he became a Kiwi international, playing 7 tests from 1991–93 and scoring 50 points. He played for Wigan from 1990–95, becoming the fastest player to reach 1000 points (93 games) in British league history; totalling more than 1900 points in all. He joined the Auckland Warriors in 1995 (5 games, 46 points).

measuring the newcomers

You can't get much done in life if you only work
on the days when you feel good.

Super League bosses argued it wasn't right to have so many teams in the Winfield Cup, and their theory had plenty of supporters. To have 20 clubs in the 1995 competition really was stretching reality. But those misgivings had always been aimed at the preponderance of Sydney clubs in the competition—11 in all, counting Penrith—with too many of them struggling financially and poorly supported by the fans.

The criticism from Super League people and others wasn't targeted so much at the efforts to take the Winfield Cup to new frontiers. This was the year when the big selling point was the four newcomers—the Western Reds from Perth, the North Queensland Cowboys from Townsville, the South Queensland Crushers from Brisbane and the Warriors from Auckland. Significantly, three of the four—the Reds, the Cowboys and the Warriors—are all in Super League's scheme. So, apart from the usual guessing games about likely grand finalists, the other interest centred on how the four new teams fared and where they ranked in the realm.

From the very opening night of the season, they made a powerful statement, the Warriors all but toppling Brisbane and then the Western Reds doing even better by overcoming St George. By the end of the 15th round, the Warriors had 16 points, the Western Reds 14, the Crushes 9 and the Cowboys only 4, holding up the bottom of the competition. But none of the expansion teams had played each other. Round 16 changed that as the Warriors started a run where they played all the new clubs on successive weekends.

From the outset, John Monie maintained the best feature of the draw was that his team didn't have to travel to Perth. So, for the Western Reds, it was the trip from hell right across Australia and the Tasman to the Warriors' cauldron at Ericsson Stadium.

A typical dart from dummy half produces a crucial try for Warriors hooker Syd Eru against the Western Reds.
Nigel Marple (Fotopress)

"I always believed it was a game we'd have to play well to win, regardless of the travel factor," says Bell. "They were able to put together a very good team."

The inclination was to associate the Reds with the wild man of their side, former Australian test forward Mark Geyer. But they also had another ex-Australian test player in Brad Mackay, as well as Kiwi loose forward Brendon Tuuta, and in the backs, other off-season imports from England in Leeds' former All Black centre Craig Innes and his centre partner from Wigan Barrie-Jon Mather, plus former St George fullback Mick Potter.

In the first half at least, it was the ordeal Bell had anticipated, as a Jeff Doyle try gave the Reds a 6–0 lead, answered later by another Syd Eru special when he blasted out of dummy half to lock the score up at halftime.

But the Warriors transformed the match completely in the second forty minutes, following Monie's game plan strictly as they relentlessly worked the ball around the ruck area to keep the Reds rolling back. The backline class did the rest, as five more tries were scored, four of them in a fourteen-minute surge, to take the Warriors out to 34–6. The Reds scored late, but at 34–10 the first battle of the expansion teams had been decisively won.

A tragic sight for the Warriors as Frano Botica ends his season with a broken leg. Western Reds second rower Mark Geyer offering some consoling words.
Nigel Marple (Fotopress)

"We knew they had a very good forward pack and that we had to contain them, so we worked at that, knowing our backs would be able to do the job for us," says Bell.

"When we opened up, we played some great rugby league, very professional, and a follow-on from what we'd done against Gold Coast. I would have settled quite happily for a win of any type against the Reds, never mind one as good as we achieved.

"It was the game that was going to settle which of the newcomers was the best and they'd arrived talking about it being their most important game of the season. But we needed the points just as much."

The victory carried a terrible cost, though. Tony Tatupu, who was shaping as one of the Warriors' most potent weapons in the quest for a play-offs spot, had his season ended when he broke his right arm in a tackle. And it became a double tragedy when Frano Botica broke his right leg falling awkwardly in a crushing Mark Geyer tackle; it made for shocking viewing watching television replays of it.

"It was sad to lose Tony because he'd become a very dangerous player for us," says Bell. "And for Frano to be out for the season was, of course, a bitter blow which I knew was going to affect us in a major way. Our goalkicking had been a problem until he arrived. Now he'd just started getting that right for us and we'd lost him.

Second rower Denis Betts fends off Western Reds captain Brad Mackay in the Warriors'
34–10 victory at Ericsson Stadium. Ross Setford (Fotopress)

"I wasn't far away when Frano was dumped and then suddenly I could see his leg facing one way, his foot the other. I knew straight away he was gone. What didn't help was that Frano stumbled as he was about to be tackled by Geyer but, despite what some people were saying, there was nothing wrong with the tackle itself.

"Actually both Frano and Gene [Ngamu] seemed to run into Geyer a lot when they had the ball. Probably the two lightest guys on the field and they were both taking on Geyer—not the best thing to do."

Bell was now relishing the loose forward's role, providing the same consistency and reliability he had in the centres. "You need a steady player at loose forward," he says. "Someone to make his tackles and make the hard yards." The by-product could be seen in the combination which quickly showed up between the Wigan trio in the forwards, a certain telepathy was obvious as Bell worked in with Denis Betts and Andy Platt.

Platt, in fact, was again the Warriors' stand-out forward, and stand-out player, as his direct, ground-gaining runs kept the Reds back-pedalling in a victory that the Aucklanders certainly enjoyed—and then savoured.

"All the players and partners got together for what was going to be a few drinks," says Bell. "But I got home at 4.00 a.m. with the sort of head that reminded me why I don't do that sort of thing very often.

"I knew I was getting too old for it. A lot of the guys meet up after a game on a regular basis but I don't because I can't handle it. It has to be right, and after we'd beaten the Reds it seemed like a good time to have a bit of a blow-out.

"I like to have a good time and believe you should live life to the fullest, but I think some of the guys have to realise that there's a time to let loose. For some of them, they treat that as all the time. You need to find a balance.

"I look at the draw and, if we've got a Sunday game followed by a Friday night game, I know there's not much time, so I'll definitely look after myself for that week.

"If I do go out for a reasonably big night, it will be the night that we've played. I might go out for a meal early in the week, but after Wednesday night I wouldn't go out again if we had a Sunday game. That's the discipline I've set myself and it works best. I don't allow myself any excuses or reasons for having a bad game; if I went out late in the week, I'd be creating a likely reason for a bad one.

"Players the world over are all the same. They like to go out, only a lot of them never seem to find the balance required."

Dean Bell needed that balance for the next of the newcomers, the Crushers, with the venue Suncorp Stadium. Bell's not unlike coaches who always strive to find reasons why the opposition deserve respect. With the Reds it was easy enough to find. And sifting through the results unearthed enough information to let the Warriors know the Crushers shouldn't be easily dismissed either.

"They were always going to be hard when you realised they had beaten Norths, Newcastle and Penrith, three teams that had beaten us convincingly," says Bell. "I also knew Tony Kemp had to be watched because he'd really improved his skill level when I'd seen him in England and on tapes of the Crushers' games."

Bell was so right about the Kemp factor. He unleashed an impressive repertoire of skills to keep the Crushers right in the game. Two Sean Hoppe intercepts, beautifully taken as usual, plus a sweet Richie Blackmore try had the Warriors out to an undeserved 16–4 halftime lead.

But early in the second half, Kemp's capers helped the Crushers close to 16–10, with the Warriors looking exceedingly brittle and likely to concede points at any time. That they were able to escape was due essentially to a smart interchange. Phil Blake came on and, in no time, scampered from dummy half to create a buffer at 20–10, later improved to 22–10 with a penalty.

"It was an awful performance all around, and certainly my worst personally," says Bell. "We were making so many errors, fumbling balls, throwing silly passes, missing tackles. I mean, we had a decent lead at 16–

4 and did everything we could to throw it away. We did no more than hang on even though the winning margin was 12 points in the end."

Bell found some time to put his Leeds coaching hat on after the game. There'd been some talk that Kemp, who was bound for Leeds, was having second thoughts about the deal.

"But I was determined to keep him at Leeds so I asked him to meet me at our hotel after the game," says Bell. "To my relief, I found out he was really keen to come to Headingley, which pleased me, because I was sure he could give Leeds a lot of direction."

A win which almost felt like a loss was also further tarnished by a dreadful reserve grade effort. They were showing signs of falling apart as they were literally crushed by the Crushers 54–16.

"We'd come out of the match with no injuries, which was a relief because the way the reserves were going we couldn't afford any at all," says Bell. "John had told us in a team meeting the night before the game that the reserves looked disinterested.

"It must have been a difficult time, though, because some of them would have been wondering whether they were going to be cut and others already knew they were being released. That makes it hard to get motivated.

"I knew what was happening. John asked me to sit in on a recruitment meeting once so I could observe what was going on and I heard the coaches talking about who they wanted and who they felt hadn't measured up.

"Some of them had probably signed up for maybe even three years, but were being let go after one. That's disappointing for them, although I guess there were a lot of players who hadn't kicked on."

The Warriors did kick on when they returned to Australia a week later, all the way to Townsville's Stockland Stadium, home of the North Queensland Cowboys who had won just two games all season.

A win should have been a certainty there. It didn't look like one when it was 0–0 at halftime and 4–0 to the locals straight after the break. But then it all happened in a near repeat of the razzle dazzle the Warriors had used to kill off South Sydney a few weeks before.

While the match was reasonably insignificant in the bigger picture, two of the year's better tries were scored that Saturday night. Richie Blackmore, as he had done against Cronulla, again flicked out a miracle ball in traffic for Sean Hoppe to race onto and bedazzle the Cowboys' defence with a super finish.

And John Kirwan also slipped a nice ball in the tackle to lay on Greg Alexander's try, one of six on the night, only two of which were converted. Botica's absence was certainly hurting.

Still, a 28–10 win completed the trifecta for the Warriors over their expansion rivals. There could be no argument about who was the best of the newcomers and, in the process, the Warriors had helped their points tally along nicely to 24, to lie sixth in the competition.

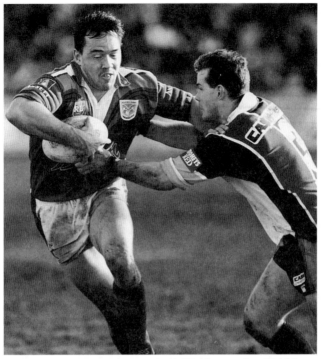

*Centre on centre as the Warriors' Kiwi international Richie
Blackmore tries to shove off Western Reds opposite and former
All Black Craig Innes.* Nigel Marple (Fotopress)

There was ample encouragement, too, in their strike power. To that stage, they ranked third behind only Manly and Newcastle in the points scored category (487), while they were the most prolific try-scorers with 91.

The Penrith loss apart, the Warriors had met Dean Bell's pre-match expectations on 4 June when, before the clash against the Tigers, he'd told his players they had every chance of stringing a lot of wins together. They'd made it six in a row with the Cowboys, in fact there were only two losses in the 13 matches since they were beaten by Manly almost four months earlier.

But a genuinely successful season wouldn't hinge on that record. It would rest on the four games left.

man of steel

Physical pain can't stop you if your mental outlook is strong enough.

In a career so studded with awards, accolades and never-ending success, Dean Bell is hard-pressed to single out one moment or achievement above the rest. After all, he has a fair-sized catalogue of special moments or highlights—his test debut in 1983, his first test win over the Australians that year, captaining New Zealand, his first season at Wigan when Graham Lowe coached them to almost everything, his first Challenge Cup win in 1988, captaining the Auckland Warriors...and so much more—too many to recount right here. But if he's not restricted to one single choice you can bet Bell will soon gravitate to his 1991–92 season with Wigan for a few of the best moments of his career.

Wigan's dominance of English league's trophies reached the upper stratosphere as the Challenge Cup stayed at Central Park, so did the first division championship, and this time the Premiership Trophy was Wigan's as well. Yes, what is known as the spring treble had been completed for the first time. Records don't have any chance of surviving for long with this super team in existence.

That wasn't the half of it either. After losing to Salford in their Regal Trophy semifinal on 30 November 1991, Wigan never lost another game all season in putting together a staggering run of 25 straight wins.

And still that doesn't fully explain why 1991–92 should be perhaps the best season of them all for the one-time freezing worker who started his rugby league career so many years earlier for Manukau in Auckland. No, the special achievement for Bell was that he was Wigan's captain for the first time in such a glittering season. He hoisted the first division's Championship Trophy when Wigan clinched it against Bradford Northern at Central Park on 11 April. He hoisted the Challenge Cup when Wigan retained it against Castleford at Wembley on 2 May. And he hoisted the Premiership Trophy when Wigan regained it against St Helens at Old

The third leg of the 1991–92 treble is clinched as Wigan captain Dean Bell shows off the Premiership Trophy, sharing the victory dais with Steve Hampson, Martin Dermott and Billy McGinty. Dean Bell Collection

Trafford on 17 May. And still there was more, as captain Bell collected one of the individual awards he coveted most in the game—the English season's Man of Steel.

Small wonder then that 1991–92 is a special season in Bell's life but, among such an array of successes and achievements, two in particular stand out for him.

"Lifting the Challenge Cup at Wembley, that was just everything," he says. "It's really one of the best things you can imagine. I know I'm looking on the negative side, but there was a worry about being captain at Wembley. I didn't want to be the first Wigan captain not to lift the trophy at Wembley in that run we were on. When I got to do it, it was such a relief. Ellery Hanley was a very hard act to follow as captain and I didn't want to fail after him.

"And there was the Man of Steel. That's really sought after. I was in with a chance of the first division Player of the Year title and I thought that was my best chance. It was announced first and when I missed out I was gutted. But the announcement that I had the Man of Steel, that was a fantastic moment for me."

For all that, the 1991–92 season was one which might have been rather difficult for a new captain. Not because he was captain, but because he was captain of a Wigan team which had lost the influential Ellery Hanley, bought by Leeds in a record transfer deal.

"I always thought it was only a matter of time before he went to Leeds," says Bell. "He lived so close to Headingley that it made sense, and Leeds have always had enough money to buy players.

"At the same time, Wigan do have a record of not holding on to even the best players if they think they're possibly getting on a bit, or are even just fractionally past their peak. I didn't think Ellery warranted getting rid of at that stage but obviously the directors were looking to the future. They had a young Phil Clarke there to take over.

"Jack Robinson [Wigan chairman] believes that if you have older players in the camp and there's a decision to be made, the coach will pick the older player instead of the less experienced one. So Jack's philosophy is to get rid of the older players to give the younger ones a chance of coming through. It's hard to argue with it the way it's worked at Wigan."

It left Wigan down on a drawcard player, and the directors are often as concerned about the commercial aspects of players they buy as they are about their pure footballing ability. With Hanley gone so early in the season, they scouted about for another big name and soon had the Widnes wonder Martin Offiah in their sights. In just four seasons at Naughton Park, since being signed for the 1987–88 season, the freakish talents of the man called Chariots—or Great Balls—had netted Widnes 181 tries in only 145 games!

Offiah was allegedly out of sorts at Widnes. "You could never be sure what was going on at Widnes," says Bell. "Who knows whether he was unhappy? I think he couldn't see a lot of future there and maybe he wanted a bigger stage. His talents deserved it. He had done fantastically well.

"It wasn't until January that we got Martin. He'd been staying away from Widnes, not training or playing. There was always talk that he was coming to us but it was a really drawn out affair. When he signed, I was delighted, and all I could think was, 'Great. This guy will score a million tries at this club.'

"He's the sort of player you love to hate. As an opposition player, you just want to get hold of him and crunch him in a tackle. He plays up to the crowd in a big way, usually after he's scored, so you're probably not in the best of moods when that happens and I guess he riles you a bit the way he can carry on.

"I realise he's good for the game. You need showmen like him and while that's not the way I behave, good on them to those people who do.

"There might have been resentment from some players about Martin, but if he can sit on his wing doing nothing for 79 minutes and then in the last minute run 100 metres to score the winning try he'll do me. That's why even at certain times when he lost form he was always a threat.

"Other sides played to him, but we covered for that. He's not a defender.

He's not a regular rugby league player. He's an exception, but what an exception. The Wigan directors also bought him for a commercial factor—to get bums on seats. I'm not sure that side of it really worked, but his strike power was unbelievable."

And that it was. In a severely shortened season for him, he made just 15 appearances but scored 30 tries!

Martin Offiah was undoubtedly the biggest buy of the year for Wigan. The biggest in history, in fact, with a record £440,000 transfer fee involved in his signing, Ellery Hanley's transfer fee having been a then record £250,000 only four months earlier. But Wigan did make other high quality purchases as well.

More integral to Wigan's all-round success—despite Offiah's exceptional try-scoring rate once he arrived—was the big Australian and Queensland centre Gene Miles, signed from the Brisbane Broncos. Monie had every confidence in Miles being the man he needed to replace the damaging Kiwi centre Kevin Iro, who'd joined Graham Lowe at Manly. Those who knew Miles well and had seen him play extensively knew Monie's assessment of him was spot on.

But a rugged start for Miles in England didn't always convince the directors, especially after they saw him in Wigan's Lancashire Cup semifinal loss to St Helens.

"It was Gene's first game for us," says Bell. "He brought a thigh injury with him but still wanted to play, and unfortunately he was very ordinary. He struggled for a month and the directors were on John's back about why he'd bought him. But didn't he make them eat their words! Gene was magic. A sensational player."

Wigan also bought another former international, ex-Kiwi winger Sam Panapa, who, as a test winger, had a smart try-scoring record for the Kiwis during his short international career.

"They asked me about Sam and I told them he was a player who was there or thereabouts back home but seemed to lack just a little something," says Bell. "But then the previous season I saw him playing for Sheffield Eagles and he looked a completely different player to me. I certainly gave him my support."

That faith wasn't misplaced either, as Panapa made 34 appearances, including nine off the bench, scoring 11 tries. Bell had also put in a recommendation for Warrington forward Billy McGinty, whose purchase was worth it as well, although he achieved some notoriety in Prime Minister Major's presence after the Challenge Cup final later in the season.

Wigan were able to count an endless string of superb results throughout the season, but two victories were truly remarkable, both in semifinals of cup competitions.

In the Challenge Cup semifinal at Bolton Wanderers Football Club, Wigan astounded themselves and totally demoralised Bradford Northern by winning 71–10! And in a Challenge Cup semifinal! Extraordinary stuff. In all, they scored 13 tries, five of them to Chariots.

But still more remarkable was Wigan's Premiership Trophy semifinal only a week after the Challenge Cup final. In front of the Central Park fans, Wigan went on an orgy of scoring against Leeds, winning 74–6—with Offiah providing the perfect 10 himself. Yes, 10 of the 14 tries went to one man alone. "Unbelievable game. Even now, I say unbelievable," says Bell. "We just couldn't and didn't do a thing wrong. This game and the one against Bradford were absolute freak games.

"To be involved in a match with a player who scores 10 tries himself is an unreal experience. It happened to me twice at Wigan—Shaun Edwards did it the next season—but against Leeds all I wanted to do was to help Martin to 10. I wanted to see it happen.

"I don't recall giving him any tries when he was all but over the line, but I do remember giving him a few passes to put him away. Some poor young kid was marking him in his debut. He's never been the same since.

"Shaun Wane, my good friend, was playing for Leeds then and his call in that game to his players when they had the ball was, 'Let's slow the play the balls down!' I laughed. What a call. Normally you're asking for quick play the balls but here he wanted to do all he could to slow the game down, and therefore slow the scoring down."

There was no way of slowing the scoring down when Frano Botica was on the field in his second season with the club. In his debut year, he'd provided 324 points, in year two he improved that to 364 points.

It seems unfair that a season as glorious as this had any debits. What it had were a couple of misses; Wigan beaten in the semifinal stage of the Lancashire Cup and making a third-round exit in the Regal Trophy. No one cared though, because in John Monie Wigan had landed another superb coach who had already brought them unprecedented success.

"I was feeling very comfortable under him. He's very methodical; a deep thinker about the game. He lives and breathes the life of a coach. If he didn't have it, I don't know what he'd do because he needs it so much. Lowie could do other things in the game, like television work and working for Super League or whatever, but that wouldn't do John. He has to be involved in coaching.

"We saw his qualities as a coach coming through that year. He is cool and doesn't get too wound up. He can't see any benefit in getting too emotional and I've certainly learnt a lot from him about how to handle people and players.

"During my time the game has changed. John was more American Football oriented in a way, like Jack Gibson. Lowie was very big on the motivation aspects, where John wasn't. He was in to the players motivating themselves while he himself spent a lot of time studying videos and analysing football and footballers."

In his fifth Wembley final, but first as captain, Dean Bell leads Wigan onto the field
with Joe Lydon, Frano Botica, Gene Miles and Martin Offiah lining up behind him.
Frank Orrell

Monie brought still another major success to Wigan in the 1991–92 season, although it was a title showdown the captain couldn't play in—the World Cup Challenge against Penrith at Anfield when Wigan won 21–4.

"In the Hull game I pulled my calf muscle," says Bell. "It was quite bad but I was really determined to play and I thought I could get away with it by having an injection on the night. So I lay on the bench, got an injection in it and jogged on the spot. Still not right. Had another one. Still not right. I ended up having four or five injections. You shouldn't have them anyway, but to have so many was not good at all.

"Time was running out and I had one more, jogged on it and thought that was it, that the painkiller had hit the spot. By then it was time to warm up outside but, as I ran onto the pitch, I felt my calf pull with the second step I took. It wasn't going to work and I didn't play.

"But something I'll never forget, and this showed the spirit in the club, was that all the players put in some of their own winning bonus money to give me the equivalent, which was about £2,000 for that game. All I had wanted to do was to play the game because I'd missed the first World Club Challenge against Manly in 1987. That was one heck of a gesture from them."

Prime Minister John Major in the Wigan dressing room with captain Dean Bell after the 1992 Challenge Cup final. He gained a new appreciation of pineapple rings on his visit. Frank Orrell

Martin Offiah was very much the talk of Wigan's season and he had everyone talking even more after his first appearance in a Challenge Cup final at Wembley. Facing a willing Castleford, including Kiwis Richie Blackmore and Tawera Nikau, Offiah's two tries fired Wigan to their fifth straight success in the big one.

"His wizardry helped us a lot that day," says Bell. "Teams weren't necessarily catching us up but they were making inroads and they were also working out how to handle themselves on the big occasions. It was two Offiah specials that basically made the difference in the final."

There was more than a tinge of sadness that utility Sam Panapa couldn't be given a place in the 15-man squad for the final, although he did travel to London. Bell had total sympathy for the first-year Wigan player.

"I felt sorry for Sammy," says Bell. "He was unlucky not to be involved and I gave him my spare Wembley jersey. He'd done such a good job for us all year.

"You sometimes wonder whether guys like Sammy are destined not to play in the big games. He was always Mr Fixit, but while sometimes versatility works for you, other times it counts against you. I didn't mind giving the jersey to Sammy because I knew he'd appreciate it, even though it's not as good as having his own. Just in case we didn't make it to Wembley again, he had something."

If Panapa had this reminder of his first trip to Wembley (even if not quite in the role he'd like), Prime Minister John Major also had a lasting memory of his day at the Challenge Cup final. He visited the Wigan dressing room after the game to meet the players and talk, and Wigan second rower Billy McGinty certainly provided a topic for discussion.

"Billy had a round piece of foam with a hole in the middle of it which he'd used to dress a knee injury," says Bell.

"The Prime Minister was moving around the dressing room talking to people and Billy, being the larrakin that he is, put his willy through the hole in the piece of foam and left it like that when he started talking to the Prime Minister.

"At the same time, a lot of fruit was being passed around to the players, which they like eating after the game. The combination of that and what Mr Major had seen made him look down at Billy and say, 'I don't think I'll ever look at pineapple rings in the same way again!'"

one of the greats

Denis Betts

You can imagine what it must have been like for me starting at Wigan. There I was, signed as a professional on my 17th birthday to play for one of the greatest clubs in the world.

But, of course, what struck me was suddenly being among so many of the great names of the game, players who were on the way to becoming legends, if they weren't already. There I was with guys like Ellery Hanley, Andy Gregory, Andy Goodway, Shaun Edwards, Graeme West, Joe Lydon and, of course, Dean Bell—just so many stars.

Dean, Ellery and Andy Goodway were the ones I aspired to be like because I could see they had the drive and commitment I would need to match if I was to be successful in this sport.

Other than the football aspects, Dean made me think about being a better person, about becoming a good person. I'm not the first to say it, and I won't be the last, but the one quality Dean Bell has is character. He also has class.

When you want to be like somebody, you have to follow their footsteps because you realise that, at the end of the day, when all the trophies have gone and everybody's stopped patting you on the back, the one thing you're left with is you. If you've got class and character, you'll go on in those years after being a footballer. You'll survive. That's why Dean will, because he has class. He'll always be somebody, not just an old broken-down footballer.

At Wigan, I could have chosen to follow a number of people, but I chose to follow those who stood out to me. Dean was one of them. Andy Goodway and Ellery Hanley were others.

My attitude was, if I want to be somebody, I want to be somebody who's going to be around for a long time and have plenty of respect. So, I'm not going to be a rebel and go out drinking to get everybody to like me that way. I'm going to work and put the time into training—I'm going to be like Dean, basically.

I was quite a limited rugby league player when I started at Wigan because I didn't have a background in the game. So I had to work hard to overcome my lack of ability; the way to do that was to learn off others and I learnt off Dean.

I was willing to listen and Dean was willing to tell. There has never been anything selfish about him. But, if I forget all about the football, having played with him and all of that, what matters to me most is that I can call Dean my friend.

Of course, I'll always have memories of him as a footballer too. Once, against Leeds, we were taking a bit of stick deep on defence, when we were awarded a penalty. Dean had the ball, tapped it to himself while everyone else was messing about getting back on defence slowly—and then took off. He stepped one man and then swerved to beat another on the outside, beating him for pace to score in the corner. I was still left standing in our own quarter thinking, 'Shit! Look at that.' He was always going on about how he didn't have any pace any more, and he went and did something like that.

When it really mattered, you could count on Dean. He was always there. The captaincy didn't change him. The whole time he was at Wigan, he was always the same as a player. He's not a shouter, he's not a bawler, he's not a pointer. He performed by doing the work to motivate those around him.

One of the great things he said to me was, "Be the one to inspire somebody else, don't let yourself be inspired." In other words, you do the work and others will follow.

I loved being part of the first year for the Warriors, and can't think of anything better for Dean either in what was his last year as a player. He deserved everything that came his way in 1995. Dean did what he has always done, that was trying to be the best he could on the field and all the rewards came to him. He got all the recognition in his last season at home and he deserved everything.

His last match against Brisbane wasn't ideal. We were all down and I'm sure Dean expected more from himself. But at the end of the day he's clever enough to sit down and know he gave his best, and that the Warriors' first year was a phenomenal success no matter how you look at it. He provided the grounding that is going to make the Warriors a very good side.

And when we do start winning things in years to come, Dean will derive great satisfaction out of being part of that building process. He'll deserve it, too, because not many players give as much as he has.

Denis Betts started his Great Britain test career in 1990, playing 25 tests (5 tries) to the end of 1994. He also played 10 tour matches (4 tries) and played for Wigan from 1986–95, making more than 250 appearances. He appeared in seven Challenge Cup final victories from 1989–1995, winning the Lance Todd Trophy in 1991. He signed a long-term contract with the Warriors, starting after the 1994–95 season ended.

the home straight

Lots of people know how to be successful, but very few people know how to handle success.

By the time the Warriors entered the Winfield Cup's danger zone—those last few rounds to sort out delicately balanced play-off spots—Denis Betts was more than rugby league's marathon man. He'd started his final season at Wigan in August 1994. By mid May he was winding it up in glory, seeing the club sweep everything available as he played the outstanding role in the Riversiders' final title success of the season, the Premiership Trophy showdown. It was all capped for him by being named the Man of Steel.

But before Betts knew it, he was on the training pitch with his new club, the Auckland Warriors, set to be his home for four and half seasons. And he was still on the training pitch at the start of August, about to complete more than 12 months of football which still had four weeks to run.

Heading towards 60 appearances in that period, he had to summon that little bit more as the Warriors eyed the tantalising possibility of making the Winfield Cup play-offs in their first season. Since the Sydney Tigers encounter, he'd played his part in putting the Aucklanders into the top eight, but they wouldn't stay there if they failed to have a solid last four weeks in the minor premiership.

Dean Bell hadn't reached the same point of exhaustion as his former Wigan team-mate. He hadn't been through the ringer of another strung out English season. But he was still feeling weary, realising his body was barely staying with the pace of Winfield Cup football as he was forced to subsist on anti-inflammatory pills to combat a chronic knee problem.

The prize for the first-year captain and his players couldn't be missed. If they won two of their last four games, they'd very likely make the final eight, but they might need three to be perfectly safe.

That was the straightforward side of it. The difficult part was the draw itself—St George at home, the Bulldogs away, Canberra at home and

Brisbane away. No other side had a schedule to compare with it.

While the Warriors had worked their way to sixth on points differential, their hold was more tenuous when the programmes for the other teams were analysed. The Bulldogs were also on 22 points, with the Aucklanders, but with a worse points for and against record. Their draw was far more comfortable, though, with Gold Coast away, the Warriors at home, the Crushers away and the Cowboys at home. After the certainties—Manly, Canberra, Brisbane, Newcastle and Cronulla—they would unquestionably be the sixth team through.

So it rested with the Warriors (22), Wests (20), Norths (18), St George (18), the Roosters (18) and possibly the Western Reds (18) for the remaining two positions. The draw legislated against Wests and the Reds (and so it proved), while the Roosters also had a difficult run, including the Western Reds away, Newcastle at home and Cronulla away.

That left St George and Norths as the most logical chances to tip the Warriors out, but the Auckland side could render all the calculations pointless if they maintained their better form.

The bare statistics said they could. They'd won six on end and were comparatively free of injury concerns other than the players they'd already lost in Botica and Tatupu. They'd learnt to win consistently, without always performing consistently. And that in the end was the rub as they prepared for the Brian Smith-coached St George, a match which had generated exceptional anticipation from the public. Monie always had well-justified fears about the Dragons.

"John warned us we'd be coming up against a side with recent finals experience," says Bell. "They'd played two grand finals in recent times and they were in a win-at-all-costs position if they were to make the play-offs."

The worry was always the St George forwards, depending on who they put on the field. In the end, their pack was an awesome one, with Jason Stevens, Nathan Brown and David Barnhill in the front row, Scott Gourley and Gorden Tallis in the second row and Wayne Bartrim at loose forward. Put them together with their halves Noel Goldthorpe and Anthony Mundine and St George had a unit which could be too much for any side, if they got it together.

Well, they did get it together, with destructive consequences for the Warriors, although at halftime the game was easily retrievable. A late try to Richie Blackmore had cut the halftime margin to 14–8; if the Warriors could hold it that way and score first after the break, they might have the win they wanted.

Those theories took just the first seconds of the next 40 minutes to be obliterated as the hungry Tallis scored one of the most astounding tries by a forward from 60 metres out. Dean Bell doesn't accept that the game had gone then, but it certainly made a noticeable difference, because the Warriors

*Centre Richie Blackmore across for his try in one of the very few bright spots
in the Warriors' shattering loss to St George.* Ross Land (Fotopress)

showed no indication they might be able to recover from it. In fact, they
went the other way; their game deteriorated so drastically that St George
carved and shredded their defence with nonchalant ease to race to a 47–8
lead before being checked by a last-minute Warriors try to Stacey Jones,
stopping 50 being posted and ending it at 47–14.

"What didn't help us was that while we were pushed at times in some
of the games leading up to this one, we weren't actually stretched," says
Bell." "We basically did just enough to win in many of them and, as well
as that, we hadn't faced a really strong side for some time. No side had
been asking us many hard questions, and when St George did we didn't
have the answers.

"We had enough warnings about St George from John but, once again,
we found a side whose enthusiasm accounted for us, just as Norths,
Newcastle and Penrith had done earlier in the year.

"Perhaps we should have used the ball more than we did to get away
from their forwards but, when you face an enthusiastic side, that doesn't
always work out. You've got them in your face all the time."

Bell himself had them right in his face, bordering on illegally so. "They
were a very niggly side. I copped an elbow from Jason Donnelly and also
one from Nick Zisti. I think John was contemplating a citing for one of
them.

"When I was at Wigan, I was king hit from behind once against
Castleford. John's never been keen on citing players, but when he saw
that one on video he regretted not citing the player concerned because it

The Warriors' former All Black winger John Kirwan tries to evade his St George opposite Nick Zisti during the dreadful 47–14 loss at Ericsson Stadium. Nigel Marple (Fotopress)

was so blatant. So when he saw the elbow on me against St George he thought about it twice. I'm glad he didn't do anything in some ways. I wouldn't be keen unless something really bad had happened. In saying that, though, there's only a centimetre or two in it being your jaw.

"I always worry about blows to the throat from a forearm or elbow after what happened to Lani Latoa [the North Harbour player who died after a blow to the windpipe in a pre-season game against the Warriors' reserve grade team in 1995]. I've seen a lot of good elbows thrown at players in my time but you never stop to think what damage they could do. What happened to Lani Latoa shocked me so much. You never take the field thinking you're going to die. You might expect to get badly injured at some stage, but not killed.

"It didn't soften my approach, but it frightened me all the same and made me think. You've got to try and protect yourself as well as you can when you're running with the ball, but sometimes players do use their forearm or elbow to deliberately cause injury."

The St George display was easily the worst home showing from the Warriors all season, prompting a mass walk-out by spectators well before the end.

The Tallis try was the shocker of the lot, both for its timing so soon after halftime and for the way the Warriors' defensive screen completely failed to cope with his marauding run.

"John pointed out later that our designated back row forwards weren't getting out to where he wanted them on defence, out among the centres," says Bell. "I was meant to be patrolling the right side where Tallis busted us but what I was doing was lining up inside the likes of Stacey [Jones], Greg [Alexander] and Phil [Blake] because I didn't want them closer in taking on the big forwards. John explained that he, in fact, did want the smaller guys in around the ruck area to work hard trying to cut down their forwards."

Too often the captain had been unable to offer a reason for other lame displays and he was as befuddled as before about this one. "You don't like to say it, but I think we might have given up in that game, thrown up the white flag. We just folded so badly."

In the face of what soon shaped as certain defeat, it seemed fair to assume the Warriors might go for a little damage control. After all, the points for and against equations were important and too often the Aucklanders, when they lost, lost alarmingly easily.

"We probably don't think about it consciously, but perhaps we should have because the points are so vital at this stage in the event of teams being level," says Bell. "All the same, I don't think the call, 'Hey, think about the points difference' is strong enough when you're looking at a big loss. It's far better to say, 'Let's play for pride.' Then the points business should look after itself.

"But it was embarrassing and no one likes to be embarrassed. I couldn't blame all the people leaving the ground early. They had every right to. At least in other games when we'd lost at home, we'd been entertaining. Maybe not quite so much against Penrith, but there was no entertainment at all against St George."

As the mediocre became the frightful for the Warriors, coach Monie was even motivated to take Denis Betts off, an admission that not even he was making the grade on the day.

"And Denis was really depressed afterwards because he hadn't suffered a defeat like that for a while," says Bell. "Despite the loss, Andy [Platt], Denis and I went out with the girls for dinner and Denis was in a foul mood all night.

"He's a fairly placid sort of guy, but what rubbed it in was that he got dragged off. Not that Andy and I helped either by consciously winding him up about Gorden Tallis being a really good second rower. We kept that up for a couple of days. People would come and talk to us to say how well St George had played and, if Denis was there, we'd say, 'Yeah, that Tallis made a real difference didn't he!'

"Of course, I'd have Denis Betts any day. He'd pretty much had a do-what-you-want season in his last one with Wigan. Now he had to front up to this, where he'd come up against a player he'd heard a lot about but hadn't played against before.

"We still worked hard for our success at Wigan but Denis found he had

A strange experience for Warriors second rower Denis Betts—taken off to sit on the bench during St George's hammering of the Aucklanders.
Nigel Marple (Fotopress)

to work much harder in the Winfield Cup for success, for breaks and tries. It doesn't come easy at all. I think he was coming to terms with it and I know he'll explode in 1996 after having a break."

The one swift but pointed observation Dean Bell had made about the Warriors' exhibition against St George was that it wouldn't have given Bulldogs coach Chris Anderson a lot to focus on.

The Warriors were once again in the position where they had to revive themselves after a shocker. They'd also have to do so with some critical differences in their line-up.

Tea Ropati, one of the Warriors' best all year, was out with a rib injury, meaning Bell reverted to the centres. Logan Edwards went into loose forward, Tony Tuimavave to the second row and Stephen Kearney to the front row.

But when Edwards was a late defection with a mystery virus, Monie played some interesting selection games. Initially Hitro Okesene was promoted to first grade, suggesting he'd go into the front row and force a reshuffle of the back three but, on the eve of the Friday night game, Monie came out of left field and put Gavin Hill in the front row instead. He reasoned Hill was up against his old club, which should have driven him on, and it also gave the side a fair goalkicker.

The coach was right both times. A spectacular Warriors start saw Greg Alexander across off a Stacey Jones pass after two minutes and then Hill plonked the conversion over from the sideline. No player was more inspired than Jones, while the Warriors' forwards blanketed the Bulldogs set to have the visitors 16–4 ahead at halftime.

Everything kept happening for the Warriors after the break too. They defended outstandingly to protect their lead and then stretched in the last quarter as the two players off the interchange bench made all the difference.

Phil Blake had come on in the first half and scored a try almost immediately. Late in the second half, Willie Poching, set to leave the Warriors, emulated Blake by scoring a try himself and then making one for Blake to finish. At 29–8, the Winfield Cup newcomers had manufactured their best display of the year.

"It all came down to making up for what happened against St George. Our dignity had taken a battering then, but here we were a week later turning it all around completely. It was hard to figure it all out sometimes," says Bell.

Sport's delightful uncertainty was in evidence again. So was the Warriors' trend of oscillating between the diabolical and the magical from one game to the next. It's as if they needed a wake-up call every now and then to remind them how to play football; but 30-point and 40-point wake-up calls become a little expensive in the Winfield Cup, as would be shown in the last two rounds.

wembley to warrior

The main ingredient of stardom
is the rest of the team.

Of all the great names that have graced Wembley on Challenge Cup final day, one has been constant over the last 50 years—Lance Todd. His name lives on, linked permanently with the most sought-after of player awards, the trophy given to the player of the day in the Challenge Cup final.

Lance Todd gives New Zealand league yet another link with the grand event, a link which has been so powerful on the playing field since the early 1980s. He toured Britain with A.H. Baskerville's famous New Zealand All Golds side in 1907, the first league tour in history.

Todd also provides another Kiwi tie-up with Central Park. After playing three tests for New Zealand, he signed for Wigan in 1908 and played in one Challenge Cup final, although he was probably better known as a rugby league commentator. Todd was killed in a car accident in 1942 and the Lance Todd Trophy was introduced four years later.

But, for an award commemorating a New Zealander, it had precious little in the way of Kiwi benefactors, or Australian ones. In fact, apart from his fame as an outstanding Wigan player, Ces Mountford boasted the singular achievement of being the only New Zealander to win the Lance Todd Trophy (in 1951). The Australians had only two players honoured, in Brett Kenny and Graham Eadie in the mid 1980s.

Considering the avalanche of New Zealanders involved in Wembley finals since Hull's glory days in the early '80s, some success might have been expected. Certainly in his first three appearnces, Kevin Iro must have been better than a close runner-up at least once; three times on end, Iro had scored two tries in the final and not been honoured.

Finally in the 1993 final—and his sixth—Dean Bell corrected the imbalance, perhaps the injustice, two days after his 31st birthday. He was not playing with the No 3 jersey on either, but the No 13.

After six attempts, Dean Bell landed one of the most treasured awards in the game, the Lance Todd Trophy as man of the match in the 1993 Challenge Cup final. Gerard Webster

"Having played in so many Wembley finals, I'd made it my aim to win the Lance Todd Trophy," says Bell. "As a player, it's an honour you want to win, although it's not always so easy for players in some positions. This time, being at loose forward, I was naturally more heavily involved and a lot of play came my way."

In fact, Bell did finish up in the centres before halftime, when Joe Lydon was replaced, but it was while at loose forward that he made his first telling impact.

In perhaps the most exciting and drama-packed final in the Wigan era, Widnes winger John Devereux lost the ball in a tackle, Martin Offiah picked up and his overhead pass to the fast-following Bell laid on another Wembley try for the captain.

And, after leading only 14–12 at the break, it was Bell's pass soon after which put substitute Sam Panapa over for what proved to be the crucial try in a 20–14 win, an act which ultimately provided Bell with the romance of again being the winning captain, as well as the man of the match.

This, though, was a final which had its touches of sporting romance for those who have the slightest sentimental streak. After the cruel luck of missing the 1992 final, former Kiwi winger Sam Panapa was rewarded this time, underlining his immense value by being able to go into the forwards. It was the perfect day for Panapa—his first run in a Wembley final, the added bonus of a try (and there have been few more delighted try-scorers) and a winner's medal.

But even more romantic was Kurt Sorensen's first appearance at the famous stadium. The former Kiwi forward had played for Wigan as a youngster, but had established himself in the English game with Widnes since the 1984–85 season. Yet, for all the success Widnes had, they had failed to make the Wembley breakthrough, agonisingly falling at the semi-final stage three times.

So there was rich reward for Widnes in 1993, but especially for Sorensen as one of the game's true warriors. The origins of his first grade career could be found 20 years earlier at the Mt Wellington club in Auckland, but here he was at 37 on the biggest stage of all. Like Panapa, his debut had a try-scoring touch as well, a stunning one, too, for the old man of the side, as he charged 20 metres, scattering would-be defenders Steve Hampson and Frano Botica on his way to the line.

To watch the victory lap after the match was to see two players who clearly didn't want it to end. Panapa had more than his share of time holding the cup as he and his team-mates acknowledged their fans, and Sorensen was anything but a glum-faced loser. A smile was ever-present, and the look of sweet satisfaction as he took everything in; it wasn't lost on his former Kiwi team-mate.

"I was really happy for Kurt that he made it," says Bell. "So many good players never play at Wembley in their whole career, which is why I never take it for granted, even though this was my sixth one.

"I talked to Kurt after the game and he was just pleased to have been part of the day. It didn't matter to him that Widnes had lost. This was a day he'd dreamed about and he didn't want to forget anything about it."

For one of the rare times since the reign began in 1988, this final really was a genuine contest, as Widnes twice had the lead, first through an early try to Richie Eyres and then when Sorensen scored.

But a final which had its share of sentiment and football quality also had its seedy side, courtesy of two Widnes players. Eyres earned everlasting shame 15 minutes from fulltime when he was ordered off for use of an elbow to Martin Offiah's head. It had to be a red card. It was only the second ordering off in a Wembley final, and the first since Leeds centre Syd Hines was marched in the 1971 final against Leigh. But there should have been a second ordering off soon after for former Wigan player Bobby Goulding, whose shocking high shot on Wigan winger Jason Robinson brought only a caution.

Widnes scrumhalf Bobby Goulding is way too late as Dean Bell runs on after scoring his try in Wigan's 1993 Challenge Cup win at Wembley. Dean Bell Collection

"There's no question Goulding should have gone," says Bell. "His high tackle was worse than what Eyres did, but I think the only reason he stayed on was because the referee didn't want to have two players sent off in the same match, and in a Challenge Cup final at that." Goulding was punished retrospectively when he was fined on a charge of misconduct.

Wigan, after letting Hanley go, had started John Monie's last season at Central Park by selling scrumhalf Andy Gregory to Leeds, while the problem child Goulding had gone to Widnes in the off-season, meaning Shaun Edwards and Frano Botica shared the scrumhalf's role. The major new off-season buy wasn't a player in the super star category but a wonderfully steady centre in Andrew Farrar, who replaced Gene Miles.

"John wanted Gene to come back and he was really disappointed when negotiations broke down," says Bell. "I think it might have been more to do with a financial argument. The directors probably thought they could get Farrar for a lot less than Gene Miles. He wasn't a Miles, but Andrew was a very good pro—very strong—and he played a lot of football for us."

None of the personnel changes disrupted Wigan's relentless roll early in the season, aside from losing the Charity Shield opener to St Helens and being well beaten 22–8 by Brisbane, a depressing experience for Bell, who had finally made it on to the field for a World Club Challenge.

Captain and coach savour retaining the first division
championship for the fourth season on end.
Dean Bell Collection

Until Christmas, Wigan had just one other defeat in 20 matches—a one-point defeat by Hull—but in the traditional 27 December clash with neighbours St Helens there was a feeling of helplessness as Wigan were unbelievably massacred 41–6. So when Bell went through the 40 pointers with the Warriors two years later, he wasn't totally unfamiliar with them, despite Wigan's perception as a side which never had embarrassing defeats.

"St Helens' trademark is usually brilliant one minute, awful the next. This time it was pretty much brilliant all the way," says Bell. "We were behind the posts for the umpteenth time and I said, 'Whatever you do, don't get ordered of, but let's get back there and just go for it!' From the kick-off, Kelvin Skerrett threw an elbow out at Jarrod McCracken and got sent off! He blamed me, but he obviously hadn't digested my message about not getting ordered off."

The trophy successes flowed despite that carnage at Knowsley Road. Wigan had earlier beaten St Helens 5–4 in a rugged Lancashire Trophy final and beat Bradford Northern to collect the Regal Trophy. The points-scoring achievements were astounding as well. Shaun Edwards with 10 tries in a 78–0 win against Swinton, Hull beaten 42–0, Leeds 31–6 at

When the Bell family numbered three—Jackie and Dean with son
Kurtis, later to be joined by their daughter Chloe.
Dean Bell Collection

Headingley, Salford trounced 70–6 and Leigh 50–0, all of which helped Botica to an extraordinary season. He kicked a Wigan record 184 goals in the season in scoring a record 423 points in all. And Dean Bell also broke a barrier by scoring his 100th try in English league, including those he'd scored years earlier with Carlisle and Leeds.

The first division programme had its occasional hiccups, though, with losses to Warrington, Bradford Northern and Castleford, leaving Wigan vulnerable to lose the championship to St Helens.

There was also a major disruption in the Bell household. At midday on 17 February 1993 Jackie produced Chloe, a sister for Kurtis. Of course, fate dictated that football would intervene on the same day. By three o'clock Dean was on the team bus to Hull and scored two tries that night in a 42–0 win. But, the crucial match of the season came on 9 April. Wigan was at home to Saints, but with a side ravaged by injury. Despite the odds, Wigan managed an 8–8 draw and then clinched the title in their final outing, beating Castleford 25–18, but taking the crown only on the basis of a better points for and against record after Wigan and St Helens had both finished on 41 points.

With the Challenge Cup also gift-wrapped for Monie in his last season, Wigan could ensure themselves everlasting fame by also snaring the Premiership Trophy at Old Trafford. But again St Helens were the spoilers, winning 10–4 and preventing a Wigan grand slam of the five major trophies.

An almost unheard of defeat for Wigan in a final failed to detract from John Monie's astonishing four years at Central Park, when they completed the Challenge Cup-first division double each season and dominated the other competitions as well. Few dared to imagine he could out-Lowe Graham Lowe, but he'd done so comfortably.

By mid-season, though, it was known his time was up, that he'd be quitting the club, having signed a lucrative contract to take the Auckland Warriors into their first Winfield Cup campaign.

"I knew John was considering the Warriors job because Peter McLeod had been across," says Bell. "They wanted John, but I really didn't think John would want the job. I imagined he'd go back to Australia to one of the major clubs, but he obviously wanted the challenge."

He also wanted a captain and one day he told Bell, "I want you to come back and be captain." Dean Bell thought it was no more than idle chatter, that maybe Monie was joking. He'd never been more serious, as the Wigan captain would soon find out.

dean the man

Va'aiga Tuigamala

When I decided to switch to rugby league, it wasn't simply a case of packing my bags and heading to Wigan. A lot of thought went into it; and one of the things that swayed me was the New Zealand influence at the club.

I've always been a mad follower of New Zealanders doing well in their particular sport, and rugby league was never an exception throughout my rugby union days. I made a point of following the British rugby league competition and the fact Sam (Panapa), Frano (Botica) and Dean (Bell) were all at Wigan was a major attraction.

I also used to watch Dean a lot when he was still playing for the Kiwis, and he always stood out as a role model for everyone, both with the way he played and his leadership. But, until I arrived at Wigan, I'd never met him before—and when I finally did, I got a bit of a shock!

The club trainer had me in the gym for a strength test, and I couldn't help hearing some giggling from the back of the gym as I tried to push some weights. Much to my surprise the people who were laughing at me were guys like Andy Platt and Betts—and, most of all, Dean Bell. It was quite an embarrassment to me, because I knew those guys worked and trained and played with weights. They loved them. Coming from a union background, I thought I was quite strong but they showed me up. And all Dean could do was giggle at me as I struggled!

He did come and shake my hand, though. So did Frano and Sam, and that was the beginning of our friendship. The three of them did so much for me when I started out in league.

I wasn't able to play with Dean that much before he joined the Warriors (after the 1993–94 season), but I now count myself fortunate to have played with and alongside one of the greatest rugby players of all time.

I owe so much to the three New Zealand guys for helping nurse me into rugby league, especially to Dean. His long injury spell that season meant I could spend a lot of time with him, giving me an ideal opportunity to pick his brains. I've never seen anyone so professional about his game; he played it even when he was off the field injured.

That's why I'll never forget sitting with him watching Wigan's Challenge Cup tie against Hull that season. Wigan were 21–2 down at one stage and we looked at each other, both of us lost for words. I had enough time to say a little prayer before the second half, telling the Lord I didn't travel all this way to watch this team lose.

I kept watching, and also watched Dean, who seemed to be waiting patiently. When we scored the winning try in the dying seconds (to win 22–21), I jumped up yelling and screaming. I couldn't hold back my emotions. But when I looked down at Dean, he was still dead quiet. I felt a bit embarrassed and for about five or six seconds nothing was said. Then all of a sudden, he turned around, smacked me and shouted, "Yeah!" I thought, "Far out!"

Really, though, he's someone you admire and respect, and the way he recovered from his groin injury that season freaked me out. Most rugby players I know would have walked away from the team with an injury like that, and wouldn't return until they were fully fit. But Dean was there throughout, still knowing his role and position in the team.

He took the time to give when I started, and he certainly gave unselfishly when it came to tips. Much of the reason why I achieved so much in a short time in league was because of Dean Bell. He doesn't expect any rewards for it. It's a personal thing I'll always hold on to, just like my union days when guys like John Kirwan, Michael Jones and Joe Stanley helped me.

The best advice Dean Bell gave me? Well, maybe not advice, just the comment the first time I got smashed, "Welcome to the real world!" Nice one, brother! One thing he did say was, "Be yourself, go out there and enjoy yourself. Do what you know is best."

He's a true original, the same on the field as off it. His professional attitude and the way he prepares himself is always thorough. His team talks were nothing over the top, just straightforward and direct, but meaningful to the players. Shaun Edwards said he'd play alongside Dean for anything and, when a player like Shaun says that, you know you're dealing with someone special. I soon found that out for myself.

It was a sad, sad day for Wigan when he played his last game for the club, because he was at the forefront of Wigan's revival, helping pull the club through. They call him Dean *The* Man around these parts and it's so true. He is The Man.

Va'aiga Tuigamala was an All Black from 1989–93. In his 39 matches for New Zealand, including 19 tests, he scored 14 tries (5 tries in tests). He represented Auckland from 1988–93, appearing in 48 matches and scoring 28 tries. He switched to league after the All Blacks' 1993 tour of England and Scotland, beginning his Wigan career in January 1994 and scoring a try on debut against Widnes. He was selected for Western Samoa for the 1995 Rugby League World Cup.

the final act

I hate losing more than I like winning.

Fate delivered the Warriors the unkind blow of opening and closing their debut year against the Brisbane Broncos. Neither occasion produced an Auckland victory, but it was the safest of bets which match the newcomers prefer to remember.

Their opener at Ericsson Stadium on 10 March had been a mind-boggling experience, when the three-point loss bothered no one. But the finale at Brisbane's ANZ Stadium was a mind-numbing experience, and the 38-point loss bothered everyone; the Warriors' season ending as ingloriously as it had opened gloriously.

The Broncos' faithful didn't care, of course. They were drunk with delight over a high-quality display which had torn the Warriors apart 44–6 to put Brisbane in the mood for the Winfield Cup play-offs. All John Monie's men wanted to do was to scramble off the park as quickly as possible and hide in shame in their dressing room.

Even during the game, Warriors' players were undoubtedly feeling for one man alone—Dean Bell, their captain, who in his farewell appearance was being forced to endure another exercise in humiliation. Hearts went out to him as the torn and frayed Warriors slunk off the field as anonymously as possible, but Bell didn't want anyone's sympathy.

"John Kirwan said to me after the game, 'Gee, I feel sorry for you.' I said, 'Don't worry about it. I've got too much out of the game to let one day like this get me down now.'

"John said he still felt the team let me down, but I didn't think that at all. I felt we let everyone else down as well as ourselves.

"Before the game I said to everyone, 'Let's be a bit selfish today and go out and play for ourselves, play with a little pride in our own performance.'

"And at the team meeting at the hotel before going to the ground I said, 'I don't like talking about negative things before a game, but I have one concern and that's the fact we haven't handled the heat before. We seem to get tired and drop off the intensity in our tackles. We start using our arms. If we do it against top teams like Brisbane, Manly, Canberra and so on, they're too strong and they're going to break tackles. We have to put our bodies on the line'. I thought if I said that they might think about it on the field and push through the problem. That certainly didn't happen.

"The opening 10 minutes set the tone and, the way the game is played under the 10-metre rule, you have games like this. They just get right away from you and it takes so much to stop their momentum."

Ideally, the Aucklanders could have done without the high-impact end to the year. In a perfect world, they would have secured a top eight spot before the 22nd and last round of the minor premiership. But it had come down to this, down to one match which could have put them in the elite. At least they had a chance—beat Brisbane and they were in. Lose and they might still have a chance.

Which was just how it worked out. As the Warriors were wallowing, North Sydney were adrift of Gold Coast; if the result stayed that way, the Aucklanders could still make it despite defeat at ANZ Stadium—that was until the Sydney Roosters began to carve up the Sydney Tigers.

That victory for the Roosters would put them level with the Warriors on 24; and the points the Roosters were scoring against the Tigers, matched against the points the Warriors were simultaneously conceding against the Broncos, had dramatically changed the points differential to the extent that they favoured the Sydneysiders. They'd therefore go into the top eight ahead of the Warriors. That was until it was all rendered rather academic. Norths scrambled a draw against Gold Coast to also finish on 24 points, but with the superior points for and against figures of the three teams.

The top eight race had been on a knife edge for weeks but, in the final run-in—and it was admittedly a demanding one—the Warriors had manufactured only one win in their last four outings.

"After we'd beaten the Bulldogs, we still had to win both of our last matches the way it was. Otherwise it would have come down to points for and against, which is just what happened in the end," says Bell.

To be fair, expecting victories over either Canberra or Brisbane, let alone both of them in the space of a week, was in the territory of dreamland. There was merit in a gritty display against the Raiders at Ericsson Stadium that celebrated—and that still was the right word—the last home game of the season. Two flashes of Laurie Daley inspiration were enough to pluck a 15–8 win, a result nearly everyone was certain had ended the Warriors' top eight hopes there and then.

But two days later it had all changed. South Sydney, the unlikeliest of all teams, opened up the race again by drawing with North Sydney, to leave the Warriors one point clear in eighth place and the knowledge that winning in Brisbane would end all arguments.

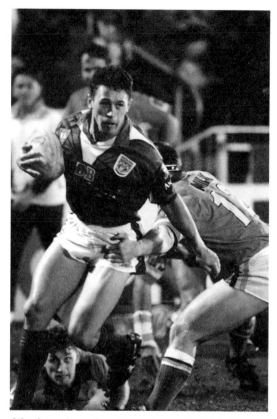

*Warriors winger Sean Hoppe leaves Brett Mullins on
the ground and runs through David Furner's tackle en
route to his 19th try of the season against his old club
Canberra.* Nigel Marple (Fotopress)

That the Warriors failed to respect their reprieve in fashioning such a limp display in Brisbane devastated coach John Monie. Not because a play-offs spot had gone, more because his players made so many criminal errors with the football, and without it. He'd set his sights pre-season on a 10th place finish for the Warriors, adding anything else would be a bonus. The bonus didn't come, the anticipated placing did and perhaps that simply heightened the belief that the season hadn't run quite well enough.

"We were terrible against Brisbane, and also against some other sides, but I think we have to appreciate the strength of the game in Australia," says Bell. "The fact is they do have so many outstanding footballers and some of them were a little too good for us."

As Bell told John Kirwan, he's had too many memorable moments in the game to dwell on the last 80 minutes of his playing career. Or the last 160 (that saw the Warriors miss their objective) for that matter .

Farewell New Zealand. Dean Bell acknowledges the Ericsson Stadium fans after his last outing on New Zealand soil. Nigel Marple (Fotopress)

And if there were team-mates and others who felt for him during his last outing in Brisbane, the man himself will far more readily recall and cherish the farewell he was given at Ericsson Stadium, both before and after the Canberra game.

"It was only about 30 minutes out from kick-off that John let on what was going on," says Bell. "He said, 'Steve [Kearney] you'll be leading the side. Lano [Bob Lanigan], you stay with Dean and he'll come out a minute later.'

"John hadn't told me earlier because he knew I'd say no to it, that I didn't want that bullshit. Then I thought about it and realised that it was a nice honour after all the years I'd been playing the game. And later I found out that Jackie had known about it for a couple of days.

"I found it very emotional going through the guard of honour, although it didn't change anything about me for the game. I was still hyped for it. I believed all that would happen would be a presentation after the game. It's nice to be thought of like that after 16 years playing first grade football.

"The start had been so memorable for me at Ericsson Stadium and it was a great way to end it as well."

If the season had a depressing finale on the field, there was on-going excitement off it as the Warriors' recruiting plans began to take definite shape. The biggest of a number of moves was Matthew Ridge's signing, an enormous coup and an expensive one as well. Ridge's Super League-contracted Manly team-mate Ian Roberts was also being connected with the club and there were signs that Canberra's two Kiwi front rowers John Lomax and Quentin Pongia were interested. Throw in some heavy work being done on signing All Black centre Marc Ellis and the recruitment drive was helping overcome the pain of on-field performances.

"To get Matthew Ridge is just a great signing," says Bell. "He impressed me so much in 1995 after I hadn't previously been too convinced about him. It also said a lot for the club that, in its first year, players like Ridge, Pongia and others were wanting to come to the Warriors. How many good players wanted to sign for Canberra, Illawarra or Newcastle after their first year? You wanted to stay away from those places."

But the hunt for players, or perhaps the players' chase for clubs, is an aspect that runs right against the grain of the working class values instilled in Dean Bell through his upbringing in South Auckland.

"What disappoints me is the attitude of some of the players," he says. "A lot of them are asking for ridiculous amounts of money. It has become a player's market—and good luck to them if they get the money—but the ones who really annoy me are the players who sign contracts and then change their minds. A contract should be a contract.

"You can look at Ruben Wiki, Henry Paul and Frano Botica. All of them had contracts with the Warriors that they wanted to back out of or change. Disappointingly, too, they're all New Zealanders. I believe once you sign a contract that should be it.

"A lot of times at Wigan I didn't even sign a contract. We often shook hands on it. That's the way I operate, but, whatever we agreed, I abided by that. If everybody abided by their contracts we'd have none of this trouble with people opting out of contracts mid-term and so on.

"There might be circumstances sometimes when a deal might be done, but really, if the price has been set, that's it. It should be like a builder giving you a price for a job. That should be it."

Dean Bell might wonder about the motives and methods of some of today's players, but in a year which ended on a downslide he was totally excited about the playing talent the Warriors introduced and developed to Winfield Cup standard.

"One that really pleased me was obviously Tony Tuimavave," he says. "He was such a major bonus, giving us strength in the back row, and he should be even better for it in 1996. He's gone from starting as just another player to one who's now a role model for others in the club, which is an achievement on its own.

"Tony Tatupu was another; a gamebreaker with so much skill and a player we desperately missed for the most important part of the season. Hitro Okesene was another who began outstandingly, fell back for a while as he learnt to adjust to Winfield Cup football, and then finished strongly.

"Syd Eru came to us from Wellington via Perth and he had some very big goals right from the start. He wanted to take Duane Mann's first grade

*No Warriors player excited Dean Bell more than scrumhalf
Stacey Jones, here shadowed by second-rower Denis Betts as
he dashes away for his try against the Western Reds.*
Ross Setford (Fotopress)

spot, and he did. One of the quickest dummy half runners I've seen and obviously a big mover for us.

"Tea Ropati was a stand-out all year, which mightn't have been anticipated at the start of the year, but he was so wonderfully consistent for us and deserved to be judged our player of the year. Two others who really impressed me were Gene Ngamu and Sean Hoppe.

"But, if I had to single out just one player, that would have to be Stacey Jones. I haven't seen a player with such a big heart in a long, long time. He has skills, and they're only going to improve, but what he has already, and what sets him apart for one so young, is that heart, that desire and those lungs. His work rate is phenomenal. If some hard yards were needed from dummy half, Stacey would jump in and do it over and above all the other work he already had to do."

Dean Bell may feel he's left the club with some wonderful talent set to explode, if it hasn't already, but, more to the point, is what Dean Bell left the Warriors.

Actually there was an unlikely legacy, maybe not entirely his own doing, yet still surely a reflection of his influence as captain; and also a signal of how far he has developed as a player and leader since his sometimes hot-headed days at Manukau, Eastern Suburbs and Wigan.

He had troubled the judiciary on occasions in both Australia and England, his combined suspensions adding up to a fairly lengthy holiday from football activity, but in year one the Warriors outstripped the other 19 Winfield Cup clubs by being the only club not to have a player appear before the judiciary. Referees' boss Mick Stone was moved to write to the Warriors complimenting the players and coaching staff on their exemplary record.

Bell could take credit for that, but, above all, he left the Warriors with his most special legacy—and that's football played with heart and soul. Football played with attitude. And no one does that better than him.

a leader of action

John Kirwan

A look at the rugby league world today shows a fair collection of All Black backs who have switched from rugby union since 1990 who at one time or another were All Black team-mates. John Gallagher's now retired, but Matthew Ridge, Frano Botica, John Schuster, Craig Innes, Va'aiga Tuigamala, John Timu and I are all contracted to the 13-a-side code.

What I do know is that, in making the switch, three of us—Frano, Inga and me—have certainly had one major benefit the others haven't enjoyed. That's an association with Dean Bell, a player and captain I had contact with for just his one season with the Warriors. But one season was more than enough.

I have a philosophy that if you hang around champions, a lot of their stuff rubs off. When I first went to the Warriors' gym, Dean was really helpful and I started training with him; I soon realised why he's such a champion and such a leader. He does that little bit extra and he never gives in.

Some of the greatest leaders I've been associated with in my football career have been leaders of action. Dean's one of those—his actions speak louder than words, although he still has the words to go with them when needed.

With his experience, he had plenty of tips for me. He knew when to tell me and what to tell me without loading me up with too much advice. It was the little points which were so invaluable. There's also an honesty about him. If you haven't played well, you can go and ask him and he'll tell you straight from the hip what you did or didn't do.

What you learn to respect is that Dean is exceptionally hard on himself, in setting standards for himself. I roomed with him on occasions and learnt how harsh he can be, while he's still honest enough to know that if you work hard on your game, you make it. I found him very similar in his philosophies to me, so we got on really well. I've always been critical of myself by focusing on the errors I make, rather than thinking about the good things.

It's very difficult to sum up Dean in words because it's so much to do with actions with him. You quickly admire his leadership qualities, his basic ability to go hard and get into it; when the team needs it, he lifts the guys. In that way, he's a lot like Buck Shelford was with the All Blacks, but he also says the right things when he needs to.

I also enjoyed him off the field; going out to dinner together with Andy Platt, Denis Betts and our wives. It was nice meeting him and getting on with him; too soon it was sad to see him leaving, but it was time for him to move on and I'm sure he'll make it as a coach.

It was a special year for me, achieving my goals of making it to first grade and playing a lot of games at that level. I've absolutely loved it. I know Inga has really enjoyed it at Wigan as well. After all, the nice thing for Inga and I is that we've been getting the ball and running with it so much more now. When the Warriors played Canberra, I received the ball 18 times—18 times! That was great.

Great, too, was the feeling of playing at Ericsson Stadium. I guess the crowd could have made life uncomfortable for me just starting in the game, yet throughout they were really understanding. The support was fantastic.

But when I assess my first year in league, I know Dean Bell, either directly or indirectly, contributed so much to me reaching my targets. He expects so much from himself—like 100 per cent all the time—and he expects exactly the same from everyone else. You just have to be influenced and inspired by that attitude.

It was nice, too, to be part of his farewell when we played Canberra, in what was his last appearance in New Zealand. I was quite emotional myself because it was a big night. I know as a player you don't like that sort of stuff. You feel a bit embarrassed.

But when Dean looks back over his career, he should be pleased to look back on that night. It was fitting. The least he deserved.

I knew he was a great player before but my respect is right up there for him after my first year with the Warriors. When I sit back in 10 years and recall some of the great people I've met, he'll be one of them.

John Kirwan was an All Black from 1984–94. His 96 appearances included 63 tests, the New Zealand record until Sean Fitzpatrick bettered it in 1995. He has the All Black test try-scoring record at 35 (the next best is 19) and his 67 in all games for New Zealand is also a record. He made 141 appearances for Auckland from 1983–94, scoring 104 tries. He retired from rugby union at end of the 1994 season. He rejected an initial offer to play for the Warriors in late 1994, but then signed in March 1995.

not so cool "joe cool"
The greatest of all faults is to be conscious of none.

Dean Bell loves night football. He reckons there's a certain magic about it. The atmosphere always seems more vibrant, the action that much sharper and, all round, there's more edge and excitement in a night game.

A night early in the 1993–94 English season certainly served his nocturnal appetite. In a tingling contest, Wigan dismissed Leeds 32–18 for their third straight first division win at the start of the season.

A chant started up, "Deano! Deano!" Something was brewing.

Television cameras came onto the field, evidently zeroing in on Dean Bell. And then there appeared a man carrying a red book. *The* man, Michael Aspel. *The* red book. The *This is Your Life* book. It was 10 September 1993 and a night that promised to be a whole lot different than any other Friday night football match Dean Bell had played.

"I thought he [Michael Aspel] had come on for Ellery or Shaun or someone like that," says Bell. "And when he came to me, I thought he's got the wrong guy. I said, 'What's going on?' It was like a bit of a nightmare because I was so stunned.

"There was just no indication to me that anything like this was going to happen. Jackie did a sensational job of keeping it quiet for six weeks, and normally she can't hold her water let alone hold a secret.

"The programme producers, as I found out afterwards, were fairly anxious during the game that I might get injured and carried off, or ordered off. It all depended on me finishing the game and standing up at the end."

For Dean Bell, it was a night like no other with his mother and father there—Cameron was still coaching at Carlisle then—his sister Tracey, uncle Ian (Bell) and cousins Clayton (Friend), Wayne (Bell) and Glen (Bell). Glen was still playing for second division Dewsbury, having previously been on Featherstone Rovers' books.

Only a few weeks before, Bell had scaled another peak when he was confirmed as the first man to lead the Warriors into their Winfield Cup debut season in 1995. Bell had hardly been back in New Zealand since the 1988 World Cup final. In fact, his only visit had been earlier in 1993 when he was, ironically, a guest for Graham Lowe's *This is Your Life* television programme shown live in New Zealand. And it was that visit which won him over to the Warriors' cause. So what with that and his own *This is Your Life,* the new season—Bell's last at Wigan—already had a glow about it.

The immediate post-John Monie era at Wigan also had an exciting look about it with their major off-season buy. Having used Gene Miles and Andrew Farrar as one-off options since losing Kevin Iro, Wigan now went domestic for a more permanent centre and landed Gary Connolly from St Helens.

"Jack Robinson told me they were trying for Paul Newlove and I said, 'Go for it.' I said he should do everything to get Newlove," says Bell. "Then Connolly came on the scene, although I told Jack that my preference was for Newlove. I wasn't so sure about Gary but he was the one we got and, in the end, he was just so good. Better than I ever thought. He's so durable and he really surprised me, but I think coming to Wigan made all the difference to his game."

What wasn't anywhere near so promising was the coaching appointment Wigan had made to replace Monie. Perhaps Wigan had been spoilt with the Lowe-Monie era, but the choice of John Dorahy, the former Australian international who had coached at Halifax in 1989–90, did seem more than strange at the time.

"Everyone was surprised when he was appointed in June 1993," says Bell. "I had met him the previous season as he was coming out of the Wigan boardroom. It didn't click with me then that he was there for an interview for the job.

"He seemed the most unlikely guy to appoint. We were expecting another big name, someone like Tim Sheens. Dorahy was a surprise not just to the players, but also to the fans. He didn't have a significant coaching background, although I have to admit I went to Leeds from the Warriors without coaching experience. It was just that you expected a lot more from Wigan with John Monie being such a tough act to follow."

Early losses to Featherstone Rovers and also the touring New Zealand team weren't necessarily read as warning signs that all might not be well, but there was soon an uneasy atmosphere building up at the club.

"When John arrived, he changed everything. Even the moves we already had he was giving different names," says Bell. "Why would you change the names of existing moves? The most fundamental thing, he'd have a different name for. I thought I should give him a chance at first, although we were uncomfortable with him straight away. Shaun Edwards doesn't tolerate fools and he lost it with Dorahy straight away, saying to me, 'What's this guy trying to do?' He couldn't stand it."

If Bell was prepared to give Dorahy some leeway initially, he changed his attitude after Wigan's away match against Castleford, a game which was played the day after the second test between Great Britain and the Kiwis. As Wigan had four players involved in the test, they could have sought dispensation to have the fixture held over.

"But John wanted to believe he could cope by using the replacement players. He was kidding himself, because we were absolutely done. We had a whole lot of kids out there," says Bell.

'Done' was barely accurate. Castleford won this match 46–0! Bell was not involved, after suffering a groin injury two weeks earlier. An injury that was to haunt him all season and all but wreck his farewell to Wigan.

"Some of the remarks being thrown at John after the game had finished were really offensive," says Bell. "People were shouting, 'What a f...... waste of money. I come all this way and you turn up this shit. Why didn't you call the game off?' I was a bit angry. I agreed the game shouldn't have been played, but John shouldn't have been abused like that."

Shaun Edwards, who had been installed as captain in Bell's absence, and Martin Offiah, pulled out of that match, claiming that they had injuries from the test. But they failed to travel on the team bus as required and were both fined and told to play reserve grade.

"After that defeat, John really slagged off Nigel Wright in the press," says Bell. "That didn't go down well with the players. Nigel wasn't playing well, but the coach shouldn't have gone public with his criticism the way he did.

"Because Shaun hadn't turned up for the bus, John took the captaincy off him. John offered the club captaincy to Andy Platt and Andy said, 'Have you spoken to Dean about this?' Andy was prepared to fill in while I was injured but he wasn't about to take it on fulltime. The fact was John hadn't spoken to me about it and he was naive if he thought Andy wasn't going to tell me."

Bell, and Platt for that matter, had more than a feeling that some strings were being pulled behind the scenes. Bell certainly detected some people had a "Dean's signed for the Warriors" attitude, meaning they believed he wouldn't be exerting himself for the Wigan cause anymore.

"The fact was I had given the club the chance to hit me with a counter offer when the Warriors were on to me," says Bell. "I didn't make up my mind about the Warriors straight away and, if Wigan had come up with an offer, I may well have stayed, I don't know. All they would say was, 'We'll see how you go during the season.'

"I was 31 and they weren't prepared to commit themselves when I thought I'd at least get an offer. That's when I began thinking I was on the outer, that maybe I would be going the same way as Ellery and Andy [Gregory]. It gave the ego a bit of a blow that I wasn't offered an extension."

But once the season was underway, and Bell's status had been settled—

that he was a Wiganer about to become a Warrior—what he saw as efforts to take the captaincy off him were beginning to irritate.

"I confronted Jack and he denied there was any conspiracy to oust me as captain. I spoke to John Dorahy, who also denied it. I told John I knew he'd been talking to Andy, yet he denied that to my face, claiming Andy had it all wrong. I was wasting my time. I couldn't figure out whether Jack was in on it or not, although the directors are usually in thick with the coach."

There was more and more discontent on the training pitch as well. Because he couldn't do ball work with his groin injury, Bell was being fed updated reports by Andy Platt. The sessions were, the players said, too long, while the training effort leading up to the Regal Trophy final against Castleford was, in a word, terrible. So was the performance in the match, Castleford 33, Wigan 2!

"On the way back to Wigan, we had a function to attend," says Bell. "We didn't often lose like that and I felt like a few drinks that night. So Andy and Angela and Jackie and I ended up sitting together. We get on well together as couples and, when we got to the function room, there was only one table left, well away from the rest of the players.

"The next morning Jack Robinson called Andy and I in to see him about not sitting near the rest of the players! By then Andy had also signed for the Warriors, so Jack was reading more into the fact that we had been sitting together.

"It got worse, though, because Jack told me he now doubted my loyalty to the club. Did I blow up! I just gave it to him, saying, 'How dare you, after what I've done for this club. You can question many things, but you can never question my loyalty.' And he followed up by saying, 'I know it's hard for you because you can't go out and prove it.' 'Prove what? I don't need to prove it!' He was obviously getting at the fact I was injured, but that simply had nothing to do with the matter."

What it did have more than a little to do with was the whole Warriors issue. It was around this time that Robinson had been labelling Monie— the man who'd brought Wigan so much success—the root of all evil, accusing him of trying to bring the club down by buying all the best players.

Castleford, for whatever reason of fate, kept cropping up as the club figuring in Wigan's strife. After two earlier defeats, the two sides were set for a Challenge Cup semifinal clash in March.

"The players had lost confidence in John by then," says Bell. "And, before the match, John said he wanted everyone to write down the 15 players they thought should be picked for the match. It told us this guy had no confidence at all about picking a team. That's his job and he's asking us? Some players refused to do it."

This unusual practice manifested itself in an odd chain of events leading up to the match.

"First John told Andy he couldn't pick him in the side," says Bell. "I think that was more to do with the Warriors situation, that Andy was going, and it was a chance to play Neil Cowie and Kelvin Skerrett who would both be there the next season. I thought that stunk. You pick a team to win a match, you don't think about next year. The result was that Andy wasn't even in the squad.

"John wanted to know who I would play out of Andy and Neil. I told him it would be Andy. 'Why?' he asked. 'Because he's a better player.' He said I was right and, the next morning, he'd named Andy on the bench. By the afternoon training run, it had changed again, John telling Andy, Kelvin and Neil that he was going to play all three of them! So in two days, Andy had gone from not playing at all, to on the bench and then into the team."

This time there was no disgrace, though, as Wigan won 20–6 to earn a spot in their seventh successive Challenge Cup final, but it did little to disguise a situation which had become unmanageable.

"I tried to come back for that Castleford match only to find I wasn't quite right yet," says Bell. "But it did mean I was helping out and training and one day John said to me, 'I wish I'd come to you earlier.' He must have said that two or three times and all I could think was, 'Why didn't you?' Because in all that time I was injured I was never approached to do anything, apart from one time. He didn't use me in any capacity. That made me feel even worse."

The real damage was coming on the field now, though, where Wigan were beginning to struggle in the first division race. There had been an unexpected defeat by Wakefield Trinity before the Challenge Cup semifinal and, after it, the outlook darkened as Wigan dropped games against Hull and Sheffield Eagles back-to-back, then Hull Kingston Rovers and Bradford Northern also back-to-back. The 10–6 loss to Bradford was, in fact, Dean Bell's comeback match after around four months laid up with his groin problem.

"Jack came to my house early one morning when we were having the losses and asked me what was going on. 'Simple', I said. 'The players don't have any confidence in the coach.' Eventually he agreed there were problems.

"It reached the stage where, a couple of weeks before the Challenge Cup final, Jack wanted me to come down to the club to meet with John. I think Jack used me a fair bit to do his dirty work for him. 'Go on Dean, tell John what you've told me about the way things are going.' I told John the players didn't have any confidence in him, that they weren't responding to him. I told him straight and he was taken aback a bit.

"Jack asked me to become assistant coach and I turned it down, maintaining there was room for only one coach in the Wigan set-up and I wasn't prepared to do it. Then he said, 'What about if you were the coach, with full reins.' I said I'd take that till the end of the season, on the basis I thought they were going to get rid of John. Only they didn't.

"So when I took my first team session, John Dorahy was less than a metre behind me—literally that—and right on my shoulder. I said to the guys, 'Right, we'll go back to all our old moves, all our old calls.' And John was right there! I had a really uneasy feeling and, after a fair bit of the session, I saw Jack and told him it wasn't going to work, and to let John have the job and see it out.

"I wouldn't say he's a bad coach, but what we needed was what was best for the club, and John wasn't that man. That's why I wanted to help. I was going to the Warriors at the end of the season but, at the end of the day, I wanted to help Wigan until I finished there."

Wigan defied the odds by beating Oldham 50–6 in their final match—yet again taken to the very end—to win the championship, although it was again decided on a points for and against basis after they'd finished level on points with Bradford Northern and Warrington. The title success almost became more famous for Dorahy's tasteless comment in a television interview afterwards when he said, "To all the doubters—suck!"

Playing a role for Wigan against Oldham was former All Black winger Va'aiga Tuigamala, who had signed with Wigan in January and had celebrated his debut against Widnes with a try. Bell, having seen Botica develop so well, was just as excited about Tuigamala's rapid transition and his awesome strength with the ball in hand.

Difficult as the season was proving for the more seasoned players with a coach they didn't want, they weren't about to let it ruin their plans to extend their Wembley run to seven wins, and for Bell to be the winning captain for the third time.

"But the build-up to the final wasn't the best and to be honest John had to make some difficult decisions," says Bell. "He left out Jason Robinson and Martin Hall, Hall replaced by Martin Dermott with Inga [Tuigamala] in instead of Jason, I don't blame him for those. They're decisions a coach has to make and live by them. At the end of the day, he was vindicated, we won and both of the players went well."

Wigan were indeed on song again at Wembley, scoring four tries, two to Lance Todd Trophy winner Martin Offiah to match the two he scored in the 1992 when he also won the Lance Todd. And, for the second successive year, Sam Panapa came on as a replacement and scored. With five Frano Botica goals, Wigan gained a 26–16 result.

But the mood behind the scenes was anything but celebratory. "At the after-match dinner there was a real tension in the air," says Bell. "Andy and I were acknowledged by the directors with champagne, that being our last Challenge Cup final, but John wasn't acknowledged at all in any way. So he and his family walked out of the dinner. It was very awkward.

"And on the coach trip back to Wigan the next day, there was some pushing and shoving going on between John and Jack. That was it for

John Dorahy, and Graeme West came in to finish off the season.

"After all that, after questioning my loyalty, Jack asked me to take over the coaching! He wanted me to change my mind about going to the Warriors and to take on the Wigan job. It would have been the easy way out, but I wanted to go to the Warriors. I'd made the commitment and I didn't want to think I'd regret anything about going home. Of course, it was the right thing to do."

Equally right was the way Dean Bell finished eight exceptional seasons with Wigan, a period when he saw the club enjoy more than 20 title successes, including the Challenge Cup seven times and the first division six times, and had never been on a losing side in a final.

It wasn't his happiest season at Central Park. He was hampered by injury, restricting him to only 16 appearances and not one try, and frustrated by coaching strife. But Bell could leave the club knowing it was in much, much better shape than when he arrived as Graham Lowe's big buy in 1986. And he could also leave knowing he was going to one of the most challenging assignments of his career—home to Warrior territory.

champion player, champion bloke

John Monie

I'm not a person who likes to let emotion take over in sport, and I'm not one to dwell on personal highlights either. But there was a special moment for me as the Warriors' first season wound down.

It was the night of our last home game of the season against Canberra, when Dean Bell played his last game in New Zealand. After I'd spoken to the team, I went across to the stadium early to catch a little of the Maori warriors and then to watch the team coming on to the field, followed by Dean a minute later.

To see him come through that guard of honour flanked by the Maori warriors, our development players, the reserve grade players and then running onto the field—that was as emotional as I've ever felt at a game. I felt proud, I felt sad, I felt excited. Every emotion imaginable at that moment. To me, that was one of the highlights of the season.

And then to have it followed a week later by the performance against Brisbane was such an anti-climax. We were given a really good hiding; we had a lot of bad players and a lot of players who missed tackles. But the thing that struck me when I looked at the video was that the quality of Dean's performance, in his last match, was right up to his usual level. Once again he gave his all and that's a lesson everyone else has to learn from him.

A word that is used a lot when talking about Dean is "uncompromising". He has that inner toughness that the players warm to. They like playing with him.

It's a tough game that we play and plenty of guys look for short cuts, but to me Dean was always up front. He never took the easy option. If the job had to be done with a bit of guile or skill, Dean could get it done. If it had to be done with bloodymindedness or brute strength, Dean could still get the job done. He is a man for all occasions, which is a rare mix.

He was also a player who would always play injured for me. A lot of players will go on the field with an injury but their performance and effort won't be the same. With Dean, he didn't just play, he played well.

There were many games in which Dean showed that attitude, but there's one at Central Park that I'll always remember most. He had a head clash with Steve Hampson which cut him open on one cheek and above one eye. I'll always have the memory of him, as he was going off the field, walking past the players, his fist clenched, saying, 'I'll be back. Don't slacken off.' He had both cuts stitched—and then went straight back out on the field to see the game out.

I knew him from when he'd played for Eastern Suburbs, when I was coaching Parramatta, and he hadn't been outstanding. His discipline wasn't what it should have been either, with a couple of suspensions.

At Wigan he'd had a couple of problems too. When I arrived there, I told Dean what I expected from a player, that I didn't like cheap shots and crap in the game. Once I explained that to him, to me it seemed that he moved up to another level with his discipline.

Knowing the Dean Bell I came to know at Wigan, I believed it was simply Dean's destiny to come back and lead the Auckland Warriors. I knew New Zealanders hadn't seen the best of him and didn't know the Dean Bell I did. I wanted to bring that Dean Bell back to Auckland to show the people what a great rugby league player and great person he had turned into since being away.

People couldn't help warming to him. They could see the complete footballer and classy man he'd become, and the person he has become outside football is the important part in this. He's cultivated that.

That's one of the good things about coaching. You can see qualities in people, help them develop those qualities and then see the reward when a guy like Dean comes back to say, 'Now, this is how you play, and this is how you conduct yourself off the field.'

When we sorted out our choices for the Warriors' first player of the year award, Dean was there in the last three. It was very close. If you conduct any poll—the best player, the toughest player, the best trainer, the top personality—Dean Bell will be in the top three of all of them. As ever, that's testimony to his character. You come to expect it.

John Monie started his coaching career at Parramatta, first as reserve grade coach (1981–83) and then first grade (1984–89), winning the premiership in 1986. He coached Wigan from 1989–93, completing the Challenge Cup-first division championship double each season. He also coached Wigan to an unprecedented treble in 1991–92—the first division championship, Challenge Cup and Premiership Trophy. He quit at the end of the 1992–93 season to take up a job as Auckland Warriors coach. As a player, he made 50 first grade appearances for Cronulla-Sutherland (1968–70).

---

out of juice

The greatest pleasure in life is doing what people say you cannot do.

When Dean Bell hauled his battered and battle-scarred 33-year-old body—and shattered pride—off Brisbane's ANZ Stadium on 27 August 1995, he was as certain as he could be that he'd played his last game of top grade football.

After a first grade apprenticeship with the Manukau club in Auckland, Bell found professional footballing life of a sort in sometimes bleak Carlisle in the winter of 1982–83. Close to 13 years later, he'd graduated to the highest levels as a paid footballer, playing a combined total of almost 400 games for New Zealand, Wigan, Eastern Suburbs, Leeds, Carlisle and the Warriors. And yet, despite choosing a coaching future at Leeds, there were still whose who wanted him to continue playing—and at the top level too.

The Kiwis had hobbled through their domestic test programme with little credit, coach Frank Endacott grappling with a side which just wouldn't gel. He was missing the leadership he wanted; not just in a captain, but also a loose forward of sufficient quality. All season, Endacott had seen the obvious answer at every training session and every time the Warriors played, well every time except three matches in mid-season when injury interfered. The man he wanted for the No 13 jersey—Tawera Nikau—wasn't available and there just didn't seem to be any other options. Finally, Frank Endacott could resist it no more; he confronted the man he needed, Dean Bell.

"Frank pulled me aside at training near the end of the season," says Bell. "And he said, 'I'm totally serious here, Dean. Would you be available for me for the World Cup, because you'd solve my loose forward and captaincy problems?'

"I was taken aback a bit and made a spontaneous response, 'Thanks very much, Frank. But no thanks.' I didn't want to think about it too much, because if I did I might have changed my mind. I knew that would have been the wrong thing.

Dean Bell, 1992–93 vintage, the way he was in more than 250 games for Wigan. Dean Bell Collection

"I just think that's gone. If they were looking for answers, I thought they needed to look for some of the younger players coming through. Quite apart from that, there was my job with Leeds to think about. It wouldn't have been fair to them and I don't think it was the way for New Zealand league to go.

"I felt Frank thought he needed to ask me. I knew my name had been bandied about in some quarters, but it was nice to be asked by the Kiwi coach to play."

But it was really asking rather too much too late in the day. It might have made for an amazing end to an amazing career. To quit after leading your country at the World Cup must have had some appeal, but Bell wasn't about to be lured by such sentiment. Besides, he'd made his commitment to Leeds, and Bell has shown throughout that he's not one to backtrack on an agreement.

Dean Bell, 1995 vintage, the way he was in one season back home for the Warriors. Andrew Cornaga (Photosport)

During the 1995 season, Bell seriously contemplated one more year of football until coaching ambition offered more long-term scope. Warriors coach John Monie still wanted him as a player, although with a niggling reservation.

"If Dean didn't get the coaching job at Leeds we certainly would have signed him for another season," says Monie. "Whether his body would have held up for another season, I don't know.

"I always say we let our champions retire too early, but maybe Dean had squeezed the orange dry. He was struggling with his knee, his right thumb had been broken quite a few times, he had an elbow that kept swelling up all the time. So, he nursed himself as much as he could through the latter part of the season, virtually living on anti-inflammatory pills."

Monie may well have been right. Bell himself readily concedes he might have found one more year one too many. But the one year he had back home—his first full season here since playing for Manukau in 1984—was educational for all concerned. It completely revived Bell's confidence in the game in New Zealand; and it gave New Zealanders the chance at last to find out why he had become such a legendary force in England.

The recognition came too. He'd barely been back in New Zealand when in November 1994 he was named the Maori sports personality of the year ahead of All Black Zinzan Brooke. He was also inducted as only the seventh Kiwi immortal, joining Tom Baxter, Des White, Ron Ackland, Roger Bailey, Kevin Tamati and Mark Graham. And when the Warriors had their first annual awards dinner, the moment couldn't pass without a special presentation to their first captain.

Bell's one-year stay with the Warriors was over all too quickly, showing in bald statistics that the team had won 13 games on the field and lost nine. They beat just two of the eventual top eight sides—Cronulla-Sutherland and the Sydney Bulldogs—while competing with Manly, Canberra and Brisbane the first time, but being ruthlessly exposed by them the next time, with the same applying against Newcastle, St George and North Sydney. The Warriors looked after the ninth-placed Roosters and lost only twice to teams who finished below them, Illawarra and Penrith.

"For most of the year we gained credibility and that's one of the main achievements I'll take when I look back on my year with the Warriors," says Bell. "That was my major concern, because so many teams before us had failed to achieve anything like what we did in their first year in the competition. In fact, nearly all of them had major struggles.

"I think the other aspect was that we were entertaining, and too often that's overlooked when analysing the performance of sporting teams. Entertaining the public is all-important. They're the people we're trying to please. They're coming through the gate and paying our wages and we delivered a lot in that respect, including some of the best tries of the year.

"In fact, the game that keeps coming back to me is the very first game against Brisbane. I've been a winner mainly and that was a loss, but the sheer magnitude of that night and how we performed meant so much to me.

"But there were negatives, too, and essentially those were the big defeats, the times when we didn't just lose but embarrassed ourselves. Those were the negatives that concerned me the most."

Those shockers were easy to find—Illawarra (40–28), Norths (48–10), Newcastle (48–6), Penrith (34–16), St George (47–14) and Brisbane (44–6). All that could be said was that they were never nilled on the scoreboard.

The upside was certainly the entertainment factor. The Warriors scored 101 tries, many of them dazzlers, with outstanding winger Sean Hoppe the chief beneficiary. His 19 tries put him right near the top of the competition's try-scoring chart.

And while Bell was well aware of the flaws on the field, he couldn't find too many off it.

"Administratively the club had some problems earlier in the year but they learned quicker than we, the players, did," says Bell. "They're so professional, and Ian Robson, what a guy to have to head your organisation. He has so much charisma and I can't speak highly enough about his professionalism. He must take a lot of credit for what goes on.

"John Monie handled the year just as I'd expected him to. As usual he was very calm and so professional. It was very different for him though. He had to learn a lot about so many players he knew little of. For me, though, it was like a typical year under John at Wigan in the past."

Dean Bell would like to emulate Monie's cool approach now he joins league's suit and tie brigade as the gaffer at Leeds. He has had much to do with so many coaches, and particularly Graham Lowe and Monie, but the coaching trip is one into the unknown for him. And at only 33, he's also giving the game one of its youngest coaches at this level.

"There's so much more involved in it, especially on the man management side," says Bell. "You can't go into the coaching game with too many fixed opinions on how to run a team. You need to be flexible. Because I'm from the old school, I will find the greatest difficulty adapting to players who don't have the same sort of attitude as me."

What Bell immediately found about the job was that it exposed him to one of the most demanding, and often delicate, aspects of coaching— looking out for and persuading players to sign.

He didn't directly have an involvement in the chase to snare Jonah Lomu's signature, but he had to be kept briefed. And when Frano Botica finally decided he wasn't going to stay with the Warriors after all, Bell was on the trail for his signature as soon as he returned to England.

"The Jonah business just dragged on and on," says Bell. "Phil Kingsley-Jones made visits to Headingley and Alf Davies [the Leeds chairman] went to tremendous lengths to put a good proposal together.

"Alf asked me at one stage, as we waited and waited, whether I wanted to pursue it. I had some doubts because we had such a huge amount of money tied up in one person and I wondered whether we wouldn't be better off signing five or six other players instead.

"The more I thought about it, though, the more I realised he'd be a sensation as a footballer, and then, of course, there were the commercial considerations. What was more important to me was the matchwinning qualities he'd bring into the team.

"In the end, we had to put an expiry date on the offer because we had to know whether the money would need to be spent elsewhere. We covered everything, not just the money. There were issues like his family to consider and I stressed to Alf that we wanted Jonah to know we wanted to look after him first and foremost. It wasn't just a case of throwing money at him.

"The most indecent amount of money was involved. The figures quoted [around $4.5 million was the ballpark figure] weren't at all far from the mark. He decided not to come, but he might change his mind in four years and want to try league."

By then Dean Bell wants to be well-settled as a rugby league coach, although he doesn't imagine coaching will sustain him as long as playing

The Challenge Cup heads for the heavens after Dean Bell's first Wembley final as Wigan captain in 1992. Varley Picture Agency

the game did. And the thought of him returning to Ericsson Stadium as coach isn't inconceivable either, perhaps as Monie's successor.

"Coaching could lead to other things, who knows," he says. "I've got an open mind. If it works out and coaching suits me, I guess it's possible I could look at coming back to the Warriors as a coach if that's on."

The most harrowing adjustment will be going from fulltime player to fulltime coach, and whether the withdrawal symptoms, coupled with the possibility of poor results from his players, will persuade him to play sometimes for a club whose colours he wore as a player in 1983–84.

Footballers' retirements regularly have a habit of leading to comebacks and it might be that Bell's retirement becomes slightly qualified at Leeds.

"I don't want to play again, that's my feeling. I definitely couldn't say I won't—but I don't want to. I'll do my best to resist the temptation."

And when Dean Bell says his best, it pays to believe him.

statistics
Dean Bell's fact file

NEW ZEALAND—TESTS

	Matches	Tries	Points
1983			
v Australia	2	-	-
v Papua New Guinea	1	3	12
1984			
v Great Britain	3	1	4
1985			
v Australia	3	1	4
v Great Britain	3	2	8
v France	2	-	-
1986			
v Australia	2	1	4
1987			
v Papua New Guinea	1	2	8
v Australia	1	-	-
1988			
v Papua New Guinea	1	-	-
v Great Britain	1	-	-
v Australia	1	-	-
1989			
v Great Britain	3	-	-
v France	2	1	4
Totals	**26**	**11**	**44**

*Dean Bell captained New Zealand in four tests in 1987–88, winning three and losing one.

TOUR MATCHES

	Matches	Tries	Points
1985			
in England	5	-	-
in France	3	2	8
1987			
in Australia	2	2	8
Totals	**10**	**4**	**16**
Overall for NZ	36	15	60

PROFESSIONAL CAREER

	Matches	Tries	Points
Carlisle			
1982–83	23	11	33 *
Leeds			
1983–84	22	4	16
Eastern Suburbs			
1985	15	5	20
1986	14	2	8
1988	11	1	4
Total	**40**	**8**	**32**
Wigan			
1986–87	42	22	88
1987–88	20	10	40
1988–89	33	15	60
1989–90	33	10	40
1990–91	37	11	44
1991–92	33	13	53
1992–93	39	15	60
1993–94	16	-	-
Total	**253**	**96**	**384**
Auckland Warriors			
1995	19	3	12
Clubs Total	357	122	477
NZ Total	36	15	60
Overall	**393**	**137**	**537**

Other Teams: Rest of the World, Oceania, New Zealand Residents XIII, New Zealand Maori, Auckland, South Island, Cumbria, Manukau.

Tries worth three points in 1982-83.